Heidegger, Kant

&

T I M E

Heidegger, Kant

&

TIME

CHARLES M. SHEROVER

With an Introduction by

WILLIAM BARRETT

Indiana University Press

BLOOMINGTON / LONDON

SECOND PRINTING 1972

Copyright © 1971 by Indiana University Press

Library of Congress catalog card number: 74-135011

ISBN: 253-32720-2

Manufactured in the United States of America

Published in Canada by Fitzhenry & Whiteside Limited, Don Mills, Ontario

To JOHN, *whose friendship*

means much

CONTENTS

[vii]

I N T R O D U C T I O N

MEMORY IS THE MOTHER OF THE MUSES. So speaks the old Greek myth, and in our time it has become necessary to give fresh attention to the Greeks and their myths. Naturally, they were not talking about routine memory—the process by which the items of the past are hoarded and tallied in the uninspiring fashion of a bookkeeper. Essential memory is something very different: an encounter between present and past in which the past becomes fully alive and the present gains its depth and meaning out of this dialogue. From such an encounter, the Greeks held, came the vision that enabled the artist to create his world. But we need not, on this point, restrict ourselves merely to artistic creation. Philosophy itself gains its vitality and meaning only when it lives in communion with its own past.

The point is worth laboring because today we seem on the way to becoming a civilization without memories. Items of culture are used up and discarded like the consumable products of industry with their built-in obsolescence. The young generation, however considerable its other virtues, acts often as if the world had only begun a few years ago. Even the most sedulous of youth's admirers have been occasionally frightened at their lack of a sense of history. Philosophy itself has not escaped this prevailing blight of forgetfulness. In some quarters a student can go through his entire graduate studies, obtain the degree that will be his union ticket to

teach other students in turn, and know chiefly the current periodi-
cal literature on his subject. A half dozen articles, researched in
detail, can suffice for a thesis. One well-known philosopher remarked in a candid moment that, as far as he was concerned, "philosophy began with G. E. Moore." He was smiling as he said it,
but he was serious. The smile, I suspect, was to indicate his toler-
ance in going back as far as Moore. Unfortunately, this cancella-
tion of the past does not make philosophy more contemporary;
it only makes it more blind—and therefore less relevant, to use the
current jargon. Like the rest of our civilization, philosophy becomes buried beneath the debris of immediacy.

Heidegger follows another path: he philosophizes always in
dialogue with the past. That the German word *andenken* (remember, think on) and *denken* (think) are obviously linked has itself
been one of the themes of his thought. This preoccupation with
the past does not mean that he merely gathers his ideas from dead
thinkers as if these ideas were so many pieces of fruit simply hang-
ing there to be collected. As if, for example, one could understand
what Kant meant by the synthetic apriori unless one had also strug-
gled with this problem on its own terms! The dialogue, rather, is a
process by which one persistently tests one's own thinking in contact with the thought of the past. In that process too, a current of
ideas is released from the past philosopher and becomes vital
again in the present. What the dead thinker was struggling to say,
what he said only haltingly or incompletely or sometimes even
unconsciously, comes alive as a question still troubling and perti-
nent for us today. Such dialogue does not aim at a "correct interpretation" in the usual sense of a synoptic and more accessible
version of a past system. It is an adventure in thinking, not an
effort at reduplication. Its view can even be quite partial, restricting
itself to a single theme that it seeks to extricate from the past philosophy in order to think it through once again.

For Heidegger, dealing with Kant, this theme is the central
importance of time in the Kantian philosophy. At first glance, this
looks like a likely enough choice for Heidegger, for whom the
question of time and of Being, and their essential relationship,
has always stood at the center of philosophy. But to pursue this
theme through the text of the *Critique of Pure Reason* would seem

[x]

a rather odd strategy in view of the fact that Kant is not usually considered as one of the time-oriented philosophers like Hegel or Bergson. His view of time, after all, is shaped by the simple concept of Newtonian time, which is foreign to the true meaning of becoming. Nevertheless, time does enter at the most crucial spot in the *Critique;* and the fact that it plays so important a role for a philosopher who is commonly regarded as not time-oriented, should provide all the more convincing indication that the question of time is central to philosophy. The witness, after all, has no antecedent bias and so his testimony is more believable.

Time, for Kant, invades the traditionally timeless sanctuary of the apriori. The full significance of his Copernican Revolution emerges as a rather startling reversal of Platonism. Plato had also located the problem of time at the center of philosophy, though in a sense quite the opposite of Heidegger: philosophy must provide an escape from the bondage of time. Beyond the Heraclitean flux there must be stable and changeless objects. The fact of apriori knowledge—the quasi-divine power of the human mind to know necessary truths that go beyond our limited experience—seemed to provide the evidence for these objects. Such knowledge was possible because the mind had access to the Ideas, eternal essences beyond time and change. Kant turns these schema upside down: a concept is not a Platonic Idea outside time but a rule for the synthesis of experience within time. Take Kant's famous example "$7 + 5 = 12$." To know this I must be able to count through seven units, hold them in mind, count through five units, and count through the whole collection. Anticipation, repetition, retention— all are parts of an essentially temporal process. Moreover, the fruitfulness of this arithmetical truth lies in its relation to future time; it allows me to anticipate future experience; I know whenever the counting is done that it *will* turn out in this way.

Modern axiomatizations of arithmetic (like Peano's) do not get around Kant's contention. Such axiomatizations permit us to replace the original proposition with an equation with twelve identical strokes on each side of the equality sign, thus:

$$1+1+1+1+1+1+1+1+1+1+1+1=1+1+1+1+1+1+1+1+1+1+1+1.$$

But here again I have to count through the marks on one side to see that they add up to the marks on the other side. Axiomatization does not bestow upon the original proposition any certainty that it had lacked; it only embeds that proposition among others in a system that serves for metamathematical research. On the surface the reduction seems to provide us with a bare identity, $A = A$, a nugatory proposition like "a bald man is a man" or all those other examples in the inane litany of tautology with which some contemporary philosophers bombard us. In fact, "Seven plus five equals twelve" is a very different kind of proposition. If I am able to count up to twelve I can perform the iterative operation and count beyond it, and so have the number system in my grasp; if I can break twelve up into seven and five, I can break it in other ways, and so have all the necessary arithmetical operations at my disposal. With these operations and the number system the whole of arithmetic opens before me. The original proposition, far from a barren tautology, is immensely fertile. That was one of the reasons that Kant insisted that it is *synthetic*.

Apriori knowledge is only one—though perhaps one of the most remarkable—modes of human transcendence. If we turn back again to Plato, we find that this problem of transcendence is at the heart of philosophy since its beginning. But approached now from the Kantian perspective (at least the perspective implicit in the First Edition of the First Critique), the question takes on a striking aspect: Man transcends time, but through structures of time. Beyond my death I know that whenever they are counted seven and five will add up to twelve. I transcend my finite condition, but this transcendence is itself a synthesis (here in the act of counting) of time. *Man transcends time but only within time.* To understand this last proposition one would have to trace these different meanings of time back to their originative source. For this one would require a whole new ontology of human existence as finite, time-bound . . . and therefore (not nevertheless) transcendent. And that was precisely Heidegger's project in *Being and Time*.

One of the great merits of Dr. Sherover's excellent book is that it enables us to see Heidegger's thought—in one direction, at least —as an organic outgrowth from his reading of Kant. It thus helps to remove one common misapprehension that Heidegger's thought is odd, idiosyncratic, and not rooted—as in fact it is—in the mainstream of philosophy. Dr. Sherover is able to remove this mis-understanding in great part through the admirable clarity of his exposition; he has succeeded in conveying Heidegger's most abstruse points into plain and understandable English, and so has overcome the formidable barrier of terminology that has blocked so many Heideggerian interpreters. This book is in fact the clearest exposition that I have read of Heidegger's thought at one stage of its development. But beyond this valuable job of clarification, by bringing the light of Heidegger to bear upon Kant, this book is also a significant contribution to Kantian scholarship. And that means, of course, a contribution to philosophy itself.

WILLIAM BARRETT

ACKNOWLEDGMENTS

ANY BOOK WHICH SEEKS TO PRESENT A SERIOUS STUDY
owes an intangible debt to countless people who contributed to
the author's development and the explication of his thinking. In
this case, among these anonymous benefactors are to be counted
teachers, students, and friends who have compelled refinement
of the ideas expressed here as they originally subjected them to
their critical consideration.

The manuscript of this book has evolved through several
stages of thinking and writing over a somewhat extended period
of time. Had it not been for the strong encouragement given me
by James S. Churchill, J. Glenn Gray, and Bruce Wilshire, it is
doubtful whether this finally developed version of the earlier
manuscript they had seen would have been developed. In this
regard I am especially grateful to Miss Renate Fröhlich, who has
given me invaluable clerical assistance along the way. I am deeply
indebted to both Paul Edwards and Milton K. Munitz, who have,
despite their basic disagreements with the orientation of this study,
urged me to develop it from earlier drafts they had seen. Gottfried
Martin has also been as kind in his encouragement as his own
book on Kant has been helpful.

I am deeply appreciative of the interest and assistance afforded
me by two friends, with widely differing philosophic loyalties, who
have been good enough to subject an earlier draft to painstaking

[xv]

critical examination. From the numerous discussions of Heidegger and of Kant which Michael Gelven and I have had together, as well as from his specific textual queries and suggestions, much has been learned which I trust is reflected in the pages which follow. Barry Gross has raised a number of questions, which I have tried to clarify—though I doubt to his complete satisfaction. Together they have served to help me refine my own thinking on numerous points at issue and, hopefully, clarify a number of important arguments in my exposition. In addition, I also want to express my appreciation to Joseph McGeough for his help by preparing the Index and for some important suggestions he made while doing so.

To no one, however, am I more profoundly indebted than to William Barrett, who, as teacher and as friend, provoked the discussions out of which this book developed. His persistent prodding, his unflagging criticism, and his relentless impatience with terminological obscurities have combined to inspire and sustain my perseverance in trying to unravel what struck me as unnecessary abstruseness enveloping some of the more profound and important philosophic thinking of our day. Were more teachers so emphatically unmerciful in espousing the ideal of distinctness of philosophic perception and clarity of expression, while focusing on living issues of human concern, philosophic writing might well begin to speak to a wider audience; philosophy itself might then once again take up the development of that imaginative vision which, some three hundred years ago, brought about its rejuvenation as it helped to redirect the development of human civilization.

Whatever intellectual merit or expositional clarity this book may have is traceable to the wisdom of these colleagues—friends, teachers, students—who have ccontributed, knowingly or not, to the writing of this book. Grateful as I am to them all for their encouragement and helpful criticisms, the responsibility for what is and is not said here is mine alone.

Earlier versions have been previously published of some of the material contained here. I want to express thanks for the kind permission accorded me to incorporate material from three published papers: (1) Adaptation of a paper entitled "Heidegger's Ontology and the Copernican Revolution," *The Monist,* Vol. 51, No. 4 (1967) and *Kant Studies Today,* Ed. Lewis White Beck (1969), La Salle, Illinois, with the permission of The Open Court Publishing Company; (2) Adaptation of a paper entitled "Heidegger and the Reconstruction of the Kantian Ethic," Vol. V, *Akten des XIV Internationalen Kongresses für Philosophie* (1968), by permission of Leo Gabriel and Verlag Herder Wien; (3) Adaptation of a paper entitled "Kant's Transcendental Object and Heidegger's *Nichts,*" *Journal of the History of Philosophy* (1969), Vol. VII, No. 4, pp. 413–22; copyright by the Regents of the University of California, by permission of the Regents.

C.M.S.

Heidegger, Kant

&

T I M E

. . . all that is grounded is necessarily finite,
and reaches no further than its ground.

—JOHANN GOTTLIEB FICHTE

The notion of nonentity may thus be called the
parent of the philosophic craving in its subtilest
and profoundest sense. Absolute existence is abso-
lute mystery, for its relations with the nothing
remain unmediated to our understanding.

—WILLIAM JAMES

I

Prospect

WHILE THE ROMAN EMPIRE was falling apart, Augustine gave voice to the central concern of this study:

> What then is time? I know what it is if no one asks me what it is; but if I want to explain it to someone who has asked me, I find that I do not know. Nevertheless, I can confidently assert that I know this: that if nothing passed away there would be no future time, and if nothing were now there would be no present time. . . . Yet if the present were always present and did not go by into the past, it would not be time at all, but eternity. If, therefore, the present (if it is to be time at all) only comes into existence because it is in transition toward the past, how can we say that even the present *is?* For the cause of its being is that it shall cease to be. So that it appears that we cannot truly say that time exists except in the sense that it is tending toward non-existence.[1]

The mark of temporality is firmly stamped on our human acting, thinking, valuing, knowing. Each one of us finds his reality in a temporal context. Our hopes, aspirations, disappointments, fears, our thoughts, plans, recollections, joys and sorrows are all bound by time, conditioned by time, fulfilled in time. The reality of each one of us, as individual beings, is wrapped in this mysterious 'thing' or 'condition' called the temporal. "The mystery of time," as Dewey pointed out, "is thus the mystery of the existence

[3]

of real individuals." Augustine's meditation still haunts us: 'I know what time is until someone asks me and then I only know that I do not know.' Time is pervasive and the prime dimension of life; yet its nature, its 'Being' is veiled in obscurity. The nature of time comes into our own era as a 'mystery,' as a prime "philosophical problem of the first importance." [2]

Most philosophic thought has declined to face frankly the pervasive fact of temporality. Plato keynoted the subsequent development in describing time as but the moving likeness of eternity, as but a second order of reality. The philosophic tradition has followed him in this flight from the temporal to the priority of the immutable. Boas' observation is telling: "when philosophers who have dominated occidental philosophy thought of time at all, they put it on the level of appearance and left it there with contempt." [3]

It is only recently that the centrality of time in human experience has been accorded explicit recognition and brought to the center of philosophic concern. Working from leads provided by Leibniz, Immanuel Kant finally brought time out of the shadows. One of the 'dogmatic slumbers' against which the *Critique of Pure Reason* effectively warns is this failure to recognize the prime import of time as the ground of all possible experience. The concept of time is a guiding thread through the First Critique; it contributes to virtually every key concept; its pervasive role in the reinterpretation of human reason is amply demonstrated in the elucidation of each of the categories—for Kant, the foundation stones of experience itself.

From this vantage point, it is apparent that Kant's Critical or transcendental idealism was revolutionary. "Since Kant, modern philosophy has directed its efforts patiently and obstinately to recuperating—and adoring—what during the centuries metaphysics had burned, namely the *hic et nunc,* history, time and movement, contingency, experience, the sensible. . . ." [4] One of those who has followed Kant's lead is Martin Heidegger, one of the more widely discussed, if one of the more controversial, thinkers of our own era. His pursuit of these themes, emanating from Kant, is focused in his exploration of the nature of time—pronounced by one of his most severe critics as a "very acute piece of work which will remain a lasting contribution to philosophy." [5]

Much of what Heidegger has had to say has been obscure and mystifying. Yet those who have attempted to come to terms with his thought generally are deeply impressed. Even Gilbert Ryle, while expressing fears of where it would lead, described him in an early essay as "a thinker of real importance . . . [who] tries to think beyond the stock categories of orthodox philosophy and psychology." [6]

Virtually all discussion of Heidegger's philosophic contribution has been centered on his major, but never completed work, *Being and Time,* or on later essays which have generally appeared to be even more obscure and enigmatic. It is true that in *Being and Time* he set out his major themes. But, in doing so, he pursued an unfamiliar, often apparently arbitrary, method and coined a language which has often served to mystify rather than enlighten.

Yet Heidegger has made it clear that the phenomenological approach embodied in his magnum opus does not and "cannot claim to be the only one possible." [7] Indeed, he has given us an alternate approach to his doctrine—particularly to the concept of time and its grounding of the concept of Being—in *Kant and the Problem of Metaphysics,* his prime interpretive study of Kant's First Critique. His implicit claim here is that the method of existential analysis is not crucial; its unspoken thesis is that his own philosophic understanding of time can be elicited from Kant's landmark work by a reexamination of Kant's theory of knowledge and the development of its ontological implications. If this be so, it places Heidegger into the heart of the modern philosophic tradition; and if it is true that this Kant-book was conceived before his major work, [8] it suggests a more original source of his thinking.

Indeed, Kant has been described as his "spiritual father," [9] and his philosophically "immediate predecessor." [10] Problematically, the reason for a special relationship between them is not hard to see. Time was presented by Kant as the ground of all cognitive experience. Heidegger has taken up this temporal concern and enlarged its role to that of the central 'category' of human experience: time's function is not restricted to the structure of all possible knowledge; it is transformed into the key to meaning in every area of life. The meaning of the concept of time is amplified

[5]

and rethought; Kant's concept undergoes a fundamental critique and redevelopment. In the end we will see that their different understandings of time serve to define the core issue between them. Heidegger begins at the point at which Kant had left the problem; in developing it, he takes up anew Kant's original stated intent, the rethinking of the possibility, nature, and limitation of metaphysics, the grounding of which Heidegger sees as an accomplishment of the First Critique.[11]

It is then strange that the Kant-book has not received much critical attention, has been largely ignored in the debates concerning the meaning of what Heidegger has been saying, or has been cavalierly dismissed as 'bad Kant'. Perhaps this response arises from the work's inherent difficulty—due to a combination of an abstruse vocabulary, a running assumption that the reader is conversant with minutiae of the Kantian text, and its composition almost as a sketch of an argument with detailed discussion of important connecting stages noticeable by their absence.

But careful consideration of the work is not only a philosophically exciting enterprise; just because of the import of, and familiarity with, the general Kantian problematic, approaching Heidegger from a Kantian pathway makes him more readily accessible. Although this Kant-book was originally intended for the uncompleted second half of *Being and Time,* Herbert Spiegelberg tells us that it "seems to have been conceived independently and can be considered as a kind of historical prolegomena" to it.[12] As such it helps open the door to the problematic context and developed doctrine of *Being and Time* as well as of later work which, however Heidegger's changes of philosophic direction be evaluated, manifests a continuing involvement with Kantian themes.

More important, the Kant-book serves as a crucial complement to *Being and Time,* which seeks in its existential analysis to focus attention on the essential dynamics of human experiencing. Instead of approaching the objects of knowledge in terms of their utilities (as "ready-to-hand") which first bring them to our attention, the Kant-book investigates the structure of our knowledge of the objects known (as "present-at-hand"); it then seeks to demonstrate how the Kantian epistemology leads, as does the existential analysis, to the concept of Concern, which Heidegger proposes as the central unifying 'category' of human experience insofar as

[6]

it expresses the essential structure of human temporality. As such, the Kant-book clarifies epistemological questions suggested by *Being and Time* and provides epistemological confirmation (or derivation) of Heidegger's development of the philosophy of time. It also suggests that in carrying transcendental philosophy forth into phenomenologically grounded ontology—with a focus on time, temporality, and the limitations of human finitude—*Being and Time* may be regarded as grounding in broad terms the *Critique of Pure Reason*. This suggestion may seem overly bold but it should be remembered that Kant, in looking ahead to what was to become the First Critique, thought of it under the title, "The Limits of Sense and Thought," and described it as "general phenomenology" as well as "metaphysics . . . with regard to its nature and method." [13]

It is, then, the plan of this study to look at Kant through Heidegger's eyes and, in elucidating his interpretation of Kant, to take a closer look at Kantian texts than he offers in his own argument. In order to do this, it is necessary to review some basic facets of Kant's formulation of the problem of human knowledge. As Heidegger's approach is usually one of selective exposition, the review of essential Kantian arguments in the early part of this study should help toward understanding Heidegger's focus and avoiding misconceptions. Although the focus of discussion is directed to the carefully structured argument of his first Kant-book, it is urged that its force is wider, that the whole of the early Heidegger as well as the essential outline of his concept of time can be clarified by a careful consideration of his probing examination of Kant's epistemology. Hopefully, this exercise will reveal at least his original philosophic thrust, which found its culmination in *Being and Time*.*

Heidegger's interpretation of Kant is certainly not orthodox. If

---

* Some ten years later, Heidegger delivered a series of lectures subsequently published as his second Kant-book (translated into English as *What Is A Thing?*); although references to it, as well as to other writings, occasionally prove helpful, detailed discussions would only be distractive: its surprisingly welcome clarity of style, which is commendable as a standard for philosophic writing, precludes the need for elucidation; and its theme, a 'postscript' to the first Kant-book, does not add development to the concept of time, although it aids us to understand Kant by making us remember that Kant's theory of knowledge was directed to elucidating our knowledge not of persons but of things.

[7]

his new approach reveals a sharp discrepancy between Heidegger's Kant and the Kant we have been taught, the discussion at least serves to explicate the philosophic issues which Heidegger has raised. If it is demonstrated that Heidegger's conclusions are, indeed, grounded on his own interpretation of Kant, that his root conception of time can be approached in a Kantian context, this should enable us to clarify obscurities which have been engendered from his own writing in his own terms. And if it is found that Heidegger's close reading of the Kantian text yields some bold new interpretations, this result should provide a new insight into the Critical philosophy, the philosophic possibilities it still offers, and thereby a deeper comprehension of its outlook.

Although Kantian themes recur throughout Heidegger's writing, no attempt can be made here to debate whether his thought has been a harmonious development or is marked by divergent and conflicting phases.[14] Except for some later references to Kant, the emphasis here, in contrast to most Heidegger studies, is on the early Heidegger, the Heidegger who sought to face the question of the meaning of Being in terms of an essentially Kantian approach to the pervasiveness of temporality in human experience.

Any thinker attempting to pioneer new perspectives must, I suppose, coin a new vocabulary. In this regard, Heidegger's 'success' is notorious. But one justification for his modes of expression is that the insights he seeks to explore and expound require us to transcend the limitations which our language imposes on our thinking. He himself suggested that "not only most of the words, but, above all, the 'grammar'" are lacking for the new dynamic perspective he offers.[15] Indeed, Aristotle had already defined this problem when he noted that a noun "has no reference to time . . . [but] a verb is that which, in addition to its proper meaning, carries with it the notion of time." [16] Our language, which centers on non-temporal nouns instead of temporal verbs, is thus an impediment to clarity in elucidating an ontology primarily concerned with time-consuming activities instead of with substantive things.

However justifiable, Heidegger's language has indeed been a stumbling block to understanding his meaning. One virtue of the Kantian approach, just because it proceeds out of more traditional discussion, is that it permits us to view his thought with this prob-

[8]

lem minimized. In any case, if what he has to say is of significance, it must be understood and assimilated by us. For this reason an attempt is made here to avoid the use of a strange terminology and to convey what he is saying in everyday philosophical English. The translations cited are used with amendments that seem to clarify what is being said or more closely convey what I take his meaning to be. To the extent that special terms cannot be avoided, an attempt is made to clarify their meaning as they are introduced.

What brings Kant and Heidegger into one perspective is their historic function of explicating the centrality of time in human experience. Other strands of their discussions can only be permitted to intrude when they are directly relevant to this subject in focus. To do otherwise would lead to a discussion of a diversity of issues that have their own intrinsic interest but would lead us far afield.

Kant brought time into modern philosophy as a prime 'category'. Heidegger has made it central. Their inquiry into the nature and import of time and temporality is the horizon within which the discussion proceeds.

II

The Project of Retrieve

It should be made clear at the outset that Heidegger's intent is to re-think Kant's problem and his proffered solution. His project* is neither a pedagogical review of Kant's thinking nor the production of a new commentary. It is a probing for questions that have not been answered or explored in sufficient depth in order to see what new questions Kant's work suggests to us.

Kant had suggested that systematic knowledge comes from the interrogation, not the passive observation, of nature. So Heidegger's method is the interrogation of Kant in order to discover those new possibilities for philosophic development that are suggested by the Kantian achievement, an achievement which marks 'the first decisive step since Plato and Aristotle,' and which cannot be bypassed by subsequent thought.[2]

Dr. Raymund Schmidt, who edited a current German edition of Kant's First Critique (and who consulted with Heidegger along with Norman Kemp Smith in its preparation), has remarked that 'Kant is much more often read today out of historical than out of systematic interest.'[3]

Heidegger does not have an antiquarian interest in Kant; his interest is what Kant has to say to him, what Kant has to say to

---

* This technical word *Entwurf* is not, as Heidegger has explained, a plan of action as much as it is a way of actuating possibilities; in this context, the actuating of the philosophic possibilities which he sees the Critical philosophy as offering.[1]

the philosophic problems and concerns of the present day. Kant's prime interest, as he sees it, was to secure a firm foundation for rethinking metaphysics. He starts from Kant because he finds parallel interests, because he regards Kant as the one thinker who "was more alert to the problem of metaphysics than any other philosopher before or since," because Kant's development of the transcendental method makes possible a secure foundation for ontology.[4]

In effect, he seeks to maintain a dialogue with Kant, to discuss points that strike him as crucial. He believes that Kant has more than mere historic interest, that Kant's thinking has crucial relevance—in what it says, suggests, and overlooks—to present-day problems. Heidegger's concern is to bring Kant-as-philosopher back to life, as a spur to his own thinking through a sharing of thought.

It is only this kind of return engagement with a thinker that can make him live in and for our own thinking. To deny the validity of this kind of effort to reexamine Kant, or any other thinker, in terms of present questions and concerns is not to honor his effort but to consign him to the dusty shelves of a philosophic museum.

It would seem that this intention is one which Kant would have honored and encouraged. Heidegger seems to have taken inspiration for this effort from Kant's own defense of the First Critique:

> Thus, the *Critique of Pure Reason* may well be the real apology for Leibniz, even in opposition to his partisans whose words of praise hardly do him honor. It can also be an apology for many older philosophers about whom certain historians of philosophy, for all the praises they bestow, speak the purest nonsense. They do not understand the *intentions* of these philosophers . . . and are incapable of *looking beyond the language which these philosophers employ to what they intended to say.*[5]

Heidegger does not go nearly so far as Kant's statement suggests. He contents himself not with what Kant "intended" to say but with the import he sees in what Kant did and did not say concerning the problems with which he dealt. From his critical study of Kant's Critique, he derives suggestions for rethinking implications he finds there. In doing this he is making Kant relevant to his own concerns, bringing him back to life by revivifying the philosophic possibilities that are uncovered. He is 'retrieving' him.*

Although Heidegger concerns himself in the Kant-book with a retrieve of Kant as a prime source of his own thinking, it is important to note that he does not limit the idea of a retrieve to any one philosopher. What is essentially involved is the intent to rethink a problem with those who thought it, to take from earlier leads suggestions of alternative development. In *Being and Time,* for example, he is concerned not with the retrieve of a particular philosopher but of a problem, the problem which he describes as the question of the meaning of Being. One may, in view of his early contact with the thought of St. Augustine, suggest that the central concern of a large part of Heidegger's thought is an attempt to retrieve the problem enunciated in the opening quotation of this book, the problem fully summarized in the title of his major book, the problem of the connection between Being and of Time. By the retrieve of a philosophic problem, then, there is to be understood "the disclosure of the [basic] possibilities concealed in it . . . thus preserving it in its import as a problem" for us.[7]

In the retrieve of a particular thinker a certain 'violence' is to be expected. But such a complaint, which he is quite clear in anticipating, misses the point. His intent is not the mere repetition of what Kant had already said, but the elucidation of what he "did not say, could not say, but somehow made manifest."[8] It is, as Heidegger suggests, a "question of examining Kant's efforts to penetrate the dimension of . . . his search for the source-ground of the 'fundamental sources of knowledge' by clarifying the preliminary insight which served him as a guide."[9] It is thus irrelevant to object that Kant is being approached from a new context, subjected to possibly strange criteria or that novel implications are seen in what he had worked out. The task of a retrieve is not to chronicle the past but to wrest out of it a deeper comprehension of our present situation and the possibilities for development it yet offers. The real question of concern is whether significant phil-

* Heidegger's actual word is *Wiederholung,* derived from the verb *wiederholen,* which means literally 'to hold again.' Its usual translation into English as 'repetition' incorrectly suggests a mechanical repeating and does not convey the dynamic 'fetch-back' sense of what is meant. Consequently, I have followed Richardson in using the French derivative 'retrieve.'[6]

osophic insights emerge, or new directions for philosophic development are brought forth, from such an encounter between two thinkers.

Such a project seeks what is still relevant or suggestive in the work of an original thinker from a bygone era. This, in fact, is an attempt to assimilate one's past, to give active recognition to the fact that our culture, our thinking, is essentially historical and comes out of a development which has brought us to the problems and concerns of today; it is to suggest that the problems of present concern are, perhaps, not entirely new, that earlier thinkers may possibly help shed new light on new versions of old problems. Emerson once admonished us to "honor truth by its use"; Heidegger would add that if there is some truth or true insight in a past thinker—or else why do we honor him?—we should use it in terms of present perspectives. We should make his truth our own.

In Heidegger's studies of Kant, then, we expect no pedagogical critical commentary, no external combing for textual inconsistencies; necessarily involved is the attempt to enter *into* Kant's thinking, to rethink the problems *with* him. From the outset, Heidegger's dialogues with Kant are, indeed, from the orientation of Heidegger's concerns. He interrogates Kant with his own questions, questions which he feels were of concern to Kant as well, questions about the attempt to find a new foundation for metaphysics, questions concerning the meaning of Being and of Time, and the consuming question concerning the 'and' between them.

III

The Retrieve of Kant

ANY THINKER functions within a given horizon; this means, from the point of view of a philosophic analysis, that he approaches any problem with certain presuppositions.[1] Heidegger's basic presupposition is acceptance of the general formulation of Kant's problematic and resolution concerning the nature of human knowledge. His inquiry is within its context and the amendments he proposes are within its essential framework.

In generalized terms, Heidegger does not question the prime features of Kant's transcendental idealism. He accepts and seeks to refine them by carrying through some of the analyses which only have meaning within the context of Kant's orientation. This is to say that the only way in which to comprehend what Heidegger is doing is to see him as a Kantian disciple, a disciple who is often quite heretical but whose heresy is essentially within the household of the Kantian way. His dialogue with Kant, his interrogation of Kant, is not an assault from outside; his examination is conducted within the boundaries of the reservation.

Kant, it will be remembered, began the First Critique with the observation that "though all our knowledge begins with experience, it does not follow that it all arises out of experience"; our sense impressions are but the "raw material" of experience.[2] Taken alone they are meaningless because they are without order or in-

ternal relation. In order for our knowledge to have attained the
organization that constitutes it, in order to explain the fact of
science, some other source must provide the principles of universality and necessity, the principles according to which these myriad
sense impressions are rendered into the coherent experience we do,
in fact, have.

Insofar as these operational principles for the organization of
sense impressions are not derived from those sense impressions,
they are, according to Kant, presupposed by our experience and
are thereby apriori,* i.e., not merely "independent of this or that
experience, but . . . absolutely independent of all experience."[3]
These apriori principles are prior to any possible coherent experience—prior in the sense of logical presupposition and not of temporal sequence. They ground experience, make its coherence possible, and cannot be derived as merely probable generalizations
from sensory data.

The elucidation of these apriori principles is a task of transcendental philosophy. The term 'transcendental' must be sharply distinguished from 'transcendent' although both share the general
meaning of 'going beyond the immediately given.' Kant uses the
term 'transcendental' primarily in two senses: (a) in contrast to
'transcendent,' which refers to what is completely beyond experience, "transcendental signifies those apriori elements which underlie experience as its necessary conditions. . . . The transcendental
is that which by conditioning experience renders all knowledge,
whether apriori or empirical, possible"; (b) as 'transcendental
knowledge,' it refers *not* to the knowledge of objects but to our
knowledge of those apriori conditions of our cognition of them.[4]

This term emphatically does not suggest an otherworldly focus;
it does refer not to the content of knowledge but to our *mode* of
knowing, of having knowledge. The word 'transcendental' is
thus used to emphasize that aspect of the mind which is independent of the passive, purely receptive tabula rasa characterization emphasized in classical British empiricism. The term was used
by Kant to emphasize the active and creative contributions of men-

---

* In order to avoid confusion in quotations, etc., concerning the different ways
of printing the word 'apriori,' I have used the form of one unhyphenated
unitalicized word throughout.

tal processes to any knowing-experience. What is to be established as transcendental provides the justification or grounding of any particular knowledge we may attain.

The use of the word is itself justified because it means 'going beyond' any particular bit of knowledge to its ground, to those organizing characteristics of our mode of cognition which makes that particular knowledge possible. In Heidegger's discussion this reference to the transcendental elements of experience is usually expressed by the substitution of the noun 'transcendence' for the adjectival 'transcendental.' The essential Kantian meaning is retained although it is expanded as the conception of experience is expanded to include, but not to be confined to, purely cognitive experience.[5]

In the Kantian formulation there are then two kinds of knowledge: (a) the transcendental knowledge—of those apriori principles which constitute the act of knowing, and (b) empirical knowledge—which is always a synthesis of raw sense impressions as molded or formed by these apriori principles.

The specific apriori principles which provide Kant with the organizational ground of empirical knowledge were presented by him as the 'categories' or 'pure concepts of the understanding'. They are those forms in terms of which we relate and order the chaos of raw sense impressions into meaningful cognition. The chief epistemological concern of the Critique is the demonstration of how these apriori concepts are necessarily applied in the construction of a coherent experience of sense data and, equally important, restricted in their validity to that sense experience.

There are then two elemental constituents which are synthesized in any particular human cognition: the apriori concepts or categories and the apprehended sense impressions themselves.

Kant termed our mode of receiving these impressions with the German word *Anschauung*. Unfortunately, it is habitually translated into English as 'intuition' and this standard English rendering causes all sorts of unnecessary confusion. Its more literal and correct contemporary translation would be 'outlook,' 'looking-at,' 'visualization,' or 'beholding'; its German root is the verb *anschauen,* which means 'to look at'. Strictly speaking, 'intuition-*Anschauung*' applies only to visualization, even if figuratively. But, as Smith pointed out,

Kant extends it to cover sensations of all the senses. The current term was *Empfindung*. Kant's reason for introducing the term intuition [*Anschauung*] in place of sensation was evidently the fact that the latter could not be made to cover space and time. We can speak of pure intuitions, but not of pure sensations.[6]

By focusing not on sense data but on intuitive receptivity, Kant threw the emphasis on the 'how' of experience in terms of our capacity for it rather than on the 'what' in terms of its specific content. Taken in this way, the word 'intuition,' as used in a Kantian context, does *not* contain the notion of instinctive feeling or mystic insight or hunch that often characterizes its current ordinary usage. It should be taken as 'view,' 'out-look' (in its literal sense), or 'perception' (in the broadest sense) as *immediate* knowledge; its concern is not a matter of feeling or conceptual reference but of immediate (i.e., *un*mediated) apprehension of a perceptual object. Its use, as distinct from sensation, throws focus on the *how* rather than the *what* of our apprehending of things. This use of the term is, to some degree, consonant with its historic meaning in the English language and this consonance offers whatever justification there is for the continued use of the term.[7] Kant himself confirmed this interpretation and also clarified the matter when he said:

> In whatever manner and by whatever means a mode of knowledge may relate to objects, *intuition* [*Anschauung*] is that through which it is in immediate relation to them, and to which all thought as a means is directed. But intuition takes place only in so far as the object is given to us. . . . Objects are *given* to us by means of sensibility, and it alone yields us *intuitions;* they are *thought* through the understanding, and from the understanding arise *concepts*. But all thought must, directly or indirectly . . . relate ultimately to intuitions, and therefore, with us, to sensibility.[8]

Intuition is, then, always particular and represents a concrete individual whole; it is always immediate specific apprehension in contrast to thought, which is always general. Intuition always conveys immediacy of apprehension of particular, specific objects which appear to us.

Generally, but not consistently, Kant designated an 'object' as given to us by sensibility and received in intuition as an appearance, viz., insofar as it is undetermined sense perception. When the content of this intuition has been interpreted by the categories, it is usually referred to as a 'phenomenon'; often the word 'representation' covers both.[9] These, it must be emphasized, are but analytic distinctions; they are merely logical distinctions within an essentially unitary cognition and are not to be taken in any sense of sequential order.

In order to make an unambiguous and emphatic distinction between empirical knowledge as such and our knowledge of the apriori grounds of that knowledge, viz., transcendental knowledge, Kant used a simple word in a special sense: the word 'pure (*rein*).' 'Pure' focuses attention on and underlines the fact that the word is used as nonempirical: 'pure' means independence of particular experiential content; it refers to the pre-empirical and is "the absolutely apriori."[10] Its use signifies what is held to arise out of the mind itself without derivation from, and as the logically prior presupposition of, any possible particular experience. Thus 'pure intuition'—which might first seem to be an impossibility—refers not to any specific empirical awareness but to the essential characterization of *any* empirical awareness (e.g., the forms of space and time). 'Pure reason' (which is in the title of the Critique) thus means pre-empirical reason, "reason in so far as it supplies out of itself, independently of [particular] experience, apriori elements that as such are characterized by universality and necessity."[11] A 'pure concept' is a category of the understanding, viz., a concept produced out of the mind itself and contributed as an ingredient of experience, but not extricated from it; an 'empirical concept,' in contrast, would be an aposteriori generalization from specific experiences.

We thus are only able to have (a) knowledge of things as they appear to us, i.e., empirical knowledge which necessarily embodies a synthesis of (1) sensory intuitions and (2) apriori organizing concepts, and (b) transcendental knowledge of the ways or 'forms' in which sense impressions may be apprehended and of those apriori concepts themselves by means of which our cognition of these apprehended objects is organized. We do not and cannot—and this is an essentially basic theme of the Critical philosophy—have any knowledge of things as they may be independently of the way in which they can appear to us; we cannot know things as they are in themselves apart from the ways in which they can be known. Insofar as we will be concerned with examining Kant's formulation of the structure of the two kinds of knowledge we *do* have, this realm of the things-in-themselves will not engage our prime attention.

If one shares this conviction of Kant's—as Heidegger does—that cognitive experience is based not on mere passive perception of physical objects but on the perception of entities as they appear to human sensibility and are interpreted, *in* the process of perceiving them, by means of apriori universal principles or categories which we 'impose' on these raw perceptions in order to cognize them— a crucial problem of the objectivity of empirical knowledge looms before us. If the world we seek to know is not merely 'out-there' but is, as we come to know it, in every sense an interpretive construction of the human mind, we face the question of just what it is that we are talking about when we talk about objects, things, entities.

Kant's problem was to establish, alongside this subjective 'prison' of the subjective constituents of all knowledge, the possibility of meaningful objectivity in the kind of knowledge we do have or can possibly obtain. His method was to bring to light those constituent elements in any empirical cognition which are not the 'given' data but are the apriori principles, organizing categories, or pure concepts contributed by the mind. Insofar as these are seen as embodying necessary universality and universal necessity, Kant believed that a complete explication of their nature and employment would elucidate the nature of cognitive objectivity in the kind of knowledge which we, as human beings, are able to have.

Dependent upon definable constituent aspects of human thought, human knowledge is thus limited by definition to the context of the capacities and modes of data-organization of human cognitive processes. This is to say that Kant sought the ground of human objectivity in a conception of the nature of human reasoning, in a conception of the nature of man. Heidegger, working within the context of Kantian thought, is in full accord; despite their somewhat divergent conceptions of just how the nature of man is to be delineated, there is agreement that knowledge, and what knowledge can provide, is necessarily rooted in human nature, however human nature be finally described.

Now Kant's avowed motivation in exploring this essentially epistemological problem must be recalled. Deep in that same human nature within which the possibility of knowledge is grounded, Kant found that concern with metaphysical questions was a prominent and "natural disposition" [12] common to all human thought. Reflective human reason, he noted, 'is burdened by questions which it is not able to ignore because they are prescribed by the nature of reason itself; and also it is not able to answer them because they transcend all the faculties* of human reason.' [13] The realm of these magnetic and yet unanswerable questions is the battlefield of metaphysical disputation. These metaphysical concerns have evoked passionate controversies of speculative opinion. The persistent raising of these questions has not been dampened by the historic lack of determinate answers; this unsatisfied persistence, then, would seem to confirm the belief that this metaphysical bent is deeply imbedded in that same human reason which is the source of human knowledge.

This persistent metaphysical questioning led Kant to raise the crucial question, "How is metaphysics, as science, possible?" [14] Concerned to end idle debate, the Critical philosophy was explicitly developed to provide an answer to this question; Kant's method, characteristically, was to determine the proper *limits* within which a rigorous metaphysics could be developed. As Lewis White Beck has pointed out, Kant saw that "the proper business of metaphysics is *Grundlegung,* not *Erweiterung,* laying the foundations, not expanding the wings of the edifice of knowledge." He reminds us of Kant's insistence that "the task of the metaphysician 'consists in discerning whether the task [of inquiring into the hidden qualities of things] be within the limits of our knowledge, and in stating its relations to conceptions derived from experience. . . . To this extent, metaphysics is *the science of the boundaries of human reason.'* " [15]

---

* Although the word 'faculty' is used throughout, it must not be forgotten that it is a translation of the German *Vermögen,* which as a verb form means 'to be able, to have the capacity or power to perform an act.' The English noun 'faculty' should then be understood in the nonsubstantive sense of an inherent capability, not as some kind of thing.

Kant's clearly declared goal, then, is the refounding of metaphysics as a rigorous discipline which can "finish its work and bequeath it to posterity as a capital to which no addition can be made. Since it is a fundamental science it is under obligation to achieve this completeness." [16] The First Critique is then, by explicitly defined intent, a deliberate attempt to provide a foundation for systematic metaphysical inquiry. Its method is to establish the ground of possibility for objectivity in human cognition so that the inherent limitations and proper modes for the legitimate employment of human reason may be defined.

Heidegger thus does no more than simply take Kant at his word —as concerned to ground metaphysical thinking. This is the essential Kantian problematic which he seeks to retrieve. His task, he announces as the opening statement of his own study, "is to explicate Kant's *Critique of Pure Reason* as a laying of the foundation of metaphysics. . . ." [17]

At the outset he accepts the leading Kantian themes: the formulation of the problem of knowledge, the grounding of its possibility in human nature, the describing of limitations and thereby the finitude of human reason, the radically new Kantian orientation embodied in the Copernican Revolution. He follows Kant in seeking to discover the ground of metaphysics from an examination of the nature and inherent limitations of human knowledge and the kind of objectivity that it is able to attain. Although Heidegger's formulations will finally go beyond the Kantian inquiry, both find the foundation of valid metaphysical thinking in the nature of human reasoning, in the question: 'What is man?' [18]

Heidegger also follows Kant here by declining to build a metaphysical system. Rather he seeks to trace the outline, the "limits and design of the intrinsic possibility of metaphysics" [19] itself. He follows the precedent of the First Critique—in declining to fill out the content of valid metaphysical doctrine, in confining this inquiry to seeking out its foundation. *Being and Time* is in large measure this 'filling out'; for this reason, Heidegger's Kantian inquiry serves not only as a historical but also as a systematic prolegomena to it. In like manner *Being and Time* can be regarded as providing the ontological grounding of the general nature of the Kantian epistemology; for Heidegger suggests that to the extent that the First Critique contains within itself the grounding of metaphysics, the foundation of metaphysics will have been firmly established in the process of interpreting Kant's work.

His interest in Kant, then, is not primarily as an epistemologist but is in accord with Kant's own understanding of the intent, purpose, and justification of the Critical inquiry as providing the foundation for rigorous metaphysical inquiry. Heidegger's interpretation of the Critique is thus explicitly keyed to the problematic of laying the foundation of metaphysics.

Because Kant's road to the foundation of metaphysics is that of an essentially epistemological critique, so Heidegger seeks out of Kant's theory of knowledge that ontological region which serves as its ground. Starting with the problematic posed by the Copernican Revolution, the focus is on the transcendental imagination Kant had posited at the center of any cognitive act. By means of a rigorous exegetical study of the prime 'moments' of Kant's doctrine of the transcendental elements in human knowledge, Heidegger examines the relationship between the transcendental imagination and experiential time which Kant had placed together at the center of the possibility of cognition. Only after this careful textual study can we move on with assurance to the broader philosophical implications which result from his analysis.

In a real sense, the structure of his Kant-book parallels that of *Being and Time* (and to some extent that of the Critique itself). The first major division of *Being and Time* is an analysis of the apriori elements constituting human existence generally; its second half seeks to 'dig' to a deeper foundation which grounds that analysis. So here the first task is an analysis of Kant's analytic of human cognition, the "execution" of the Kantian retrieve; the second major division displays the "results" of the retrieve, the broader ontological foundation for the possibility of human knowledge which Kant had been concerned to define.

As Heidegger follows Kant through the first part of the Critique, so I follow him (bringing in other essays as they are relevant). Only in this way can we consider the evidence he presents for the conclusions he urges on us.

In this philosophic journey Norman Kemp Smith's admonition

might well be kept in mind: "It is always safer to take Kant quite literally. He nearly always means exactly what he says at the time that he says it." [20] This not only describes Heidegger's handling of the Kantian text; it is also good counsel for the reading of Heidegger.

I V

The Copernican Revolution

as Ontology

THE REVOLUTION which Kant had wrought is summed up in the Copernican Revolution. It is Kant's central issue; in it are focused the various strands of thought and the entire problematic Kant had sought to resolve. Heidegger's ultimate Kantianism is to be seen here; for deeply rooted in Kant's Copernican Revolution is Heidegger's insistence on ontology as the central concern of philosophic reflection.

Quite clearly Kant envisaged the task set forth by the Copernican Revolution to be one of metaphysical concern. As he said in the First Edition Preface of the First Critique, "In this enquiry . . . I venture to assert that there is not a single metaphysical problem which has not been solved, or for the solution of which the key has not been supplied." [1] Virtually the entire Second Edition Preface would support Heidegger's claim—in full awareness of the contrary tradition—that to ignore Kant's metaphysical problematic and the context of the Critique is to misinterpret the work from the outset. [2]

Kant's Copernican Revolution reversed the 'common-sense' view of the relationship between the knowing subject and the object known. Just because it locates the ground of any knowledge of any subject within the knowing subject, Kant's revolution represents, as Heidegger recognized, the first serious attack on the traditional approach to insight into the nature of things by focusing on that which is to be known.[3] For Kant, in contrast to the Aristotelian tradition, thought does *not* know the thing itself without any intermediary;[4] thought merely structures what sense intuition 'reports.' The concept is *not* "necessarily in conformity with its object";[5] the Copernican Revolution proclaims the reverse: it is the object that, to be known, must conform to the knowing requirements of the knower. One need but review the opening chapters of Aristotle's *Metaphysics* to note the complete reversal of orientation. If one recognizes Thomism as a "continuation and amplification"[6] of Aristotelian realism, one can surely appreciate the force of Gilson's relevant insight: "Today our only choice is . . . Kant or Thomas Aquinas. All the other positions are but halfway houses. . . ."[7]

Kant has thus brought us to the point where the ground of the presence or absence of an object in knowledge is to be seen within the nature of the knower; he thus opened that new philosophic gateway through which we may proceed to seeking a "metaphysics of the subject."[8] The Critique offers us the insight that for us to have any particular bit of knowledge we must employ the cognitive apriori concepts which "prior to the object being given"[9] define that knowledge as, indeed, possible. For something to be an object of our knowledge it must conform to the conditions of our knowledge which permit it to be cognized by us. For something to be regarded as an existent thing, the apriori constitution of our knowing processes—the transcendental laws governing the synthesizing operation of our immediate apprehensions and our pure concepts or categories—must 'permit' it to be recognized as such.

To take an empirical perceptual example, our ears can only 'hear,' i.e., have an immediate awareness of, sound waves of between 50 and 15,000 cycles per second. We have, by mediated inference, reasoned that there must be other sound waves, and we make simple dog whistles geared to the sound-reception capabilities of canines, but not of men, so that dogs can be summoned home without disturbing men. For the normal human, that sound which his dog can hear, he cannot. For the human who is concerned neither with his wandering dog nor with scientific sound-wave investigation, that sound which his dog hears cannot enter his immediate sound perception and thereby it cannot exist or be or have being *qua* heard-sound for him. For any sound to be, as such, in the sense of *immediate* sensory intuition—which both Kant and Heidegger have emphasized as necessary to the empiricism of experience—it must be within the range of our possible auditory perceptive capacity. Thus, if I say, "I hear a whistle," I am claiming that the sound of the whistle exists for me,* that it has being* in my present *immediate* experience; it may be presumed with certainty that the sound *is** within the range of human, if not canine, auditory capacity.

The be-ing of any object within our experience thus justifies the presumption that it conforms to those cognitive conditions which render experience of it possible. It can be described as coming

---

* Two German forms of the infinitive verb 'to be' are essential to Heidegger's discussion: *Sein* and *Seiende*. The usual translations are 'Being (abstract)' and 'being (specific thing).' Neither succeeds in avoiding ambiguity or in conveying the essential dynamic nuance of meaning. Moreover, to translate the infinitive *sein* by a noun form encourages the erroneous tendency to treat it as a 'thing' instead of an 'act' and also violates all sense of grammar. To comprehend the full force of these verb forms, it is essential to remember that the German word for 'verb' is *Zeitwort* ('time-word'—the answer to the question 'when?').

Despite Heidegger's later fascination with the form 'is,' the only appropriate translation of *sein* seems to be the literal one of 'to-be,' and of *das Sein* 'the to-be' (as suggested by Heidegger himself). For his use of these words usually conveys something of the dynamic contingency and problematic of Hamlet's question. 'The to-be' is often cumbersome; alternatively, I have rendered it as 'being-status' or by the hyphenated 'be-ing.' The hyphen conveys something of the time-binding sense of the English progressive tense and forewarns against the substantive sense of a noun. The progressive-present—which conveys temporality together with a 'spread' through time—does not exist in German; its absence seems to contribute to a number of Heidegger's circumlocutions as it is usually in this progressive sense that he seems to use forms of the verb 'to be.' Ironically, English does not extend the progressive-present to the verb 'to be' itself, and this lack contributes to some unavoidable circumlocution in an English rendering.

With regard to *Seiende,* it is crucial to note that this is a verb form; it should remind us of the Leibnizian principle that to-be is to-be-an-activity, that any existent is an act of be-ing. The best rendering might be 'existent' except for the confusion this invites with the special meaning Heidegger attaches to the word 'existence' (cf. VII, 2). Consequently, it is often rendered by 'thing that is,' occasionally by 'being(s),' more often by 'object' or 'thing' in the most minimal sense demanded by the condition that for an 'x' to be an 'object' or 'thing' it must be such for, or within, human cognition; when this qualification is lacking or not implicit, the neutral word 'entity' has been used instead. (Some translations use the word 'essent,' for which I have consistently substituted in all quotations where it would otherwise appear.)[10]

within the limitations of those characterizations which mark out the capacity for experience that we, as human beings, have. If objects must conform to our cognitive requirements to be known by us, their status as perceived or known is thereby, by definition, confined within the limitations *of what we can* perceive, of what we can know. To the extent that we can know an entity, it must conform to the transcendental grounds of our cognizability.

The meaning of the Copernican Revolution, then, is this insight that all knowledge of the particular things that are in our field of cognitive vision is dependent on the *pre*requisite for something to be, to be knowable, for us. For something to be an object for us, the way it 'appears,' and if it 'appears' at all, is determined "in advance" of that object's appearing by the capacity of our cognitive faculties to perceive it and by the manner in which we are able to perceive it, become aware of it, cognize it. Heidegger cites the famous passage from the B Preface:

> reason has insight only into that which it produces after a plan of its own, and that it must not allow itself to be kept, as it were, in nature's leading-strings, but must itself show the way with principles of judgment based upon fixed laws, constraining nature to give answer to questions of reason's own determining.[11]

What Kant had in effect asserted, Heidegger points out, was the necessity of passing beyond the constitution of the be-ing of objects to the laws of human cognition which prescribe the conditions for appearing within our experience. Before we can determine the being-status of particular things as they appear to us, we necessarily invoke the laws governing our cognition, governing and setting the conditions of the possibility of a thing to be, to be present, to come into being within our experiential realm. We necessarily invoke these cognitional laws in any cognition whether or not we are aware of them or of our utilization of them.

When we invoke these transcendental apriori laws of our possibility of how-and-what we can know, we are concerned with the condition and the nature of be-ing, of the meaning that is intended in the verb 'to-be.' We thus find ourselves entering into that branch of metaphysical thought which has been concerned with the meaning and nature of be-ing as such and has generally been termed 'ontology.' Metaphysical concern with particular or special kinds of beings was traditionally divided into theology (concerning the being-status of the divine being), cosmology (concerned with the being-status of the entities within nature), and rational psychology (the concern with the state of being of the human soul). In each of these traditional areas of concern, attention was focused on the 'whether' and on the 'how' of the particular kind of entity being investigated. Each of these areas of 'special metaphysics' is clearly and traditionally delineated from 'general metaphysics,' which is concerned with what it means to-be as such, with ontology.[12]

In coming to the portal of questions of ontology, Heidegger has suggested the import of the Copernican Revolution: instead of seeking to abstract the nature of being-in-general from a study of particular or special kinds of being, ontology or 'general metaphysics' is necessarily prior just because it is concerned with the general question of what it means to-be, what it means for any object to have the status of being within the ken of human knowledge. It is only after the grounds which render it possible for an entity to appear to human awareness, to come into the focus of human cognition, are determined, that we can legitimately discuss the particular being-status of the particular objects that meet our prime requirements for appearing to us.

For Kant these conditions for something to have the possibility of existing within our circle of awareness, of becoming manifest to us, were the apriori transcendental constituents of our cognizing 'faculties'; these transcendental conditions are to be found in the synthetic unity of our 'pure' (pre-empirical) intuition and the 'pure' concepts of our understanding. These transcendental apriori conditions are, it will be remembered, not particulars, but general, universal, and necessary. Failure to recognize the necessary priority of these apriori grounds for any cognition, Kant had suggested, was responsible for the failure of metaphysical inquiry.

Our knowledge of these pre-experiential grounds of cognitive experience is, in Kant's terminology, "transcendental knowledge." In Heidegger's reformulation, as a consequence of the reasoning just outlined, this "transcendental knowledge" is translated into the term "ontological knowledge," i.e., the knowledge of the non-experiential (or Kantian apriori transcendental) grounds for any particular thing to-be capable of being known to us.

[28]

Similarly, just as Kant regarded any empirical knowledge as a particular bit of information, and any particular intuition as the particular immediate apprehension of a particular individual object, so Heidegger has rendered this experiential particularity by the word 'ontic.' An ontic investigation, then, would be one concerning particular facts, actual specific occurrences, and empirical generalizations from them. An ontological investigation, on the other hand, as a Kantian transcendental investigation, would be directed toward the general, universal, and necessary grounds upon which, or limits within which, any ontic, or empirical, experience can occur. The transcendental or ontological is thus logically prior to, and renders possible, empirical or ontic objects or events.

An ontic discussion, then, deals with particular, individual, actual things or situations; it is directed toward the specific objects of empirical cognition. An 'ontological' discussion, in contrast, is concerned with what makes that particular experience itself possible—the general structures, pervasive conditions, limiting possibilities within which any actual experience is necessarily contained. It thus delimits those qualities or characterizations of any possible objects which may appear to us within the range of the transcendental modes of human cognition. By defining, in advance of any experience, what attributes it is possible for an object-in-our-experience to have, one thus defines the possible ways in which an object can *be* for us in the knowledge of it which we are able to have.*

What Heidegger has seen Kant as having accomplished in the Copernican Revolution, without necessarily being aware of it, was the demonstration of the possibility of real ontological knowledge. He cites Kant's own statement of the Copernican Revolution and focuses our attention on one passage: conforming our objects to our knowledge "would agree better with what is desired, namely, that it should be possible to have knowledge of objects apriori *determining something in regard to them prior to their being given.*" [13]

The "something in regard to them prior to their being given"

---

* It is here, incidentally, that Heidegger grounds another consequence of the Copernican Revolution, the reversal of the traditional priority of 'actuality' over 'potency,' a reversal inherently implicated in his conception of time (see VIII, 3).

is precisely what Kant had called the "transcendental conditions of knowledge" and what Heidegger refers to when he discusses the object of ontological knowledge, the constitutional prerequisites imposed by the human mind on any object as a condition for it to be known, i.e., to have the possibility of affirmative being-status within the horizon or limitation of human cognition.

The pure intuitions of space and time prescribing the 'forms' of any particular, or ontic, intuitions and the schematized categories and their modes of synthesis—in the Kantian scheme of things—combine to permit, or qualify, particular experiences to take place, to have reality, to be actual for us. In Heidegger's vocabulary-transformation of Kant, this is to say that these transcendental conditions of any particular possible experience are the ontological grounds of the possibility for any entity to-be, to be actual, to have be-ing for us. These transcendental conditions are the ontological constituents of any particular object, of the possibility for being-status of any thing that is *in* our experience. If we follow this vocabulary-transformation it is apparent that Heidegger has given us a fair summary of Kantian doctrine when he says, "By this Kant means: not 'all knowledge' is ontic, and where such knowledge is given, it is possible only through ontological knowledge." [14] Just as for Kant any empirical knowledge is predicated on transcendental conditions, so for Heidegger any particular or ontic knowledge is predicated on ontological conditions or qualifications whether explicitly acknowledged or unconsciously presumed. When we seek to explicate these conditions for something to-be for us, these necessary characterizations of things to appear to us, we are seeking ontological knowledge, i.e., knowledge of the transcendental grounds which are presupposed in particular ontic experiences.

The prime feature of the Copernican Revolution, then, was this insistence that for an object to exist for us, it must be conformed to the conditions requisite for knowing it:

> But this necessity expresses precisely the dependence of the empirical object with regard to ontological knowledge, and it is this dependence which will permit, in the empirical order, that the object and knowledge should conform to each other and be able to be gauged in accordance with each other. [15]

It is crucial to note that the transcendental and ontological conditions for any object to appear to human cognition are the same conditions. Viewed from the side of the perceiving subject, the conditions are transcendental; from the side of the object they are ontological. But, however regarded, their source is in us. Because the possibility of knowing the objects-that-are in our experience constitutes the be-ing of these objects for us, the knowledge of these necessary characterizations of objects as known, in advance of any particular encounter, is a knowledge of their ontological characteristics, namely, ontological knowledge. It is in this sense that the possibility of ontological knowledge, the knowledge of what it means 'to-be,' is rooted in human nature (as Kant would have put it); it is in this essentially Kantian sense that ontology becomes Heidegger's central concern.

This is to say that the Critique is not to be regarded as primarily an epistemological treatise or a theory of the natural sciences. Either interpretation would seem to reduce the Critique to merely one consequence of itself. The Critique provides for both epistemology and for science without being reducible to either. If, however, one persists in regarding it as an essentially epistemological study, then Heidegger would counter: it only can be justifiable to do so if it is regarded as a study of that ontological knowledge which is presupposed by all ontic experience (or, in Kant's terminology, the transcendental grounds of any possible empirical cognition); for we require a logically, if not temporally prior knowledge (even if preconceptual) of what it means for something to be for us before we can know that a thing *is* within our experience. By clarifying "the complete outline of a system of metaphysics," [16] Kant had directed our attention not to the particular things which we cognize but to the necessary conditions of the things that do appear to us for them to be able to appear to us.

Heidegger has thus given us a new perspective on the Critique as an ontological propaedeutic to 'every future metaphysics.' The emphasis and interpretation, as well as the implications to be drawn, are his own—but an ontological focus is neither that revolutionary nor unique. Kemp Smith, for example, has insisted that "the ontological . . . aspect of consciousness . . . must be constantly borne in mind if the Critical standpoint is to be properly viewed"; and he found the source of the Hegelian misreading of Kant to arise from a reduction of Kant's doctrine to a part of itself: "To eliminate the ontological implications of his theory of consciousness is, by anticipation, to render many of his main conclusions entirely untenable." [17] Gottfried Martin has joined Heidegger in declaring that "Kant's final intention . . . is directed toward an ontology, a doctrine of being." [18] Actually, they both go much further than Heidegger in regarding the Critique not merely as the preparation of an ontology but as already being and providing one.[19] Whatever question there might conceivably be concerning this kind of characterization, it would seem plain that it is in accord with the whole direction of development of Kant's thought; as de Vleeschauwer has pointed out,

> Considered materially, metaphysics corresponds to ontology or to the study of the whole domain of apriori knowledge without distinction of type, so that the distinction earlier established between it and transcendental philosophy disappears almost completely. This ontology can be applied primarily to determinate objects. . . .[20]

Kant had defined transcendental knowledge as that knowledge "which is occupied not so much with objects as with the mode of our knowledge of objects insofar as this mode of knowledge is to be possible apriori." [21] Heidegger has generally transformed the adjectival 'transcendental' into the noun 'transcendence.' Thus the capacity for transcendence, for going beyond particular sense data, for going beyond the given, for invoking the transcendental ground of the possibility of knowledge, is necessarily prerequisite to any particular knowledge. This transcendence is requisite to, and provides the possibility for, any ontic knowledge regardless of whether it is unconsciously invoked, consciously presupposed, or deliberately applied. When this transcendence, this capacity to invoke and utilize the transcendental grounds of knowledge is itself examined, we attain to transcendental knowledge, i.e., knowledge of the transcendental grounds of our ability to know things, knowledge of the ontological grounds of their appearing as such to us. The transcendental and ontological grounds are the same, be it remembered, the former from the side of the knower, the latter from the side of the thing that is known.

To look ahead, the confirmation of this parallelism is to be seen in what Kant had called the Highest Principle of All Synthetic Judgments, and which Heidegger regards not only as summing up the core of the Critical doctrine but as explicating the justification of his own explicitly ontological interpretation. If knowledge is to have objective reference and not to consist in empty concepts, Kant had pointed out, the "object must be capable of being in some manner given." [22] Without objects of cognition there would be no knowledge, no experience, and even our notions of space and time would be empty and thereby meaningless. The reality of our knowledge is dependent upon prior possibility; it is defined by that possibility. What we do know is known because it accords with the transcendental grounds defining the possibility of our knowing. What we do know is further dependent upon the possibility of bringing concepts into unity with the objects represented as the content of our knowledge. It is, as Kant put it, "the *possibility of experience* . . . [that] gives objective reality to all our apriori modes of knowledge." [23] This possibility of experience derives from the principles which define our modes of synthesizing representations and concepts apriori; as exemplified in the Schematism, these pure concepts are actually operative as time-related synthesizing and organizing principles of cognition.

Actual experience is formulated in empirical judgments deriving from the unification of the field or manifold in which our perceptions occur. This unification itself occurs within the limits set by apriori rules, within that experiential range defined as possible. It is from this prior possibility of a given experience that its objectivity derives. Thus, "the highest principle of all synthetic judgments is therefore this: every object stands under the necessary conditions of synthetic unity of the manifold of intuition in a possible experience." [24] Apriori synthesizing principles are possible when the formal pre-experiential conditions of apriori intuition, imaginative synthesis, and apperceptive unity are related to a possible empirical field. Thus, "the conditions of the *possibility of experience* in general are likewise [at the same time: *zugleich*] conditions of the *possibility of the object of experience*. . . ." [25]

Kant's Highest Principle, as Heidegger has rightly insisted, combines our capacity to understand the modes of our own cognition and our ability to attribute ontological characterizations to the objects we cognize. The parallelism between the transcendental grounds of knowledge and the ontological conditions for something to appear as such in that knowledge is, within Kantian terms, complete.

Our knowledge, then, of the necessary characterizations of the things-that-are for us is ontological knowledge; the capacity for this knowledge is the basic root of the activation of our capacity to go from the given in experience to the conditions of its possibility, from the fact of experience to its constituent structure within us. "Nothing in apriori knowledge," as Kant asserted, "can be ascribed to objects save what the thinking subject derives from itself." [26] Ontological knowledge is the ground of the empirical or ontic; it is recognition of the limits of our possible experience and these limits arise from the limitations which we *qua* humans necessarily prescribe to it. Ontological knowledge, then, is concerned only with those universal principles of our mental operation and their intrinsic self-imposed limitations; ontological knowledge has been taken by Heidegger to denote that immanent structure of knowledge which the human mind projects as the *pre*requisite for any experiential content.

The philosophy of the Critique is thus seen by Heidegger as a 'metaphysics of experience' in that it seeks to go beyond common sense in order to bring to light the fundamental structure necessarily present in any ontic experience. In the structural elements of human reason the Critique has sought out the apriori conditions of the possibility for us to have knowledge of what is requisite for something to-be for us. This is to say that the essential point to be extricated from the Critical doctrine is that ontology is the center of metaphysics and in Kant's landmark work "is provided with a foundation and, for the first time, revealed for what it is in itself." [27]

The central concern of the Critical inquiry becomes for Heidegger that of the nature of our capacity to go from the given to its conditions of being cognized by us. It thus demands an examination of our capacity for transcendence, i.e., our capacity to achieve ontological knowledge, knowledge of the nature and the conditions of the being-status of the things-that-are or can be in human experience. Empirical or ontic knowledge can only arise within the limitations of the transcendental (or ontological) limitations imposed by our cognitive processes. It is this concern which Kant had summed up in his quest for the possibility of synthetic apriori judgments. This question, Heidegger agrees, is the key one for metaphysical inquiry. The goal of Heidegger's attempt to reexamine the Kantian effort is to seek out the source-ground of our capacity for apriori synthesis, the Kantian source of the possibility of our knowledge. For Heidegger, as for Kant, this synthesis is what constitutes the human ability to discover, within itself, its capacity for transcending raw given data. Insight into the nature of this synthesis enables us to understand the transcendental structure of our mode of cognition, the ontological structure of things as we can know them, and thus of the possibility and essential structure of our particular empirical or ontic cognitions.

The focus of metaphysical inquiry is thus shifted from the specific things-that-are to the grounds of their be-ing for us. Focusing on this immanent ontology—what is termed in the early Heidegger "fundamental ontology"—the task becomes that of systematic inquiry into the apriori grounds of possible human knowledge. Such inquiry elicits the justification, as Kant had pointed out, of the existential assertions we can make with certainty. Metaphysics, as ontological investigation, thereby defines the possibility, structure, and possible extent of the actual specific experience we do or can, indeed, have. By defining and justifying the universal categoreal limitations on what the content of our experience can be, it proposes the necessary determinations for the character requisite for any particular entity in order for it to enter into our experience. It thus defines the ontological characterizations of the objects which are manifest to us in terms of the transcendental grounds of our capacity to become aware of them.

For Kant the possibility of metaphysics was to be found in the synthetic unity of the human 'faculties' of cognition. Heidegger has interpreted this to mean that for Kant, as for himself, "the question of the basis of metaphysics is equivalent to the question concerning the true nature of man or, more specifically, of human reason." [28] Our ability to comprehend the nature and the structure of our world is dependent on our understanding of the ways in which we can know it. Our ability to have knowledge of objects is dependent on the ways in which we can recognize them as such. The human mode of cognition is the key to what can be discerned as the content of cognition. The limitations of human cognition thus impose limitations on what can appear in that cognition. The manner in which human cognition functions determines how appearances can arise for it. The possibility of a metaphysical description of the structure of the world we know is dependent on the world we can recognize as existing or being *for us*. Metaphysics then rests on ontology, on an immanent or fundamental ontology which describes the ways in which the necessary structure of human cognition is able to recognize the things-that-are present to it, the ways in which it ascribes the status of be-ing to what it takes as real.

Kant's avowed intent was the discovery of the ground upon which a rigorous metaphysics could be built in the light of the Copernican Revolution. He pursued this goal by exploring the nature of, and the presuppositions found in, human knowledge. The characteristics necessarily possessed by any object in order for it to be within human experience were identified as those apriori constituents defining the possibility, extent, and inherent operational limitations of human cognition itself. These transcendental grounds of human knowledge thus comprise the modes of be-ing of any object insofar as it can be known. As such, they constitute the ontological determinations of any object within human experience.

This rooting of metaphysics in ontology and the grounding of ontology in the structure of human cognition is, for Heidegger, the revolutionary import of the Copernican Revolution Kant had wrought.

V

The Execution of

the Retrieve

THE KANTIAN CRITIQUE proceeded out of the thesis that human knowledge emerges from a synthesis of sensory intuition and conceptual understanding. It is, Kant had stated, "only through their union, however, that knowledge can arise." [1] Heidegger accepts this as basic and points us to the consequent questions: what is the nature of this union? what is the origin of these two components of human knowledge?

Kant had recognized but bypassed the second question. The two essential components of cognition, he observed, "perhaps spring from a common, but to us unknown root." [2] He proposed to begin his inquiry only "from the point at which the common root of our faculty of knowledge divides and throws out [these] two stems. . . ." [3] But this second question is crucial: this 'common root' must be unearthed. If, indeed, sense and thought have a common source, we can only comprehend them if we can discover from whence they spring. When we perceive their origin(s) we can begin to understand how they come to be, how they function in union. To leave their source(s) hidden or unknown, Heidegger insists, subverts the entire structure of human knowledge which depends upon them.

As Kant had left it, the Critical inquiry did not explore this common root though it pointed it out; enunciating no first principle of knowledge, reason, or ontology, it nevertheless proceeded in full consciousness of, and pointed itself toward, this unknown. Heidegger's quest is for this unknown imbedded in Kant's Critique, this unknown common root of the two elements of our knowledge; this quest animates his interrogation, and provides the criteria of emphases and of development. Why is it so important to bring the common root to light? Because, according to a Kantian epistemology, it is the source and origin of our ability to have a unified experience. In order to comprehend the things that appear to us within that experience it is necessary to elucidate the unity of sensibility and thought which constitutes cognition. We can only determine "the essence of ontological knowledge"--the apriori criteria for characterizing as actual the things that do appear to us—by comprehending the constituting structure of "the sources which make it possible." [4]

I · *Cognitional Finitude*

KANT'S PRIME PRESUPPOSITION in his explication of knowledge must be kept in mind: the postulation of human finitude as exemplified in the crucial characterization of human reason as finite. This finitude, Heidegger argues, is neither a matter of the actual limits of knowledge or of our lack of certainty; they are the results of our finitude, not its cause, and ensue from the inherent structure of human reasoning. Human reasoning is finite just because it is not self-contained or self-dependent: although it organizes the data of sensibility into coherent experience, it is not able to provide that data itself. Reason is essentially and necessarily dependent for filling its concepts with meaning on what sensory intuition reports. It cannot nourish itself. It has no other source on which to feed than the "raw material" which the senses provide for it. As Kant emphatically insisted in the opening sentence of the body of the Critique: "In whatever manner and by whatever means a mode of knowledge may relate to objects, *intuition* is that through which it is in immediate relation to them and from which all thought gains its material." [5]

From this essential empiricism with which the Critique begins, Heidegger permits no withdrawal. Whatever else a Critical doctrine of transcendence may be, it must be at least this Critical empiricism. Allowing no diminution, equivocation, or compromise of this priority of the sensory in the formation of knowledge, Heidegger's essential criticism of Kant starts here. He is to protest, repeatedly, whenever Kant seems to yield to the temptation of diluting the priority of the sensory in some kind of rationalistic formula. Whatever nonsensory elements may be demonstrated as essential to experience—and the focus on transcendental-ontological characteristics may often *seem* to obscure this – the ultimate focus of any knowledge is its essential reference to the particular perceptions or appearances represented in sense intuition.

Kant opened the Critique with the emphatic declaration of the precedence of sense intuition before conceptual thought but he promptly proceeded to the assertion of their coequality: 'Neither of these qualities is preferable to the other.' [6] His reiteration of the equal import—the dualism—of sense and thought underlies the structure of Kant's Analytic. But, as Heidegger insists, the opening statement of the Critique not only contradicts the whole theme of coequal duality; it implies that these two components of knowledge are *not* coequal. Knowledge is primarily involved in sense intuition. It is, he says, "a thinking intuition . . . [that] defines the true essence of knowledge." As Kant had said, pure concepts are only *"forms of thought* which . . . apart, therefore, from the only intuition that is possible for us . . . have even less meaning that the pure sensible forms." [7] Despite their essential interdependence, it is sense intuition, which sustains the "immediate relation to the object," [8] and not conceptual thought that provides the center of cognition.

This point is crucial. As Heidegger says, it must "be hammered in." [9] Here is the heart of Kant's revolution, the Critical revolution which repudiated rationalist metaphysics without succumbing to the ambiguities of a mere sense-data empiricism.

The Critical doctrine disavows that excessive rationalism which saw sense percepts as a jumbled kind of knowledge calling for reduction, by an analytic logic, into clear and distinct ideas. Autonomous reason is not sovereign: human rationality is essentially dependent for content upon what sense intuition can provide. The Critical comprehension of reason is that its competence is, in essence, limited and is "essentially grounded in pure intuition and sensibility":[10] in advance it is confined to the *ways* in which sense impressions may be apprehended and to the content they provide. The significance of this thesis cannot be overlooked: as Heidegger points out, "This essential definition of knowledge is the first and completely decisive blow against rational metaphysics . . . thought belongs to intuition and in such a way that it stands in the service of intuition."[11] It is for reason of this apriori radical limitation of the understanding to what can be apprehended that Kant disavowed the tradition of speculative metaphysics; it is for this reason that he dismissed the traditional doctrines of speculative reason as "transcendental illusion."

Essential to Kant's critique of pure reason is this point: cognition is essentially interpretive of sensory reports. "Cognition is primarily intuition";[12] sense intuition is essentially particular; it refers to specific objects. In sharpest contrast, a concept can only point to that object as an example of some common and general trait. The 'reality' of a particular experience emanates from the singular object that is, and as it is, reported in intuition. Just because a concept generalizes, it can*not* comprehend the particular object in its essential singularity; it can only relate it in terms of what seem to be common attributes with other objects seen as similar. Conceptual thought functions only to explain the kinds of things that are reported in sense intuitions. Concepts do not refer directly to things; they are, the Copernican Revolution asserts, merely ways or modes by which to relate one human percept to another in order to understand them.

Knowledge cannot, then, be seen as a function of thought. Knowing is not 'intuitive thinking'; it is not reducible to the connection of concepts which are merely 'fueled' by occasional percepts. "Human knowledge is conceptual judgment-forming intuition."[13] It is, first and foremost, 'thinking intuition'—for the thinking that is in knowledge is only there by virtue of its service of understanding and relating the reports of particular apprehensions. The role of thought is analogous to that of the translator who renders a particular statement comprehensible in the hearer's language: as the utterance of the translator approximates, and depends upon, what was originally given, so thought approximates in explanation, and depends upon, the particular intuitional report which it interprets in terms of a wider experience. Concepts only provide knowledge *about* entities but have no direct contact with them. Thought considers an object that appears through the *mediation* of conceptual translation; but intuition is *immediate* apprehension of the object to which the cognition refers.

Likewise, the Critical doctrine is not akin to that naive empiricism which saw concepts as confused sense impressions and called for their reduction, by an analytic logic, into clear and distinct percepts or simple perceptive ideas. The dependence of thought on intuition is matched by the finitude of intuition itself, the need of intuition for explanatory, if dependent, thought. For a divine being, an infinite intuition could yield complete knowledge. But human intuition is limited and needs conceptual thinking in order to know *what* it is that it is perceiving. It is just this need of human intuition for the translation of percept into concept that brings to light the radical finitude of human cognition.

It is precisely this essential finitude of each of the two components of the cognitive act that Kant pointed up in the famous aphorism: "Thoughts without content are empty, intuitions without concepts are blind." [14]

This essential finitude is developed with special reference to the finitude of human reason in its twofold aspect: (1) 'subjectively' from the side of the human subject, the knower, and (2) 'objectively' from the side of the object, the known.

(1) Finite intuition, i.e., sensibility, is not creative; it is receptive, dependent for its content on the object which appears to it, which "announces itself." We live amidst entities, and our sense organs offer an entity the "possibility of giving notice of itself." [15] The manner in which an entity can "announce itself" to our awareness, the way in which we can perceive it as an object, as the appearance that appears, is obviously limited in advance by our capacity for receiving these sense reports. Someone with normal color vision will see a brightly colored flower in a different way than either a color-blind individual or a dog, which only sees shades of gray. Sense experience is thus grounded in what we bring to it, in our finite modes of apprehension, in the particular ways in which the reports of sensibility *can* be received.

But mere apprehension of a particular appearance does not constitute knowledge; what is essential is what Kant described as representation by concepts. "Judgment is, therefore, the mediate knowledge of an object, that is, the representation of a representation of it";[16] only in this way does the intuitional content become meaningful. In the synthesis of intuition and understanding, the unity of the two (and the truth of the unified cognition) becomes manifest; in this synthesis, my perception of an apprehended colored shape is cognized as a brightly colored flower.

But, Heidegger insists, this does not mean a coequality of sense and thought. Intuition is dependent on understanding as the source of concepts, for the determination of what it is that is being perceived. But understanding "is even more finite," just because of its complete dependence on sense intuition for any content at all: "Finite knowledge," is then "a mode of intuition which is receptive and, hence, in need of thought." [17]

(2) As for the object, what an intuition reports is an appearance before it. For an X to appear meant for Kant that it was the "object of an empirical intuition." [18] Kant was quite clear that the appearance of an object is not something distinct from the entity itself; it is merely that thing as it is able to appear to us *qua* phenomenal object. The phenomenal appearance is merely that aspect of the object which we are able to apprehend.

Now, Heidegger points out, we are while in the act of intuiting an appearance only able to perceive some aspect of the object; the entity, aside from the way it appears to us, remains concealed, hidden from us, unknown. If I look into the dark unlighted room, I may notice a bright yellow corner of a chair which catches and reflects back the light that falls upon it from the lighted room in which I stand. But this, say, triangular appearance is not the chair; it is only because I have previously seen the whole chair that I know the yellow triangle to be a corner of the upholstered square cushion. But suppose that I have never seen the room before; all that is appearing to me, in the limited beam of light, is a triangular yellow shape suspended in darkness. If this finite vision cannot be expanded—if I can neither enter the room nor increase the light—the rest of that cushion and its chair remain concealed and unknown to my perception. I conjecture concerning them: I do infer that there is some entity there which, in this limited light, appears in a limited aspect as a yellow triangular shape.

Finite knowledge keeps the entity concealed in the process of apprehending an aspect of it in an appearing. As long as my limited vision cannot be made even less limited, much less un-limited, the appearance and the knowledge of that appearance leave the unknown context of the yellow triangle in the dark. That which is behind the appearance is the same entity as the object appearing; but it remains concealed and is not completely accessible to my recognition—just because I can only cognize par-tial aspects of the thing insofar as it appears to me. The totality of aspects of a thing can*not* be seen *at once:* e.g., to the extent that I examine the internal structure of the desk before me, I have effectively removed its external appearance from my immediate perceptual field—and to examine the internal structure of the material out of which the desk is made would necessitate destroy-ing the desk itself as originally perceived.

In any finite view of a thing, therefore, I must recognize the presence of what is *not* now being perceived. Any finite cognition thus essentially includes a 'negativing' factor—it leave 'unlighted' those aspects of the entity which are not being seen as a present appearance. To understand what it is that I *am* seeing, I must take into account the negative component, the not-being-seen that is part of the thing I am cognizing.

The essential finitude of human knowledge is then made mani-fest by two considerations: (1) we need objects as the content of thought—we cannot think without thinking about *some*thing; (2) sense intuition, which supplies this need, is finite because it cannot provide us with complete knowledge of entities as they are in themselves; it can only report those aspects of things which appear to the extent that our receptive capacity permits them to do so. Any cognition is then partial: it cannot deal with the totality of the entity and it presumes, in advance, aspects of these entities which remain hidden from our immediate apprehension of them.

If, indeed, the beginning of wisdom lies in the confession of ignorance, as I believe Socrates suggested, this beginning for Heidegger, as for Kant, lies in recognition of what is involved in the simplest sense perception of any object. This essential finitude of possible knowledge defines Kant's investigation, and all that Heidegger has really done here is to make the matter completely explicit.

Kant, it will be remembered, insisted from the outset that our knowledge of particular or ontic things, our empirical knowledge, is rendered possible, defined, and limited by the apriori structure of the two components of that knowledge, sensibility and understanding, as they are synthesized into unified experience. We bring with us to any possible experience this transcendental ground of experience—which effectively defines in advance the range of possibility within which knowledge can be had and the categoreal structure that it must have. This transcendental ground defines in advance and permits us to anticipate the possible ways in which we can describe the content of a perception, assign ontological characterizations to ontic content, frame the kinds of questions which our description must satisfy in order to be deemed knowledge.*

How then is it possible for a finite knower to be oriented toward an object and intuit something about it before it is given? How is it possible for me to know, before my friend's house comes into view as I walk toward it, that it will be one total object of my perception—though made up of separable components? that it will be seen as a finite reality, coexisting with the trees next to but separable from it? that it will appear to be made of some solid kind of substance such as wood or brick or steel? that I will regard it as caused to be there by human effort and not as a product of nature (such as a tree)? that I will be aware of the contingency of its being there (another house or no house at all might have been built in that location)? My judgment "this is my friend's house" will thus comprise a judgment of its singularity,

---

* Regarding the continued use of the phrase 'in advance' as the anticipatory meaning of the word 'apriori,' note Heidegger's explanation:

Newton's first principle of motion and Galileo's law of falling bodies both have the peculiarity that they leap ahead of what verification and experience, in a literal sense, offer. In such principles, something has been anticipated in respect to things. Such anticipations rank ahead of and precede all further determinations of things. In Latin terms such anticipations are apriori. . . . The priority of the apriori concerns the essence of things. What enables a thing to be what it is *pre-cedes* the thing as regards the facts and nature, although we only grasp that which precedes after taking account of some of the most obvious qualities of the thing.[19]

On this principle, Beck offers a perceptive delineation of Kant's transcendental empiricism: "Hume had thought concepts must *come* from experience; he was a genetic, a retrospective, empiricist. Kant taught that concepts must apply to experience; he was an anticipatory empiricist."[20]

affirmation of its actuality, of its substantial character, and its co-existence with the other houses and trees about it, of its being here before me as the effect of a number of contingent human decisions, of its necessary conformity to the laws of nature which I presume and to the laws of human cognition which I invoke in order to perceive it. More precisely, then, how must I, as this finite knower, be constituted with regard to my own structure of be-ing if, without the aid of a present perception (of my friend's new house), I am able to bring forth the ontological structure of the house, i.e., effect an ontological synthesis? [21]

In order *for me* to know my friend's new house as such, I necessarily impute to it, as a synthesis, all these general ontological characterizations of its being in advance of my perception of it; I must be able to do this in order to be able to recognize it, *qua* conforming to these characterizations when it comes into view. I must be able to anticipate what sort of thing I am seeking out, what sort of characterizations it must incorporate, so that I can recognize it when it comes into my view. I know that I am looking for a new house, not a large eagle's nest or a mound-filled meadow. How, in advance of my perception of it, am I able to demand without contradiction or doubt that it conforms by necessity to certain categoreal descriptions of what-it-is, that-it-is, and how-it-is—and how it came to be what-and-how-it-is?

The conceptual synthesis which I formulate as anticipated ontological structure of that house not only precedes any particular encounter but serves me as an instrument which describes the kind of perception that would meet its requirements. It alerts me to look for certain kinds of thing-structures and to ignore others as not being germane to my quest. It tells me what kind of perceptions can be synthesized with this set of concepts in order to yield particular, or ontic, knowledge. The full synthesis on which knowledge depends is such that the pure apriori forms of intuitional receptivity and of concepts, as well as the particular applicatory empirical concepts themselves, must logically precede any specific encounter. As presupposition of any possible cognition, synthesis of pure concepts and pure intuition is what first makes any particular cognition possible. But the question is then crucial: how can I, a finite human being within a field of entities, whose entire knowledge is dependent upon the 'independence' of those entities, "in advance pass beyond (transcend)" [22] the object as it appears to the basic structure of its ontological synthesis, when I have not created the object and am dependent upon it in order to have a cognitional relationship to it?

Kant suggested that the answer is to be found in my "finite pure reason as that which by its essence . . . 'reason produces entirely out of itself.'" [23] Kant's analysis of this finite pure reason was an inquiry into the nature of the possibility of the transcendental synthesis which makes any ontic experience possible, a transcendental synthesis of the two 'pure' components of knowledge—the pure form of any intuition and pure mode of conceptualization. This transcendental synthesis provides the defining ground of the apriori structure within which the limited possibilities of empirical knowledge are to be found.

An inquiry into the nature of this transcendental synthesizing Kant had termed a transcendental inquiry. Just so, Heidegger terms it an ontological inquiry into ontological synthesizing precisely because it is directed to the limited characterizations which may define the being-status of any particular object for me as I am able to be aware of it. For such synthesis defines the limitations of what may be experienced in the appearances of unknown entities insofar as they can enter our awareness of them; thus defined—in capacity and limitation of content—are the kinds of objects we may encounter, the sorts of things that can-be, can have being-status, within any possible experience we can have.

By the change of terms—from transcendental to ontological—Heidegger throws emphasis not on the subjectivity of this possible experience but on the kinds of things that can be within it, on the possible range of content which we are able to experience in the cognitional aspect of what he will term our being-in-the-world.* For both of them, however the change of emphasis, the systematic grounding of this synthesis, whether called transcendental or ontological, is indeed the 'prolegomena to any future metaphysics.'

Heidegger guides us in a step-by-step interrogation on each of

---

* But note the basic subjectivist ground; as Glenn Gray has pointed out: "Heidegger starts from the idealistic assumption that man's essence is completely inseparable from the world in which it finds itself. . . . What should be

the five stages in which he sees Kant as having worked out this 'prolegomena': the first is a reconsideration of the Transcendental Aesthetic, which he sees as proposing the priority of intuition before thought (see V.2). The four additional stages are seen in the first two books of the Transcendental Logic, a portion of its first chapter which seeks unification of sensibility and thought (see V.3); the Deduction of the Categories, which elucidates the possibility of ontological synthesis (see V.4); the Schematism, which grounds that possibility (see V.5); and the Highest Principle of All Synthetic Judgments, which demonstrates the identification of the transcendental and ontological (see V.6). In his five-step inquiry of Kant, Heidegger sets out the evidence for the conclusions which are subsequently developed.

Kant's Critical inquiry was framed by the principle of the Copernican Revolution and the correlative principle of cognitional finitude. Together these principles defined the ontological problematic which Heidegger sees Kant as having worked out in five stages. In each stage he sees Kant as having effectively taken a further step to bring to light the necessary structure of ontology and thereby demonstrate its essential possibility. In his examination of Kant's development of this thematic project, there is to be no slavish repetition of what Kant had said but rather a *reinterpretation* by entering into Kant's thought and proceeding by means of an *internal* critique.

The object toward which the inquiry is directed is the demonstration of the grounding of ontological synthesis in the heart of Kant's Critique, a grounding which establishes and delineates the foundational nature of temporality. Each of these five stages will be seen to have been necessary for attainment of this objective.

---

emphasized, however, is that despite all novelty of approach Heidegger is continuing . . . the idealistic tradition of interpreting reality from the standpoint of the subjective thinker." [24]

2 · *The Priority of Pure Intuition*

THE THRUST of the Copernican Revolution requires a rigorous examination of the way in which human knowledge is constituted. What is obviously of concern here is neither any specific empirical information nor any genetic or psychological description of a particular individual learning procedure. What is of concern is an elucidation of the ways in which human knowledge is essentially structured, the internal logic of any cognition, the operational procedure that is necessarily presupposed in any cognitive act. The Critique is directed to this investigation of the human mode of cognition and the ensuing limits which its essential structure imposes on its areas of competence.

Kant pursued this essential investigation of those constitutive elements necessarily presupposed in any act of cognition in the prime section of the Critique entitled, "Transcendental Doctrine of Elements." Insofar as any cognition is a synthesis of sense impressions and concepts, his problematic was the manner in which they arise and are brought to synthesis in any specific empirical (ontic) cognition. Again, the concern was not with the content but with the logical structure: in what form do we receive all data? how do we constitute specific concepts used to interpret data and render them meaningful?

If we remember that the word 'apriori' refers to that which is logically *prior* to any specific content, that 'pure' denotes the form or procedure quite aside from any content, that 'intuition' is the mode of immediate apprehension of the reports of sensibility, and that understanding is the source of specific empirical concepts—then the essential Kantian thesis becomes clear: any cognition of any object results from the synthetic unification of pure intuition (the defining manner in which impressions can be received) and pure understanding (the procedure in which empirical concepts are created); regardless of specific content, any specific empirical cognition focuses the combination of our way of receiving sense impressions and the way in which we are able to produce empirical concepts on some particular or ontic presentation. These 'ways,' be it remembered, are prior to any particular application or employment.

Kant's procedure, in elucidating the essential structure of any human cognitive act, was to examine each of these constituent or elemental procedures in turn. Just because concepts are invoked to explain what sensibility reports, Kant first examined the way in which such reports could be received; this examination constitutes the short opening section of the Critique which, following a traditional usage, he termed "Transcendental Aesthetic." This short section is followed by what is generally regarded as the heart of the Critique, the "Transcendental Logic," which examines the ways in which empirical concepts may be formed and related to the objects reported by sensibility; here he also established his justification for that application. Subsequently, in the "Transcendental Dialectic" (which Heidegger finds no need to scrutinize), Kant drew the implications of the earlier section to disavow the traditional doctrines of speculative metaphysics as beyond the bounds of what is possible for human knowledge (as distinct from speculative thinking and acts of rational faith).

Kant opened the body of the Critique by emphasizing the complete priority of intuition, the mode of receiving information, before thought or the understanding that supplies integrative explanatory concepts.

In whatever manner and by whatever means a mode of knowledge may relate to objects, *intuition* [*Anschauung*] is that through which it is in immediate relation to them, and to which all thought as a means is directed. But intuition takes place only in so far as the object is given to us. This again is only possible, to man at least, in so far as the mind is affected in a certain way. The capacity (receptivity) for receiving representations through the mode in which they are affected by objects, is entitled *sensibility*. Objects are *given* to us by means of sensibility, and it alone yields us *intuitions;* they are *thought* through the understanding, and from the understanding arise *concepts*. But all thought must, directly or indirectly, by way of certain characters, relate ultimately to intuitions, and therefore, with us, to sensibility, because in no other way can an object be given to us.[25]

In order to discover the form of receptivity, as distinct from content, he set out to "separate off from" sensibility "everything which belongs to sensation, so that nothing may remain save pure intuition and the mere form of appearances, which is all that sensibility can supply apriori." [26] By disregarding any specific content of sense receptivity, the concern is to determine the ways in which we are *able* to receive sense impressions; these 'ways' are designated as 'forms.' The forms of intuition, the system of relation in which any appearance must be apprehended, are but two, the "two pure forms of sensible intuition, serving as principles of apriori knowledge, namely space and time." [27] All appearances of objects are seen *by us* as spatial; hence space is the form of outer sense, of our receptivity of sense reports of all external objects. But *all* sense reports, as well as all thoughts, awarenesses, and objects of consciousness (including, but not restricted to, external objects) appear to consciousness in temporal sequence; hence time is the form of what Kant called inner sense.

Immediately after defining these two forms of all intuition, Kant made his ontological concern explicitly clear:

> *What, then, are space and time?* [1] Are they real beings [*Wesen*]? [2] Or are they only determinations or relations of things, but yet such as would belong to things [entities] in themselves even if they were not intuited, [3] or again, *such as only attach to the form of intuition and hence to the subjective nature of our mind,* apart from which these predicates could not be ascribed to anything whatsoever? [28]

Not *how* can we *know* them? But *what are* they?

The third ontological italicized position was affirmed. In effect what Kant did here was to carry forward the Leibnizian thesis. The Newtonian view that space and time are somehow absolute and nonrelational self-subsistent 'containers' in which things happen, Leibniz had argued, is incomprehensible because we have no way of speaking intelligibly about space and time except in terms of the relationships of things and events; consequently, space and time are not 'things' but the ways in which things are related to each other. But the Leibnizian argument presumed to talk about the relationships of things in themselves despite Leibniz' own metaphysical grounding of our knowledge of them as 'reflections' in monads. The principle of the Copernican Revolution thus carries the monadological principle forward but argues that Leibniz' stated view goes far beyond any evidence which we could conceivably obtain; the most that we can say with any degree of assurance is that space and time are the ways in which things are related *in our experience of them,* that they are the forms in which the data-content of experience is received; by this strategy Kant effectively internalized the Newtonian view and was able to explain the pervasiveness of time and space in human experience. Space and time then are brought to 'being' in the encounter between men and things *as* men meet, relate, use, and specify things. Space and time are real and pervasive within our experience but we have no way of knowing that they are somehow so beyond it; they are then "empirically real" but "transcendentally ideal" insofar as they are brought *by us* to any possible experience as the forms *in* which we necessarily can know it.

In the course of Kant's examination, then, space and time were described as forms of appearances and of sense intuitions; time, as the form of inner intuition wherein all representations, including outer representations, must be ordered took priority over space. "The ancient ontological proposition that everything real is in space and time has here been reduced to the thesis that all appearances are in space and time";[29] insofar as all appearances that are spatial must also be temporal, there is the additional crucial thesis that only some appearances are spatial but *all appearances are in time.*

Because of Kant's procedure of separate examination of the 'aesthetic' and 'logical' components of the transcendental structure of cognition, one is tempted to evaluate each aspect separately. Doing so, Heidegger argues, is a crucial error of much traditional neo-Kantian scholarship which has led to a gross misreading of the entire work; to the extent that Kant himself may have felt it possible to do so, we can only say that his loyalty to his own architechtonic interferes with loyalty to his crucial insight. To comprehend the nature of either intuition or understanding requires fidelity to its place in the organic unity of any cognitional act. Separate treatment is merely an analytic device which brings issues to view; the context of intuition's functioning—in synthetic unity with thought—needs be clarified before the full import of the priority of intuition, or the role of explanatory concepts, can be grasped. Kant did not really suggest the mere addition of two completely

[51]

separable components each of which could finally be examined in its own terms; the essential thesis, which is to be spelled out, is that the cognitive act is one inherently unitary act; its elements may be separable for purposes of analytic description, but such description is *within* the context of one unified cognition. As experienced, thought and sensibility are intrinsically related to each other; to face either, except in a very preliminary way, without reference to the other is essentially distortive.

Empirical thought is always, as representation, "directed toward what is intuited in intuition and thus is entirely at the service"[30] of intuition. If so, the meaning of receptive intuition will emerge from its interpretation by thought and the meaning of thought is tied to the nature of what sensibility *can* report. Sense intuitions, then, are always individual, particular, and temporally-framed; a concept is a general term invoked to relate selected aspects of that specificity to others in terms of generalized traits. Concepts devoid of reference to specific content are empty just because they are not *about* anything that can be in the time of human experience. If, indeed, all information comes to us in temporal form, if the function of understanding is to render it intelligible, then the function of concepts, as shall be seen, is to structure temporal experience, to structure human time.

If one remembers that the Aesthetic is merely Kant's opening, that its thrust is essentially restrictive, that both the nature of the legitimate uses of the understanding and the limitations of that usage flow from it—one can then appreciate the force of Heidegger's insistence[31] that it can only be regarded as an introductory statement, that it cannot be taken as a self-contained discussion legitimately examined by itself. Even though it is introductory it is crucial; it undergirds Heidegger's repudiation of nonintuitional conceptualization, and Heidegger's insistence is in conformity with Kant's—that apriori knowledge depends for its possibility on pure intuition, which provides this empirical ground for all cognition.

The temporal concern presents another reason for refusing to consider the Aesthetic separately. There are a number of divergencies between Kant's formulation of the concept of time here and in the Analytic which follows, where its fuller meaning is developed.[32] To some extent these divergencies stem from the fact that Kant was, in the Aesthetic, examining the purely passive or receptive aspect of mental activity whereas in the Analytic he was concerned with its active nature; in the Analytic, where the mind was examined in its role as interpreter of experience, the preliminary pairing of time and space radically receded and time dynamically emerged as the mode of all human experience and, by implication, of the objects that can appear to it.

The Aesthetic does, indeed, seek to examine the receptive side of human apprehension. But, Heidegger urges, the Kantian discussion, at least by implication, suggests that pure intuition, although primarily an act of receptive representation, is also in a sense creative. The forms of pure intuition make possible the kind of receptivity we have; they impose in advance on any conceivable object the temporal and spatial character in terms of which it must appear to us in order to appear at all. They authorize us to anticipate that any external object *will* appear as spatial—because it is the only way in which we could possibly apprehend it; that any awarenesses *will be* apprehended in a temporal sequence. Before any particular object can be seen, the apriori forms of pure intuition make possible, create the spatial and temporal character in terms of which it must appear to our consciousness. Thus, even our receptivity is not completely passive; even on this level we make an active contribution to the nature of any phenomenal appearance.

In this reference the presence of negation, of the 'not,' the idea of the *Nichts** must be brought into consideration. What is represented in *pure* intuition is not a thing (no object-that-is which appears) but yet not absolutely nothing. It is perhaps not merely a matter of chance formulation that Kant's own discussion of the two pure forms of all intuition began in terms of negation—in describing what they *are not:* not a being, not a thing or object, space is "nothing that can be represented empirically . . . [it] is

---

* The word *Nichts* is rendered as 'non-thing-ness' in the sense explicated below (V. 4) in the discussion of Kant's transcendental object. Crucial to Heidegger's thesis concerning the nature of temporal experience in particular, and fundamental ontology generally, it is urged that any judgment concerning this central concept be bracketed until it has been more fully developed.

[53]

a pure representation, i.e., that which is necessarily represented in advance in finite human cognition." [33] The representation of all things in one pervasive space is made possible by the nature of human intuition. Only because pure intuition itself imposes the essential form on what it receives is it able to receive as it does; only because of this dual nature can it be both receptive and pure, i.e., intrinsically prior to any specific content. Space intuition thus does not perceive space but perceives all objects *as in* the spatial form which it projects upon them. The essense of an intuition is that it can only represent a particular thing. Yet all spaces are seen as parts of one inclusive space and this is certainly not empirically perceived: "If this unique whole is given at once and as a whole, then the act of representation in question originates that which is capable of being represented and in this sense may be termed an 'original' act of representation." [34]

Similarly, all things are seen in experiential times, all of which presuppose the unity of all time in one inclusive representation of time as such, a representation of 'something' which we have never perceived. "Time is the formal apriori condition of all appearances whatsoever." [35] just because it is "nothing but the form of inner sense, that is, of the intuition of ourselves and of our inner state." [36] Time (as space) *is* then *not-a-thing;* it is a function, the capacity of the subject to have internally coherent experience; it is a mode of relating experiences; in itself it has no content but it is the way in which any content is to be had.

Given this temporal priority, the two otherwise separate forms of intuition—with the consequent possibility of two disparate regions of experience—are unified without any third factor being required to effect their synthesis.

The complete priority which Kant accorded to time in the Aesthetic becomes, then, a preface to the 'doctrine of the elements of human knowledge' and the guiding thread of Heidegger's analysis of it. All of our representations are ordered by us in terms of succession or temporal order. If this temporal cast is pervasive—a demonstration which the Analytic provides—it is the prime form of all human knowledge. As the universal and necessary prerequisite for, and ingredient of, experience, it is then 'pure intuition' itself: for it is *the* essential form of consciousness, of every "I think"; it is the essential form, the "single and only" [37] form in which *all* representations, without exception, are to be had.

It then becomes, so Heidegger argues, the key to transcendence, the human capacity to utilize the transcendental ground of experience in order to have a coherent experience, the capacity to have a "horizon of objectivity in general" [38] within which all experiencing transpires and all the objects which enter into our experiencing are to be found. It is, then, the form of time which is utilized in our capacity-for-experience that creates an area of possible experience in which we can apprehend objects *qua* objects, i.e., as independent of our apprehending them. We are thus able to transcend our inner subjectivity and find ourselves in a world of other beings, of objects, with which we are in constant knowing contact.[39] Insofar as time is the universal element in all experience, it is the crucial element of the transcendental ground of the possibility of knowledge itself. Much of what follows is concerned to spell out the implications of this complete priority of time: for example, the concepts which we use to describe the content of experience will be seen essentially "as ontological predicates" of the things we experience in a temporal field.[40]

Kant's 'reduction' of time as the *subjective* form of all intuition, and of the objectivity provided by it, may seem at first strange. Heidegger's emphatic underlining of its subjectivity may seem even stranger, especially in view of his shift of focus from the nature of our cognitive processes to the ontological predicates which may legitimately apply to things. As the key to transcendence and the capacity to develop a coherent objective horizon of experience, it seems paradoxical, indeed, to emphasize subjectivity as foundational to experience. Yet on reflection it is really not strange at all.

Kant's limitation of time to a subjective ground is seen by Heidegger as equivalent to

> an extension of the domain within which time can function as the anticipatory mode of intuition. . . . Time as immediately limited to the data of internal sense is, at the same time, ontologically more universal than space only if the subjectivity of the subject consists in being open to the thing-that-is.[41]

Time "as the anticipatory mode of intuition" gives us in advance the complete totality of relationships in which all appearances can be ordered. As any transcendental element in knowledge, it prescribes, as prerequisite to any specific cognizing, the limitations of possibility within which that knowing must be confined. The form of time is thus *pre*scribed in advance of any representation as *the* necessary condition, the *sine qua non,* for it to be a representation at all. The form of time is thus prescribed to all objects we may apprehend so that they may appear as objects for our cognition and to all principles of knowledge so that they may be applied to all representations and thus construct knowledge in a pervasive and essential temporal field. (As Kant had already intimated nine years before the Critique, the form of time will, in the end, emerge as the capacity of the self to affect itself by its experience and, indeed, to be a self at all.[42])

The essential subjectivity of time is, then, the source of the apriori itself in terms of which we are able to anticipate the essence of things within our experience. As Kant himself later pointed out, "the first datum which made apriori knowledge possible" is not to be found in the cognitive Principles which become the conceptual ground of explanation but "the pure sensuous intuition"[43] which invokes them. "The apriori," as Heidegger later explained, "is what belongs to the subjectivity of the subject."[44] And it is precisely from this vantage point that transcendental philosophy must proceed. Generalizations from experience can only indicate what has been or is present; subjectively grounded apriori concepts outline the areas of what is yet possible for us. They permit us to approach any new situation with determinate interpretive categories and with an apparatus by which to comprehend it.

The Aesthetic, short as it may be, is then but the introduction to the argument of the Critique; it spells out more specifically the problematic which the Copernican Revolution had enunciated. It set up the task to which the Analytic is directed. For if what is given is, indeed, given through temporal intuition and if the legitimate use of thought is the interpretation of intuitive presentation, then a new logic of applicability of thought to temporal objects is required. If all presentations are inherently temporal, then an a-temporal logic is distortive and a new time-forming transcendental logic is needed. What is requisite is a mode of thought by which we may legitimately apply non-temporal concepts to temporally perceived objects. It is to the clarification of this problem that the Transcendental Logic, which comprises the heart of the Critique, is directed.

Kant pursued that inquiry in its first part, the Analytic, which henceforth engages our attention; here he presented his reasoning concerning the ways in which conceptual thought can and may relate to temporal things and, in so doing, he outlined the theory of knowledge which Heidegger sees as providing the foundation of ontology. Before proceeding further into this inquiry, we should note what has already been established: in the process of expediting the priority of the form of time in human experience, Kant had affirmed the priority of intuition before understanding, an affirmation Heidegger regards as crucial to comprehending the Critique and its essential empiricism. The creative function of pure intuition has been taken to imply a priority of time to be fully worked out in the interpretation of the Deduction of the Categories and the Principles. Likewise, discussion of the Aesthetic has presented preliminary statements of the priority of the apriori and of the concept of *Nichts,* the import of which are pervasive and more fully elucidated in the ontologically oriented interpretation that Heidegger presents for our consideration.

The announced priority of time in the Aesthetic, then, impels us to go beyond it in order to discover the nature and fuller significance of this priority. Time will be seen to emerge not only as the essential form of cognition but as the prime mode of the kind of to-be we have, of the kind of being that each one of us is; it becomes the key to the fuller meaning of what is to be understood as the 'subjectivity of the subject' and of what Heidegger develops further as the nature of temporal experience in fundamental ontology.

3 · *Unification of Thought and Sensibility*

THE DUALITY OF SPACE and time was unified by the essentially idealist 'reduction' of space to time; this was accomplished in the Aesthetic. But no such 'reduction' was suggested for the unification of sensibility (provided by pure intuition) and thought (provided by pure understanding), both of which constitute together the integral unity of any act of cognition.

Kant's parallel presentation of sensibility in the Aesthetic and thought in the Analytic raises the question of just how these two elements are to be brought together into one unified cognition. Perhaps because the Analytic is the heart of the Critique, the interpretations of neo-Kantianism and speculative idealism sought to explain cognitive unity from thinking alone; but, as Martin has urged, "it is still questionable whether this interpretation really exhausts the Kantian philosophy." [45] Heidegger is too much the empiricist to believe that it does.

Heidegger has taken the Aesthetic to mean that intuition, the possibility of sensibility, is 'reducible' to time, the form of inner sense. He has emphasized the Kantian thesis that pure thought is dependent for its 'material' on what intuition provides; he is to protest repeatedly any attempt to treat either thought or sensibility separately—as abstracted from the organic unity which binds them together into one cognitive process. His persistent focus on the essential priority of sensory intuition then requires a nonconceptual source of this unity of sense-and-thought embodied in cognition; the unity of these two elements presupposed in any particular cognition is logically prior to each of them. Their unity is then prerequisite, not consequent.

Just as the Analytic carries forward the cognitive problem enunciated at the outset, so it also develops the problem of time. Presented in the Aesthetic as the subjective form of all apprehension, the Analytic progressively moves to the possibility of the 'objective' time-order in which objects are seen. In contrast to the Aesthetic, time is no longer generally paired with space; in the Analytic, which takes its cue from the Aesthetic doctrine of the priority of inner sense, time emerges as the unifying form of all possible experience and, thereby, as the mode of unification of the objects appearing in that experience. The problems of time and of cognitive unity are then essentially related: "Without reference to the principle themes of the Analytic, unity in general, object in general, subject in general . . . time cannot be understood." [46]

In approaching the Analytic, then, the guiding query is for the ground of the possibility of the unity of experience. If knowledge comes out of the union of sense and thought, how is this union effected? What brings these two disparate elements of cognition into the integral relationship which makes possible a unified act of cognition? The quest is for the discovery of the nature, mode, and source of the unification of experience. The intent, which only becomes explicit toward the end, is to show that time—as implicit in its role as the form of inner sense—is the basic unifying form of all representations. Time, as the form of all experiential unification, will appear as the essential principle of cognitive unity.

In what follows it should be borne in mind that the function of the Analytic, as Kant had explained it, is concerned "with the laws of understanding solely in so far as they relate apriori to objects." [47] It is concerned to develop those Principles of empirical knowledge in terms of which we understand and conceptually order the presentations of intuitional receptivity. Kant warned that the transcendental categoreal kinds of descriptions, which empirically directed Principles apply, "should be used only as a canon for passing judgment upon the empirical employment of the understanding." [48] (The confirmation of this inherent limitation is the task of Kant's Dialectic, which Heidegger finds no reason to examine.)

The Analytic, then, is concerned with the ground and use of concepts in empirical knowledge. The nature of a concept then becomes crucial; it has, Heidegger explains, the character of a representation:

> the fact that what is represented therein has the form of an element common to many—always arises from reflection. . . . Accordingly, if the act of reflection is itself a representation of unity, this means that the act of representation of unity belongs to the essential structure of the fundamental act of the understanding.[49]

A concept is not merely a way in which to subsume given particulars under a generic term. For Kant as for Heidegger a concept is "a synthesis of actual and possible perceptions" [50] which outlines an area of possible experience and is 'involved' in experiential denotative applications. The *modes* of synthesis of the kinds of concepts we use in experience are, abstractly considered, called the pure concepts or categories. They, together with the forms of intuition, are given in advance of any ontic experience; they are thereby apriori and help to constitute the areas of possible experience within which any actual experience is to be had.

In opening the "Analytic of Concepts," the first of the two divisions of the Analytic, Kant had emphasized the point that sensory intuition and conceptual understanding *together* constitute a cognitive act.[51] Having examined the way in which sensory intuitions are received, he now turned to an analysis of its one partner in cognition, viz., conceptual thought produced from the understanding. This analysis had, as its declared intent, not the examination of specific concepts but "the hitherto rarely attempted *dissection of the faculty of the understanding* itself in order to investigate the possibility of concepts apriori by looking for them in the understanding alone, as their birth place, and by analysing the pure use of this faculty." [52]

First Kant tried to derive the pure concepts of the understanding, the categories, from the traditional table of logical judgments. Heidegger joins the attack on this derivation and argues they are not, and cannot be, derived from it: if we are, indeed, concerned with the nature of our finite knowledge, we cannot forget that all thought is dependent for content upon what intuition provides. Pure concepts can only be discovered by explicit acknowledgment of their essential dependence upon pure intuition. The function of the categories is to make possible the unificatory interpretation of intuitive presentations; as such they are essentially "ontological predicates," [53] which together speak out about the to-be of the things-that-are in our experience. But this awareness of things is derived from sensory intuition and these predicates, thereby, must manifest an essential relationship to what is presented in intuition. At best, therefore, the Table of Judgments from which Kant tried to derive the categories is essentially derivative; it can only conceivably provide a convenient hint that helps bring them to light: it cannot serve as their true source. Aside from this suggestion —that what Kant had actually termed a "Clue to the Discovery" of the categories can be nothing more than that—the derivation does not require further attention here because Heidegger does, in effect, suggest an alternate source for their derivation from the doctrine of the Schematism as well as from the Principles of Pure Understanding.

Kant had addressed himself directly to the unity of the cognitive act—Heidegger's concern—in seven pregnant paragraphs designed to serve as a preface to the proposed table of categories. These seven paragraphs, as Smith has remarked, embody the fundamental ideas of the whole Deduction; Heidegger joins him in regarding them as crucial; they are fundamental to Heidegger's interpretation of the Critique as providing the foundation of general metaphysics or ontology.[54]

The full elucidation of these seven paragraphs would involve most of the ensuing discussion; they comprise, in a sense, a sequence of topic sentences, to the development of which the balance of the Analytic is devoted. Kant's seven paragraphs serve as a summary of his doctrine; they can be capsuled in eight propositions, which are enlarged upon in the following discussion:

a. in contrast to an analysis of particular concepts abstracted from experience, the concepts found in transcendental logic start with a manifold of sense impressions as reported in sense intuition;

b. these reports of sense intuition come into the focus of thought as formed by space and time, the "conditions of the receptivity of our mind—conditions under which alone it can receive representations of objects, and *which therefore must also affect the concepts of these objects*";[55]

c. in order to know what is presented to the mind by the receptivity of sense perception, conceptual thinking must connect and interpret this perceptive manifold by synthesizing it;

d. synthesis 'in the most general sense is the act of putting different representations together, and of grasping what is manifold in them in one cognitive act';[56]

e. synthesis is thus "the mere result of the power of imagination";[57]

f. transcendental logic provides the ground for this synthesizing activity which constitutes a unified cognitional response to sense-impression receptivity; the unification of sense impressions requires concepts, and the function of a transcendental logic is determination of the apriori, pre-experiential principles by which this synthesizing cognition of unified sensibility and concepts unites them into one unified act of knowing;

g. there are thus three discernible 'moments' in any cognitional act: (1) the manifold of intuition, (2) the unification of this manifold by the power of imagination, (3) a synthesis of this 'sensory synopsis' with the concept(s) that explain it;

h. as transcendental (pure, or pre-experiential), transcendental logic provides for this threefold unification of experience by introducing categories, namely, the pure concepts of the understanding, whose function is this conceptual unification of the components of cognition; these categories are derived from the Table of Judgments.

Despite the tendency to treat the two components of knowledge independently, Heidegger argues that the essential insight is that the unity of knowledge cannot be attained by mere addition. The pure concepts, the categories, are the terms in which empirical concepts are drawn; they can only be comprehended as possible predicates of the kinds of things that are experiential for us. The essential relationship between transcendental categories of conceptual organization and the pure forms of intuition in terms of which all sensibility is 'received' can only "be understood in the light of the essential unity of pure knowledge" which serves as the "foundation" of the two constituent elements.[58] If sensibility and thought are intrinsically intertwined and mutually implicatory, they are not two separate 'things' but merely functionally distinguishable aspects of a common originating act. The synthesis of intuition and thought, then, is primal, not derivative; their necessary mutual reference to each other is presupposed from the outset in the unity of any cognitive act. The fundamental question, then, concerns the nature of this unificatory source. Insofar as pure intuition was identified by Kant as time,[59] the question posed is how time and the categories (i.e., pure intuition and a-temporal pure concepts) are ultimately related to each other.

Kant himself had spoken of the " 'synopsis' of intuition."[60] Not only is the variety in intuitional presentation unified as one manifold; its content is unified, by concepts, with other manifolds. Any pure concept is a representation of a kind of unification—it represents a mode of unity in perceptual experience—and thus contributes to the unity of experience; it points out, in advance of any specific application, the kinds of syntheses which it can represent. The concept 'house' is not only applied to the unified perceptual synopsis which I organize into the representation of the red-shuttered white long object I now behold; it permits me to point out this object as an example of a concept which I have already applied to somewhat similar objects that were differently colored and shaped; it permits me to anticipate characteristics which any house I may encounter must have. The concept is thus a mode of enabling me to unify, in recollection and anticipation, a number of differently colored and shaped perceptual objects which could not otherwise be brought together into one field of cognitive comparison—brought together in terms of this general idea which encompasses its entire denotation.

Inasmuch as these two constitutive elements—sense and thought—require each other, they reveal articulations which indicate, in advance of any specific houses I may see, the possibility of joining them together in thought. In order for sense and thought to be capable of being joined together, they must have something in common, some 'overlap,' some mutuality permitting us to do so. Thus we must return to our question: how are the synopsis of intuition and pure reflective or predicative syntheses joined together into one cognitive unity?

Kant set up the problem in his introductory description of the unity of pure knowledge:

> Transcendental logic . . . has lying before it a manifold of apriori sensibility presented by transcendental aesthetic, as material for the concepts of pure understanding. In the absence of this material those concepts would be without content, therefore entirely empty. Space and time contain a manifold of pure apriori intuition, but at the same time [they] are conditions of the receptivity of our mind. . . . But if this manifold is to be known, the spontaneity of our thought requires that it be gone through in a certain way, taken up and connected. This act I name *synthesis*.[61]

But, Heidegger protests, this is "remarkably superficial. Strictly speaking, 'transcendental logic,' does not have 'lying before it' the pure temporal manifold." [62] Intuition must be primary. He suggests a revision consisting of the following propositions:

a. pure thought is dependent upon the pure manifold;

b. because thought is finite, this manifold must be brought into the range and the capacity of finite thought;

c. in order that pure intuition may be determined through pure concepts, it must be organized.

Reciprocity between intuition and thought is demonstrated in the process which Kant termed synthesis. The natural fitting-together of the two elements into synthesis, their functional unity, is the essential prerequisite for pure knowledge, the pre-experiential possibility of any empirical cognition. For empirical knowledge depends upon the synthetic union of sensibility 'reported' in intuition and the concepts of thought from the understanding.

Heidegger's analysis can now proceed to its first prime conclusion, the explication and implications of which are pervasive:

> This synthesis is the business neither of intuition nor of thought.
> . . . "Synthesis generally, as we shall henceforth see, is nothing
> more than the operation of the *power of the imagination,* a blind
> but indispensable function of the soul, without which we should
> have no knowledge whatsoever, but of the existence of which we
> are seldom even conscious." [63]

As Kant had explained, the role of the imagination* is that of bringing concepts into synthesis and it is from imaginative synthesis that all knowledge is derived. Paton sums this up quite well when he notes that "the transcendental unity of the synthesis of

---

* The German word is *Einbildungskraft,* not *Einbildung.* Smith and Meikeljohn generally translated it merely as 'imagination'; Müller occasionally as the 'faculty of imagination' although the word generally used for 'faculty' is *Vermögen.* In order to take in the full significance of *Einbildungskraft,* the literal sense of the German must be kept in mind: *ein/bilden* = 'to form in(to),' 'to form in,' 'to in-form,' 'to picture in,' 'to structure in.' The word *Einbildungskraft* must then be understood in its full literal sense as joining to 'imaginative structuring' the *kraft,* the power to do so, i.e., 'the power of imaginative structuring,' or 'the power of the imagination.' So as to avoid undue cumbersomeness, I usually abbreviate this to 'imagination' or the adjectival 'imaginative,' reserving the additional 'power of' for emphasis where needed. *Its full meaning as 'power of imaginative structuring' must consistently be kept in mind in all that follows.*

imagination is the pure form, or condition of all possible experience, whatever be the matter given to sense." [64] This is, to look ahead, substantiated in the Deduction: *"The unity of apperception in relation to the synthesis of imagination* is the *understanding;* and this same unity, with reference to the *transcendental synthesis* of the imagination, the *pure understanding."* [65]

Paton's extended comment on this introduction of the power of imagination as the unificatory factor in knowledge is very helpful:

> Kant has been criticised for failing to recognize sufficiently the interdependence of thought and intuition, and for supposing that the faculty of imagination is necessary to mediate them. I think rather that it is his critics who are too facile in their solution, or evasion, of the difficulties he is trying to meet.
>
> The fact that both thought and sense, as Kant fully recognizes, are involved in all knowledge is no good reason for confusing them: it is on the contrary a good reason why we should be careful to mark them off from one another. . . . And Kant's account of imagination as having an intermediate place between thought and sense is of permanent value. Without imagination we could not pass beyond the momentary sensum, and human understanding, as we know it, would be impossible.
>
> Furthermore the account which Kant gives of the synthesis of imagination as both empirical and transcendental seems to me to be clearly true. As we combine our senses (in accordance with our empirical concepts of objects), we also fill out in imagination the one space and time in which all objects are.[66]

There are, then, *not two* elements in cognition *but three:* pure intuition, the power of imaginative synthesis, and the understanding. But, as Heidegger points out, it is imaginative synthesis that is central; in pure imagination, pure intuition and pure thought meet together in a common 'overlap' and are able to be fused into the unity of the cognitional act. The unification of sense and thought is 'proposed' by the power of imagination; it is not a conclusion at which the investigation may halt but the proper beginning of our inquiry. What is the source of this synthesis which originates knowledge, which welds sensibility and thought into the unity of a cognition? It is the imagination which now appears to bridge the 'gap' between the two other elements—between sense and thought, intuition and understanding, time and the categories. What, then, is this imaginative synthesis and what is its origin, its source, and its essential nature? These facets of the question take us immediately into the heart of the matter. For pure synthesis is not a 'thing' but an 'act'; we can only understand it by seeking out the ways in which it comes to be, the ways in which it arises.

We have passed beyond two disparate elements somehow mysteriously joined together. The imagination, the new third element, has emerged as the central unificatory agency.

But this seems strange in view of the Kantian architectonic which divided the doctrine of the elements of knowledge into the Aesthetic and the Logic. It does not seem that an originating synthesis of imagination properly belongs in either of these two provinces. And why does the question of imaginative synthesis—which becomes a central question of the Critique—first arise in an analysis of the concepts of 'transcendental logic'?

Heidegger seeks to justify the Kantian presentation. In these passages, he suggests, Kant has implicitly revealed the essential finitude of human thought in its inherent dependence upon the material of intuition, its inability either to provide data directly for itself or to establish a direct contact with its intuitive 'source of supply.' Here Kant has effectively raised the question of the unity of knowledge and the way in which it is to be justified; it is immediately clear that it cannot come from conceptual thought alone.

In the transition from the Aesthetic to the Analytic—before any analysis of thought itself—we are promptly made to face the question of just how sense and thought are to be coalesced into the unity of a cognitional act; prior to any examination of the understanding itself, Kant has presented us with an unexplicated introduction of a third 'bridging' element, the power of imagination as the ground of the synthesis which welds sense and thought into coherent cognition.

There are three elements in human knowledge, not two. As the enabling source of cognitive synthesis, the power of imagination appears to be more important than its rather casual introduction suggests. Just because it is the unifying center of the 'two sources' of knowledge, Heidegger argues that it is the fundamental one; because of it, knowledge is rendered possible; because of it, sense and thought, time and the categories, are able to function harmoniously together in a meaningful and intelligible way.

The nature and function of the power of imagination, then, demands elucidation. In the central role to which Kant had casually brought it, Heidegger sees the key to the fuller comprehension of Kant's thought; as the key to the nature of cognitive synthesis, he sees it as the instrument provided by Kant that enables us to explicate a fuller comprehension of the meaning of time and the grounding of metaphysics.

4 · *Possibility of Ontological Synthesis*

THE FOCUS has been on the unity of the elements constituting cognition. If I am to know that the arrangement of color before me is that kind of seed-producing botanic process which I call a flower, my perceptual receptivity of these shaped colors and the meaning contained in the concept 'flower' must be joined together into the unity of a cognitive act. For it is this unification of percept and concept that constitutes the structure of any particular act of knowledge.

If any empirical concept is merely the application of certain essential organizing categories—e.g., unity, reality, substantiality, causality, contingency—then the first problem faced is the determination of just what these essential categories are. Kant had tried to draw them, as universal functions of thought, from the traditional table of logical judgments. But he could not use them as traditionally received because their validity is confined to conceptual analysis. His task was to develop a new system of relating abstract concepts to the particular things that are perceptually experienced. This new logic of concept-and-thing relationships is transcendental just because it is originally presupposed in any particular experience, because it is the body of those organizing concepts that structure empirical concepts; embodied in any empirical concept, these categories are thereby prerequisite to the possibility of experience itself. Prior to determination of an authoritative list of organizational concepts or categories, the possibility of such a transcendental logical system must first be established and grounded.

Transcendental logic is not concerned with an analytic determination by means of which different representations are brought under a concept. It is concerned to investigate the way in which "we bring to concepts, not representations, but the *pure synthesis* of representations," [67] i.e., the manner in which our organized knowledge of the things we perceive is necessarily structured—the structure of our knowledge which is the necessary condition of its being our knowledge. Just as any particular experience is unified and known by means of the synthesis of concepts and percept incorporated in it, so transcendental logic systematically sets out the way(s) in which pure, or pre-experiential, concepts are united and brought into synthesis with the form of time which necessarily binds together any particular awareness we may have. It thus determines knowledge *qua* knowledge; it defines the nature of knowledge, the necessary condition of which is the fusing of sense and thought.

As the first full focus of his inquiry, Kant's Transcendental Deduction narrowed down to a more specific demonstration: that this unity of sense and thought is indeed possible, that pure general a-temporal concepts can indeed be necessarily synthesized with particular temporally framed perceptions; in short, that this unification and thereby our knowledge of things is possible.

The Deduction, Kant made it quite clear, was to be guided by the question: "what and how much can the understanding and reason know apart from all experience? not:—how is the faculty of thought itself possible?" [68] The function of the Deduction is determination of the rules by which apriori organizational concepts can be provided by the understanding for forming cognitive experience.

The word 'deduction,' as Kant clearly explained, is *not* a logical deduction but a justification of the uses of apriori categories. Such a justification or grounding is clearly "indispensable, [and] it must in any case be transcendental," [69] just because it explicates the necessarily pre-experiential ground of any particular experience.

[68]

The business of the Transcendental Deduction is then to ground the necessary applicability of pre-experiential concepts to particular experiential objects. It establishes the *principle of* the *general* applicability of categories as such to what is reported in perception. It thus precedes and postpones the examination of the particular modes of applicability to the Schematism and of the particular categories as they are actually operative to the Principles of the Pure Understanding. Just as the Principles develop the specific categoreal principles and the Schematism concerns itself with the *how* of their applicability in general, so the function of the Deduction is to demonstrate first *that* they are indeed generally applicable.

The problematic of this discussion is a consequent of the Copernican Revolution. All our knowledge is obviously limited by our capacity for attaining it. The nature, content, and limitation of any cognition is thus grounded in human subjectivity, in the way in which we can and do apprehend, interpret, and understand the appearances reported in intuition. *What* we can know is predetermined by *how* we know. The prime problem then arises: if all our knowledge is conditioned by our subjective grounds for knowledge, how can I have objectively valid knowledge of the particular objects I claim to know something about? It is the business of the Deduction to show that such conceptually organized knowledge is indeed possible and that its validity is limited, in advance, by the grounds of its possibility.

That this grounding or justification is essential to the plan of the Critique was explicitly recognized by Kant himself.[70] Its import is underlined by at least three considerations. First, it brings together the entire Critical doctrine into what might be called its essential nucleus. Second, together with the Schematism, it is the prime locus for development of Kant's insight into the nature of time: the Aesthetic voiced the claim that we know time intuitively as the form of all sensory receptivity; the Deduction expounds the thesis that we know time conceptually—that this consciousness of time is intrinsic to the possibility of knowledge, that time is not *merely* intuitive, but that "temporal factors are contained in all pure principles;"[71] the essential thesis underlying the Deduction is "the essential temporality of human consciousness."[72] Finally,

Heidegger is to take these two sections (the Deduction and the Schematism) as the chief ground for his own interpretation of Kant's temporalism and as the point of departure for his own development of the concept of time in an essentially temporalist ontology: the principles of Kant's grounding of apriori cognitive synthesis are also requisite for the belief not only in a unified coherent experience, but in a unified world which is apprehended and interpreted in that experience.

It is not surprising that, because of its crucial nature, this chapter was regarded by its author as the most difficult part of the entire Critique. References to its 'obscurity' are legion. Paton most graphically sums up the matter: "The crossing of the Great Arabian Desert can scarcely be a more exhausting task than is the attempt to master the windings and twistings of the Transcendental Deduction." [73] This chapter caused enough difficulty for comprehending the Critique, not to say controversy in interpreting it, to have induced Kant to rewrite it completely for the B edition. Heidegger's analysis is aimed to explicate Kant's postulation of the transcendental imagination as the center of cognition and the necessity of temporalizing the understanding itself. His discussion is based entirely on the A edition for reasons which can best be examined separately (see VI.4). He succeeds in underlining the import of the Deduction by bringing to light the pervasive implications it set forth.

Kant had opened his own discussion by postulating two sources from which all knowledge arises: (a) intuitions due to our receptivity of sense impression, and (b) concepts issuing from thought. The Critical epistemology is based on the claim that the concepts of the understanding synthesize intuitional reports into cognitions. Although the idea of a synthesizing imagination was also introduced as the second of a tripartite cognitive process, Kant's central argument was designed to establish the thesis that consciousness is impossible except within the dual partnership of intuition and thought as a consolidated or fused cognitive experience. It thus develops the principle underlying the Critical inquiry: the thesis that we bring to any experience certain "apriori concepts . . . [which] must be recognized as apriori conditions of the possibility of experience, whether of the intuition which is to be met with in it or of the thought." [74] The Transcendental Deduction, then, expounds the necessity of apriori categories as essentially presupposed components of any empirical cognition; it thus demonstrates the possibility of the cognitive experience we do, in fact, have. As such it also provides a justification of the prime doctrine of the Aesthetic and its integration with the Analytic by the principle of cognitive unity.

Kant presented the Deduction in two separate sections: (1) an introductory exploration offering a 'preview' in order to help us "over obscurity in matters which are by their nature deeply veiled";[75] (2) the Deduction-proper. Although each covers much the same ground, each should be considered in turn. Following Kant's suggestion, the Deduction-proper becomes more readily comprehensible after the 'preview' has been reviewed; Heidegger's comments serve to clarify philosophic issues they present.

Kant's 'preview' is crucial; it consists of four distinct segments, each of which faces a crucial problem. The first three center on the three aspects or 'moments' of the triune cognitive synthesis; the fourth is a general conclusion bringing some threads of the discussion together.

In turning to each in turn, it is imperative to remember that Kant did not suggest a sequence. Each aspect was presented as such for analytic purposes only. Each is but a distinguishable element of one unified cognitive process, of any single cognitional act. The *entire* discussion faced *one* question: how is knowledge, which depends on synthesis of sense and thought, possible? Each segment of the discussion faced a distinguishable aspect of this one problem; each presented the reasons for a *negative* reply to a specific question:

a. can I have a cognition without immediate sensory awareness of some temporally defined thing?—the denial is headed "i. The Synthesis of Apprehension in Intuition";

b. can I have a cognition without invoking memory of past awarenesses?—the denial bears the title "ii. The Synthesis of Reproduction in Imagination";

c. can I have a cognition without any conceptual reference?—the negative reply appears in both "iii. The Synthesis of Recognition in a Concept" and in "iv. Explanation of the Possibility of Categories";

    d. can I have a cognition without awareness of my abiding self-identity?—the answer is also divided between "iii" and "iv" and presents the doctrine of transcendental apperception.

i. The Synthesis of Apprehension in Intuition

Any experience I have begins with an apprehension, i.e., an *immediate* awareness of an object in perception; I am immediately aware of some representation. Immediate sense awareness is conveyed to consciousness in the form of intuition. For an apprehension to be an apprehension, whatever its nature or source, I must, as apprehending subject, be aware of it. Thus, any apprehension of mine—whether of an external object or an internal idea—represents a modification of my mind. Such a modification of my mind the Aesthetic ascribed to inner sense and identified with time. Consequently, the content of any awareness of mine is temporally framed. As all knowledge refers to representations, to objects 'seen,' and these are always necessarily represented in the form of time, it follows that "our knowledge is thus finally subject to time, the formal condition of inner sense." [76]

What is presented is already a unified representation of awarenesses of object(s) seen as object(s)—rather than as a chaos of color patches—in the limited area before me; the object is thus seen as an object and as being in some area or field of vision (i.e., the "manifold" of intuition). To be aware of the object which I am now seeing before me already represents the presupposition of a 'spread of time.' For my awareness is not merely of the content in the representation of an instantaneous perception; my awareness already presents to my mind a representation which first must have been 'run through and held together' in sequential order—in the order of the sequential modifications of my mind.

As I am looking at a country house, I am discerning color patches, but not all at once; no matter how I narrow the 'now' of the perception, my quickest glance comprises a sequential series of perceptions. To see this house before me 'now,' I have run through and put together several disparate 'noticings'—the white walls, the red roof, the shutters, windows, trees flanking it, the lawn and path leading to it. In the 'now' of immediate apprehension, I am seeing these separated percepts all put together in the report of the briefest possible perception: the 'I am seeing the country house' reports one unifying act of intuitional apprehension (internally ordered by the time distinctions of the few seconds which I require in order to take it all in).

This unificatory synthesis, directed as it is upon intuition without conceptual mediation, is termed by Kant the "Synthesis of Apprehension." Prior to any particular presentation this capacity makes the representation of any field and of the objects in it, as such, possible. Presupposed by any perceptual act, it is then, an apriori, transcendental, and necessary requisite for any 'raw data' to be brought into experience as the representation of any particular manifold; it is then also requisite for the apriori representations of space and time.

Pure intuition, then, is not merely the 'form' of all representations; pure intuition is already time-forming: I am "generating time itself in the apprehension of the intuition." [77] Pure intuition, as such, presupposes a time-consciousness which makes it possible to grasp immediately any object and the field of vision within which it appears; this immediate 'grasping' is the Synthesis of Apprehension and constitutes the first possibility of any awareness at all. The prime temporal doctrine of the Aesthetic was that all representations are necessarily apprehended under the form of time. The Analytic at the outset goes further: time-consciousness is necessary even for the form of time itself.

ii. The Synthesis of Reproduction in Imagination

But this immediate awareness already connects with the notion of memory and memory recall. To be aware of any thing which occupies even a minute spread of time, I must represent to myself a relationship between the immediate perception of the present moment with that of a past moment. To know that the white house at which I am now looking is one house—and not several— I require an awareness of a spread of time in order to connect previous apprehensions of that house with the white house I am now seeing at this instant. As prerequisite to knowing that it is one complete representation, I must be able to keep simultaneously before my mind my memory of earlier perceptions along with my present immediate awareness of it. Perhaps this is more dramatically apparent if the illustration is an 'event' such as a horse-race, instead of a 'thing' such as a race-horse (although a 'thing' is perceived as enduring through a spread of time). It is by means of this facility to bring into the present representation memory of earlier perceptions that I am able to have connected experience of any single thing.

In the act of bringing past apprehensions back to mind, I recall those particular past apprehensions, or their generalized representations, as I suppose them to be of some relevance to my present perception. This selective recall is itself a temporal process and is effected by an exercise of imagination. Whether I am to grasp the temporal spread within a fleeting instant or to know how to identify similar objects perceived in different temporal spreads, this capacity to unite selected past with present awareness of a thing or notion is not only an act of imaginative relating of historically separate perceptions; it is also essential that I be able to do so.

Effected by selective imaginative 'reconstruction' of past content in union with present, this synthesis provides the necessary condition for awareness of an object 'in time' and of the relationship between objects in 'different times,' between a house in present immediate perception and the house in the perception of a few seconds, days, or years ago. The capacity for imaginative synthesis of empirical perceptions is presupposed in any specific experience I may have; it is then an apriori necessary condition for experiences. Our discrimination of it is transcendental in character; as such, this reproductive (or memory-recall) synthesis establishes a necessary defining condition of experience; as a transcendental synthesis, it provides the possibility for the necessary unity of the content of appearances and underlies the possibility for the application of concepts to things.

This memory-recall synthesis is, in Kant's presentation, the one aspect of the tri-partite cognitional synthesis that is preeminently 'time-binding' in character—just because it consists in bringing a 'past' into synthetic union with the 'present' percept. It is, further, essentially temporal because all representations—past and present —are ideas in the mind, representations in inner sense. Intrinsically it is tied to the intuitional Synthesis of Apprehension, of sensory awareness, which provides the ultimate referent of any imaginative recall as of any cognition. This transcendental capacity for imaginative synthesis enables me to be aware of the connections of perceptual instants, of succession in my apprehensions; and it is necessary (as is the first phase of the cognitional synthesis) for even "the most elementary representations of space and time" as such.[78]

iii. Synthesis of Recognition in a Concept

Although it might be argued that momentary particular apprehensions may not require self-consciousness, it is apparent that memory recall does—just because the connections between past and present momentary representations are bound together by an "I think." An act of self-consciousness is presupposed in the binding together of a number of separable representations into one unified whole. Self-consciousness is presupposed in one synthesized field of awareness which unites several different successive apprehensions into one more comprehensive apprehension.

Now, Kant proceeds, if memory recall is not merely a random association of past and present perceptions but involves knowledge of that about which we speak,

> our thought of the relation of all knowledge to its object carries with it an element of necessity; the object is viewed as that which prevents our modes of knowledge from being haphazard or arbitrary, and which determines them apriori in some definite fashion. For insofar as they are to relate to an object, they must necessarily . . . possess that unity which constitutes the concept of an object.[79]

My basis for comparing present and invoked past apprehensions, discriminating the similar and dissimilar in what imagination presents, is by conceptual reference. To know that I am seeing a house and not a barn, I necessarily invoke the general conceptual meanings in terms of which I differentiate between these two similar but disparate kinds of structures. By invoking general concepts I conclude what kind of thing it is that I am seeing. Only by reference to some sort of conceptual standard do I invoke and evaluate particular memories of particular objects and reject others as irrelevant to the apprehension of the moment.

The concept, the general idea, invoked as the principle of comparison defines the content memory presents to me for comparison or coordination with the current apprehension; it further supplies the criteria for evaluating their mutual relevance. If I see before me a red-headed man and focus on the red-headed, my memory may present recollections of other red-headed beings I've seen: men, cats, dogs, birds—and I may conclude as to the variety in the class of those animals with red heads. If, however, the focus is on 'man,' my memory recalls other men with differently colored hair and I conclude that red-headed is a variable property of the genus man. The concept under which the object is seen is the 'ruling' concept which defines the necessary and universally binding relationship of apprehensions of the object or notions about it; it also directs the order in the notions I compare and the knowledge I derive from the reflection.

But such necessity of relationship is not found in the particular contingent objects I apprehend. This necessity is 'imposed' on the content of perceptions in order to make them coherent in terms of the criterion offered in the concept that is invoked. The capacity to do this is "without exception, grounded in a transcendental condition." [80] This condition cannot be my experiential awareness of my self, the temporal flow of my own inner-sense perceptions:

> For the mind could never think its identity in the manifoldness of its representations, and indeed think this identity apriori, if it did not have before its eyes the identity of its act, whereby it subordinates all synthesis of apprehension (which is empirical) to a transcendental unity, thereby rendering possible their interconnection according to apriori rules.[81]

This apriori self-consciousness is at the root of any awareness I have; it was called by Kant "transcendental apperception"; it is the "original and necessary consciousness of the identity of the self"; it is "a consciousness of an equally necessary unity of the synthesis of all appearances according to concepts," i.e., the rules by which we connect objects to each other as examples of a special kind; it is also prerequisite to "the apriori concepts (space and time)." [82]

Just as all empirical intuitions are unified under the forms of space and time, there is requisite for knowledge the unification of all appearances by the necessary unity imposed by transcendental apperception. For it is by means of this essential unity of the self that I am able to bring what I have apprehended in separate instants together in terms of one unifying coherent idea.

This triune synthesis, with its three distinguishable but inseparable aspects, represents the functional fusion of the "three original sources (capacities or faculties of the soul) which contain the conditions of the possibility of all experience, and cannot themselves be derived from any other faculty of the mind, namely, *sense, imagination* and *apperception*." [83]

iv. Preliminary Explanation of the Possibility of the Categories, as Knowledge Apriori

From the elucidation of the triune cognitive synthesis the conclusion emerges: all appearances in human experience necessarily conform to the pure concepts of our understanding as these determine the ways in which empirical apprehensions and memory recalls may be unified. It is these transcendental organizing concepts which prescribe the terms by which we may apprehend, understand, and know the things that appear to us. These pure concepts are the modes in terms of which the elements of our experience are brought together; they are the conditions defining the conditions of human knowledge and the kinds of knowledge accessible to human beings. They are the categories in terms of which we apprehend, relate, and think the objects of which we are, can be, or have been aware.

As Kant explained,

the categories . . . are nothing but the conditions of thought in a possible experience, just as space and time are the conditions of intuition for that same experience. They are fundamental concepts by which we think objects in general for appearances, and have therefore apriori objective validity.[84]

These categories are founded on "the relation in which our entire sensibility, and with it all possible appearances, stands to original apperception," [85] i.e., to the conditions of self-consciousness and the possibility of synthesis itself. The affinity of the content we cognize, of the field of apprehension, to our modes of cognizing, is constituted by what we term rules or laws. A rule is that "representation of a universal condition according to which a certain manifold can be posited in uniform fashion . . . when it *must* be so posited, [it is] a *law.*" [86]

That organized dynamic system called 'nature,' to which we look when we perceive objects, is then not something wholly independent of us; insofar as we can know it, it is rather nothing more than the unified collection of possible appearances as representations in the mind; its mode of being *for us* is dependent upon our subjectivity, upon the subjective laws structuring the appearances of entities insofar as they can appear to, and be known by, us. "The apriori conditions of a possible experience in general are at the same time conditions of the possibility of objects of experience." [87] The possibility of an object's being-status in my cognition is predetermined and defined by the extent of my abilities to cognize it.

The fact that I have experiences and can relate them to each other as sequential in one temporally unified experience presupposes my abiding cognitional identity. Any experiences at different times are ordered as *my* comprehensive experience in one comprehensive spread of time—in that one spread of time "in which all modes of appearances and all relation of being or not being occur." [88] These separate experiences are represented and connected in one spread of time as they are ordered into one experience—mine. The transcendental unity of apperception is thus requisite for the unity of experience and for the knowledge of the objects we have experienced within it. It is this thesis that the whole Critique serves to demonstrate. The objects seen as the content of our knowledge comprise the unified world, in a unified space and unified time, in which we see their to-be. The unity of that time, that space, that world of objects which we cognize, is grounded in that apriori self-consciousness which unifies all our apprehensions by means of apriori rules and which Kant terms the radical faculty of all our knowledge. It is for this reason that Kant described the "ground principle of the synthetic unity of apperception" as the "highest principle of all use of the understanding." [89]

There is admittedly much obscurity in this four-part presentation of the triune cognitional synthesis. Paton's extended comment, however, provides an important clarification of just what Kant was doing here:

> He is presupposing that the transcendental synthesis of imagination necessarily combines given appearances in conformity with the forms of thought in which that unity is necessarily manifested. . . . Most of the obscurity is, however, due to the absence of a clear distinction between imagination and thought . . . *without the synthesis of imagination thought can give us no knowledge of objects;* and on the other hand that thought with its forms is the source of the ultimate principles which control the synthesis of imagination . . . every synthesis of imagination (so far as it is a factor in experience of objects) is a synthesis 'in accordance with concepts.' [90]

This Kantian 'preview' of the balance of the Deduction presents the essential points to be re-presented in the Deduction-proper. Insofar as these prime points have emerged here, the focus of Heidegger's discussion is aimed at the 'preview.'

Heidegger has interpreted the second stage of the 'retrieve' as establishing the essential unity of pure knowledge (cf. V.3). This third stage carries the matter forward: the prime point of the Deduction is seen as demonstrating the possibility of what Heidegger is to call ontological synthesis, i.e., the synthesis of the unified characteristics of an object which define it as an object in my awareness—the synthesis of the characteristics which I must discern in order to know that they are descriptive of the object as it appears.

Intuition, or immediate apprehension, is essentially passive in character. The objects which I perceive are not created by me; as a finite knower, I always distinguish them, in any act of cognition, from my own self. If an object is to be cognitively related to me, it can only enter my possible experience of it *as* it appears within the limiting and enabling apriori forms defining my human cognitional capacity. If the object is to be met in experience, it must, as a precondition for such an encounter by me with it, be recognized as a thing that is at hand, as a thing that already is here for me to encounter. The factuality of its being-present, that the object *is*, and the ways in which it *is*, the structure of its be-ing, its to-be, must be recognized as an element within my experience of it.

The necessity of transcendence in human finite knowledge is then demonstrated in the Deduction. This apriori knowledge was termed transcendental by Kant when viewed from my cognition-possibility as knowing subject; this same apriori knowledge is on-tological when viewed from the side of the structure which the object must possess insofar as it can be known by me.[91] This apri-ori knowledge of the necessary character of a known-object is likewise prior to my encounter with it, describes its essential at-tributes of being, and is thereby ontological knowledge. This ontological knowledge is thus apriori knowledge of the to-be char-acteristics of the object, which necessarily conform to the transcen-dental conditions which frame my possibility of knowing it in the first place. In order for an object to be known by me, its own ontological description must conform to the transcendental de-scriptivity of my knowing capacity. This fact, that the ontological characteristics of the things as known are counterparts to the tran-scendental condition of my knowing them, is thus "the condition of the possibility that an object as such can, in general, become an ob-ject for a finite being."[92] This ontological knowledge thus de-fines the possibility and manner in which an object must appear in my cognition. The possibility of this ontological knowledge permits and enables me to orient myself with regard to the object to be known. In order for me to be able to comprehend the be-ing structure of my friend's new country house, I must first be able to turn toward it and establish a cognitional relationship with re-gard to it.

A finite cognitive being essentially requires this basic ability which can be described as the capacity to orient itself to the object as standing over against it. In this radically basic self-orientation to the object, the finite knower extends before himself an open domain (or free area) within which something can 'correspond' to him. To hold oneself in advance in such an open domain, to form it originally is nothing other than the transcendence which characterizes all finite comportment with a thing-that-is.[93]

This possibility of knowledge of the being-structure of the things that are encountered in experience, i.e., of ontological knowledge, is based, as Kant maintained, in transcendental terms, on pure synthesis. This prior system of legitimate ontological predicates attributable to known things, this pure synthesis, Heidegger emphasizes, offers the possibility of permitting an entity to become an object for our cognition. It organizes and grounds the unity of the inherent structure of our transcendence (viz., our capacity to go from particular momentary awarenesses to trans-momentary knowledge of the objects perceived). Pure synthesis is the base of our ability to organize our myriad sense impressions into a coherent intelligible experience of things—of things we take as independent of our knowledge. By thus going to the transcendental ground of our knowledge of objects, the façade of their complete independence has been stripped off and the dualism of an object-subject dichotomy has been bridged.[94]

Our sense impressions reporting objects, then, are 'excited' by them but certainly do not create the entities whose appearance as cognizable objects they make known. Although the entity that appears is uncreated by us, the only way in which it can appear to us *qua* object, the only way in which we can describe its essential traits of 'independence,' is in terms of the pure pre-experiential synthesis which constitutes the ways in which we receive, integrate, understand, and interpret the meanings and significance of the sense impressions we receive. At the same time we are completely dependent upon independent entities to appear within our experience in order to have any content in that experience (or, for that matter, any experience at all); and we are only able to know these objects in accord with the cognitive forms which we 'project' upon them as their objectively ontological characteristics; thus, the essentially finite nature of human reason is vividly brought to light. This pure capacity for pre-experiential cognitional categories, Heidegger continually reminds us, is, as Kant pointed out in opening the Aesthetic, in the service of those representations which pure intuition provides. The central question of the Deduction, then, is: just how can pure thought take us into the heart of the problem of that unity which characterizes ontological knowledge, knowledge of the synthesis of the requisite—of sense and thought —for an object to be for us?

When Kant insisted that it is our representations of objects that render their possible to-be for us, he made it quite clear that the representation of an object does not effect or affect the object's own existence.[95] Human cognition, to use Heidegger's term, is not ontically creative. Human knowing is finite on at least two grounds: it is limited by its own transcendental modes of knowing and by its complete dependence for content on entities insofar as they appear *qua* objects independent of, but conforming to, the specific ways in which we can recognize them as such.

As Kant asserted at the outset, human knowledge begins with specific experiences of specific objects in perception. They are comprehended *qua* interpreted by the concepts in terms of which we 'read' them. General concepts then are only instruments or tools which we utilize in order to correlate, compare, and organize the kinds of perceivings we have. Without specification a 'pure concept' is empty. It remains so as long as I have no idea of what kinds of object it points to.

As I refer a concept to varied types of objects, I begin to understand the kind of object it is that I am concerned about and also the fuller meaning of the concept itself. In bringing a concept into relationship with things, three results ensue: (1) as soon as it is related to even one object, the concept attains to some meaning; (2) the object to which I relate the concept becomes meaningful as I understand something of the kind of thing it is that I am seeing; (3) as the concept is brought to bear on different relevant objects, as the extent of its denotational reference is expanded, the concept's meaning is expanded.

The concept 'substance' as an empty 'pure concept' says nothing to me until it is thought in connection with differing kinds of possible referential illustrations of its significance. Its meaning, when I am cognizing animals and plants, is taken in the sense of 'biological substances' and is quite different from its invocation in terms of the 'things' in a carpenter's shop, such as pieces of wood or the solid iron of his hammer. Or, to take this carpenter's hammer in a gross physical example, it has a different significance as it is 'subsumed' by me under different kinds of empirical concepts as I see it as (a) a tool used to hang a picture on the wall, (b) a tool I use to build the picture frame, or (c) a tool with which to assault the picture's critic.

To comprehend the full meaning of the empirical perception of a hammer, I will see it as interpreted in terms of different kinds of conceptual frameworks. To understand what is meant by any concept, I leave it as meaningless as long as it remains an isolated abstract noun. As adjectival modifiers are added to it, illuminating areas in which relevant examples might be pointed out, the concept becomes filled with meaning as an instrument for classifying the kinds of examples to which it points me. Taken either from the object's side or that of the concept itself, the meaning of the concept develops only as it points me to certain areas of experience, certain kinds of manifolds, which it circumscribes and explains. As I come to see which adjectival modifiers I can incorporate into its range of meaning (by the criterion of specific examples), my comprehension of just what the concept can mean becomes clearer and broader. Concepts are thus functional modes of unifying awarenesses into cognitions. As they prescribe a certain mode of unifying such awareness, they are essentially anticipatory and normative in nature.[96] As concepts define and thereby limit the objects to which they are related, they define and limit themselves and their proper use and employment.

Kant's radical empiricism at the heart of the Critique, especially as Heidegger's interpretation highlights it, thus becomes explicit in its crucial import. If empty concepts can at best have only a negative value in possibly guarding against error, as Kant suggested,[97] if thought, as Heidegger puts it, is always in the service of intuition—then the sole positive value of concepts and the sole mode of their meaningful employment is to render our perceptions intelligible. In order to be meaningful a concept must refer to a kind of thing, to an object reported by intuition—for "intuition takes place only in so far as the object is given to us."[98]

A meaningful concept is ostensive; it has a denotation. The bare requirement for meaningfulness is that the concept have an object to which it refers as a relevant instance of what it 'says.'

This point is readily clear with regard to empirical concepts. But this referential criterion for meaningfulness has not been confined to empirical concepts; Kant regarded it as universally applicable to all concepts as such. But then what are the objects-of-reference of the categories which are pure, pre-experiential concepts? In discussing the conceptual element of the triune cognitive synthesis, Kant had insisted that the representation of things, the reports of intuition, are "not to be taken as objects capable of existing outside of our power of representation. What then," he asked, "is to be understood when we speak of an object corresponding to, and consequently also distinct from, our knowledge?" [99] This question arises just because "outside our knowledge we have nothing which we could set over against this knowledge as corresponding to it." [100]

What then is this thing-that-is that is represented in our representation of a general or pure concept? This object to which a transcendental pure concept refers is not empirical and therefore cannot be perceived as an object that our sensibility can report. Empirically, then, the reference of a transcendental concept as such is not a 'thing' which can appear in our experience. But what then is this unknown kind of object? Kant suggested that it can only be thought as "something in general [*etwas überhaupt*] = X," [101] a general *kind of* thing, but not a specific thing or a specific perceivable object. A specific perceived object can only be presented in and by intuition, not by thought; a representation of a specific thing invokes thought—it is not invoked by it. If *every* concept must have a referential object in order to be meaningful, if specific objects come into consciousness only through sensibility, if transcendental concepts are logically pre-experiential and cannot, as such, presume the particular ontic experience which incorporates them and which they make possible—what is the referential entity that is which gives these transcendental concepts meaning? What is that to which a transcendental concept is pointing us? Kant's answer has been a mystifying one, viz., a 'transcendental object.' Its importance is underlined by Kant's own judgment that it is *the* fundamental concept of transcendental philosophy; one important reason for this conclusion is indicated in Kant's own statement in the summary chapter "Phenomena and Noumena," where we are told, "This transcendental object cannot be separated from the sense data, for nothing is then left through which it might be thought." [102]

Paton's comment is suggestive:

> The 'something' to which we refer one appearance differs in no way from the 'something' to which we refer another appearance, if we consider it an abstraction from the appearance which is referred to it. Since *ex hypothesi* it cannot be known by means of intuition, it cannot be known at all, it can only be conceived or thought; and the concept of something in general [i.e., of its "'thingness' or 'objectivity'"], since it contains no elements derived from empirical intuition, must be a pure concept.
>
> This concept of something in general or the transcendental object is present in, or presupposed by, all our empirical concepts —when we judge that this is an animal, we judge that the given appearance is the appearance of 'something' which is real independently of our minds. The presence of this pure concept in all our empirical concepts alone can confer upon our ideas relation to an object, or in other words objective reality.[103]

We can only have receptive intuition by orienting ourselves to some specific thing that is represented to us but which we do not know aside from the perception of it. Abstractly considered, however, any representation happens to be of 'some thing in general'; if we consider *that* some thing is, without considering *what* it is, we are thinking a general thingness and not a pipe-thing or a cigarette-thing as such on the table before us. Until the 'thing-ness' has been specified, however vaguely, the representation of a 'something-ness' is not the representation of an intuitable object within our sphere of knowledge. A 'some (kind of) unspecified thing' does not exist in human experience; only particular specific things do. But the 'some (kind of) unspecified thing' is logically presupposed as a generalization of specific things—insofar as any thing that appears, appears as a thingness specified as perceivable. A transcendental concept does not, *qua* transcendental, refer to any particular specified objects; it merely renders derivative applicable principles possible; so the transcendental object (referential object of a transcendental concept) is not a particular specified object; it merely renders empirical objects possible. For a pipe-thing to be, it first, logically if not empirically, must be an example of 'thing-ness in general' before it can possibly be specifiable as a particular pipe-thing. Just as empirical objects are cognized in terms of empirical concepts (or the applicable principles of pure concepts) so the relation of the transcendental object to the transcendental concept establishes the possibility of the distinction and relationship in the first place (i.e., the distinction and the relationship between object and concept, of object *qua* objectively independent of and yet related to the concept *qua* subjective ground of cognition).

The 'some thing in general,' the *etwas überhaupt,* was thus for Kant the necessary logical referent of a transcendental concept which cannot be intuited but must be presupposed. In the world of the empirical, the intuitable, a mere 'some thing,' a mere some-entity, has no reality, no be-ing; a general *etwas* is not an object of possible empirical cognition; in human experience it is *not* a thing-that-is.*

If the transcendental object (the 'some thing = *etwas* in general') *is not* some particular thing, and yet it is not 'pure negativity,' it *is* at least a *non-thing.*[104] Obscure as this point seems to be, the peculiarities of the English language seem to augment its obscurity. It is essential to note that the two key German words, *etwas* and *nichts,* are not etymologically related as are the standard English counterparts, 'something' and 'nothing.' The whole meaning of Kant's discussion, as well as of Heidegger's, is lost if one forgets this linguistic difference. The *Nichts,* as Heidegger abundantly makes clear, is *not* to be understood as 'absolutely nothing' (*nihil absolutum*);[105] it *is* that quality of being not-a-thing in our experience; but this is not to say that thereby it must be, in the full sense of the English word, 'nothing-at-all.' For 'something' may be presupposed without its being a definite 'thing' we can

* The term 'thing' is no simple concept; it has often been used in otherwise precise philosophic discussions without care. In a Kantian context it becomes a precise technical term and means a particular object of possible experience. As Heidegger has elucidated the matter in *What Is A Thing?* it is an object within human experience legitimately describable in terms of the cognitive Principles.

perceive as such (e.g., 'a law of nature' is not a perceivable 'thing' but we nevertheless do not regard it as empty meaningless nothing-ness).

The whole meaning of this discussion, also, for Kant as for Heidegger, is lost if we forget that the point at issue is the pre-experiential transcendental ground of human cognition, the pre-experiential ground of the ontological characterizations of the things-that-are *in* our experience. These grounds, for both, are not inductive generalizations but apriori presuppositions.

As ontological ground of the specific things-that-are *for us*— as the transcendental ground of our representations of them— there is thus presumed, as Heidegger explicates the matter, not a postulation of complete emptiness but some kind of 'reality,' some kind of 'nonphysical' descriptive structure which the specific thing must incorporate in order for it to-be, to be known, to enter into our field of cognition. This presupposed structure does not come into our perceptual range and it is thereby, as such, not a 'thing' which sense intuition can report. It thus needs remain a general some-thing-ness which abides as concealed from our per-ceptual range.

Interior to every appearance there is some aspect of it which re-mains unperceived and unperceptible even while the 'surface' of the appearance is cognized. In full fidelity to Kant's transcen-dentalism, Heidegger insists on the thesis that the possibility of human cognition of objects is bound up with the necessity of according a kind of positive ontological status to that which is not open to our sensibility, to our immediate knowledge. The issue is not that of perceptibility or specificity; it is not a specific object of intuition to which a transcendental concept refers—but a generalized kind of being-ness as such, a necessity of the object's own to-be in order for it to be for us. Necessarily presupposed in any specific perception of a thing is that the thing is, that it enjoys a state of be-ing quite aside from its be-ing in our perception of it. Thus the specific object can not be reduced to a mere congeries of subjective sense impressions; these sense impressions mark out the limited range of our experiential capacity—but that limitation points to the hidden structure of the thing that is here before me, that enables it to be here and so be capable of being recognized as existent. The structure of the thing, which I cannot see, must be presumed in order that it can-be and can come into the horizon of my experience. An example might be helpful, if not taken as anything more than a somewhat symbolic illustration of the point at issue.*

When I look at a modern skyscraper, I presuppose some kind of supporting framework which maintains the building the surface of which is an appearance before me. As long as I leave the building intact, I cannot possibly see that framework no matter how closely I examine it; yet I presuppose that hidden framework in every reference I make to the building as having a positive being-status outside of my representation of it. I am as certain of the existential reality of that hidden framework as I am of the building itself or of any aspects of it of which I have immediate knowledge. And, if we want to carry the matter even further, I presuppose those modes of operational procedures of the being of nature that I call 'physical laws,' which explain to me, if I pursue the matter, just why the framework does keep the building erect in one specified place during a specified 'spread' of time.

What Heidegger has in effect suggested is that Kant's transcendentalism works with a concept of the finite human mind *qua* the center of an experiential field. Like a magnet, the field around it is structured for it by the ways in which it can become aware of what is there to be recognized and to be known. The objects it 'attracts' comprise the content of its experience. But that it can 'attract' objects, become aware of them, and the aspects of them of which it can become aware, are limited by the special ways in which it can establish a relationship with the objects about it. A 'self-conscious magnet' would not be aware of a glass paperweight but would instantly and necessarily establish a cognitive relationship to an iron decoration mounted on it; it would, however, only be aware of the magnetic aspect of that iron decoration whose color would remain 'hidden' to it. Just so, the human knower is

---

* If taken without 'a grain of salt,' going to perceptual examples as illustrative of transcendental or ontological nonperceptual theses necessarily confuses and misrepresents the point being made; a 'physical' example, taken literally, literally begs the question! The example or illustration is never the point; in a somewhat clumsy and unsatisfactory way it is like a traffic arrow which points in the general direction where the point at issue is to be found.

only able to maintain an orientation toward those 'things' in his field which meet the requirements of his perceptual capability and of the structure of the concepts in terms of which he is able to assimilate and understand the limited kinds of representations he is able to have. Just as the 'self-conscious magnet' would recognize the iron decoration of the glass paperweight in terms of its magnetic response, it would 'presume' that that decoration has a certain shape and color, which do not appear to it as its immediate knowledge—so we can only become aware of those aspects of the things-that-are in terms of the ways in which we are able to respond to their modes of be-ing. Just as the 'self-conscious magnet' would not be able to see the magnetic field with which it structures the field about it, but on which it necessarily depends for its responses to the objects in that field, so we cannot see the transcendental structure which we project onto the field about us—and which returns to us in ontological terms as the structuring of the objects which are reported back to us. But transcendental (outgoing) or ontological (incoming), that projective cognitive structuring is 'unseen' and yet presupposed in every cognition; that projective structuring is also presumed in every description (taken as objective and true) of the specific things which respond to our 'taking them in' to the extent that they are 'taken in.' *

The hidden framework, which supports the surface of the thing as it appears to me, is not a thing within my perceptual experience. More precisely, perhaps, the 'magnetic'-like structure of the experiential field which I project about me is not a perceptual thing but is necessary for my perceptual experience of any specific thing.

Yet, how do we describe these structural components of the experiential field in a terminology that seeks to remain loyal to the empirical insistence on the necessity of sensibility for any experiential content? If the cognizable structurings of the particular things that can appear to perception are not themselves things, appearances, or perceptions, yet are objectively real, how shall we designate them? They are not to be regarded as particular things-that-are, but also, they are certainly not nothing-at-all;[106] they *are*

---

* One prime reservation about this illustration is that although the magnet's 'awareness' affects its object of cognition (as distinct from its cognition of the object), no such reciprocation is suggested by either Kant or Heidegger.

non-things. If they are not specific intuitable things, they are, by
obversion, 'non-(specific, intuitable things),' viz., 'non-things.'
And, it is in this sense that Heidegger's *Nichts* would seem to
become intelligible and must be understood.*

If the structuring of the experiential field of possible awarenesses
—following the analogy of the magnet—is necessary for any
specific experiences at all, if the human mind must project itself
into these experiential structures in order to 'fetch-back' the representations which nourish its experience, if the objectivity of
experience lies in the simultaneous independence of those represented objects as they yet conform to the projected structure of the
field in which they are known—then the human mind must operate out from its center into the non-thing structure that it has
projected into the experiential field before it. The human mind
must, as Heidegger graphically puts it, hold itself out into this
area of non-thing-ness in order to be able to perceive specific
things.[107] In order to know what it can know, the human mind
must maintain itself in contact with those *dynamic* modes of
be-ing in terms of which it is able to become aware of, cognize,
and understand specific things. Knowledge of these projected
modes of be-ing is the 'ontological knowledge' of which Heidegger
speaks with increasing frequency. In order to make fullest use of
these 'lines of communication' between objects and ourselves,
which we lay out into the experiential field about us, we must
ourselves maintain these dynamic modes of be-ing that permit
objects, to the extent that these objects are in accord with them,
to be recognized and known *qua* objects independent of our
recognizing and knowing them to be.

This structuring of the experiential field (in terms of which
objectivity is defined) is that object of transcendental concepts to
which Kant obliquely and ambiguously referred as the 'transcendental object.' It is that necessary structure of the objectivity of
the particular things-that-are in human experience, as Paton sug-

---

* Heidegger could not have used the word *undinge* because a 'non-thing' is
not chimerical, absurd, or unreal. This is not to be interpreted as any kind of
reification; clearly, the *Nichts* is not a 'thing' or entity; it is a way or mode of
be-ing which is requisite for a 'thing' to become known or knowable to us.
(N.B. Kant's use of *undinge* [e.g. *CRR,* A39 = B56] is precisely in the sense of
the absurdity of an unreality.)

gested, to which the concepts of human transcendence refer. It is this projection of a determinate structure within which, or underlying which, objects must appear in order for us to become aware of them. It is this correlation of the transcendental grounds of our cognition with the structural field in terms of which we recognize the to-be of the things-that-are for us that enables us to speak meaningfully of the objectivity of the entities that appear as objects of our cognition. It is just because this structure of the objectivity of objects is projected out of the mind's transcendence into its experiential field, which is thereby defined as such, that the dichotomy of subject-and-object is obliterated without negating the pragmatic import of the distinction.

Although Kant's obscure reference to the transcendental object appeared as an unenlightening digression, the interpretation which Heidegger's discussion suggests is necessary and crucial just because his concern is to focus on the ontological structures of the entities that appear as objects to us and which render them capable of so appearing. His 'category' of non-thing-ness, as the dynamic structuring of the experiential field, hopefully throws light on the positive significance of Kant's transcendental object and suggests why Kant felt it necessary to bring it into this discussion. It also seems to clarify the manner in which the Kantian solution of the problem of objectivity, propounded by the transcendental formulation, actually succeeds.*

This discussion of the transcendental object arose out of recognition of the twofold nature of cognitional finitude seen in the cognitive limitation imposed by the transcendental grounds of human knowledge: the human capacity for transcendence, and the essential dependence of human knowledge on specific representations of specific things for experiential content. The animating query for the interpretation is for the ground of those ontological characteristics which objects must possess in order to enter our cognition and the conditions which enable us to orient ourselves to objects as they appear in our cognitional horizon. Our

* The additional significance of the transcendental object and the 'category' of non-thing-ness emerges later, as we shall see, as integral to the conception of time, the priority of possibility, and the understanding of temporal experience.

capacity to orient ourselves to objects, to let them be for us, is a mark of our transcendence. Despite its subjective ground, as the last few pages show, this origin in human subjectivity cannot be legitimately charged with 'subjective idealism'; it is rather a carrying forth of the principle of the Copernican Revolution. The task which is then imposed is the explication of the Kantian thesis that knowledge is not mere illusion.

The import of the Deduction is seen in the clarification of the ground of objectivity in an experience that ultimately emanates from subjective projection. The first two aspects of the triune cognitive synthesis—the intuitive synthesis of apprehension and the imaginative synthesis of memory recall—point directly to the subjective conditions of cognition which are required to render knowledge possible. The conceptual aspect of the triune synthesis yields transcendental apperception, the unity of the "I think" as the source of those universal and necessary apriori categories in terms of which the objectivity of human knowledge is defined.

Insofar as these categories are applied to representations of objects whose existence is not regarded as dependent upon us, they become meaningful. The alleged independence of objects is the mark that our knowing them is no mere subjective daydreaming. In some sense an unknown entity appears before us—in a way that accords with our limited cognitional power. Insofar as a given appearance calls forth certain concepts and bars the applicability of others, it imposes a limitation on the ways in which we can legitimately describe it. If I am seeing an automobile before me which a companion insists on describing as a horseless carriage, we may argue about which conceptual structure is more precise, but we would both agree that the same appearance precluded either of us from describing it as a sled or toboggan.

The 'I think' * by which I relate each of my varied experiences to each other is the source of unification which permits me to see them all as segments of my one unified experiential history. My 'I think' builds this unity of my experience by relating the 'places'

---

* Note that the *ich denke,* as the *cogito,* although traditionally translated as 'I think,' can be rendered with equal linguistic legitimacy as 'I am thinking'; this alternative rendering by the present progressive tense urges the *essential* temporality of any intellectual activity—a prime thesis which Heidegger develops.

of varied objects that have appeared as being in different parts of 'one space.' [108] Insofar as every representation is sequentially ordered in my mind, I relate them in terms of the 'one time' in which I have experienced them. Insofar as I regard these objects as not dependent upon me and as intelligible by me, I regard them as being subject to the kind of universal necessity which is prescribed by all the pure concepts at my disposal and so as forming "a whole of causally interdependent existences." [109]

Thus the conceptual side of our cognitive process imposes a twofold limitation on that process: (a) the limitation of the concepts which we may legitimately apply to given appearances, and (b) the organization of all appearances into temporal as well as spatial order. Concepts thus impose a constraint upon my realm of possible experience and define the limits of objectivity attainable in that realm.

The whole notion of the objectivity of the object itself necessitates certain limitations of conceptual description and applicability.[110] This necessary constraint and limitation, Heidegger points out, must be regarded as imposed in advance; before any particular object appears, the concept, as normative, enables us to differentiate what kinds of objects should or should not be accepted as appropriate examples of that concept. As precursory or anticipatory, a concept is thus a particular idea of the way in which diverse presentations can be legitimately unified; it thus offers a prescription of a legitimate mode of unifying separate awarenesses.

As the concepts I project are the means by which I unite diverse objects into intelligible and temporal order, the operational modes of this unification of experience are thus unified in the unificatory act expressed in my 'I think.' The unity of our representations in a unified field is, as Kant described it, dependent upon consciousness. This representational unity of my experiential field consists in positing the independence of objects from my perceptions of them. Heidegger terms this an 'act of objectification.' The object's objectivity is then defined for me by the ways in which I can 'see' and comprehend it, by the transcendental modes I have to cognize it and in terms of which I describe it as ontologically being here for me to see. This positing of independent beings, this act of objectification, Heidegger reasons, is ultimately basic; it is the fundamental act of the understanding at the base of the possibility of experience itself.

The understanding is thus the source of objectification, the source of the possibility of letting objects be objects for us. By means of pure concepts, all of which depend on this root concept of the objectivity-of-the-object, the understanding prescribes rules of necessity which permit the ordered unity of experience. The understanding thus imposes order on all of our representations and, as Kant had said, "prevents our modes of knowledge from being haphazard or arbitrary . . . [rather it] determines them apriori in some definite fashion." [111] As the source of concepts, the understanding is thus self-constraining. In advance of any presentation, it prescinds the 'impossible'-for-us from the realm of possible experience. By its rules it prescribes all possible modes for the unification of representations which may be brought together into a coherent experience. Thus, Heidegger suggests that when Kant spoke of concepts as serving as universal conditions, what was meant was that pure concepts have "normative unities as their sole content . . . they provide, first of all and in advance, the normative as such." [112] The pure concepts of the understanding thus define and set out the limits of what is possible for us, the confines of that possibility within which all human experience is necessarily confined.

If the entire possibility of the objectivity of objects is determined by the understanding, if the concepts of the understanding define the entire possibility within which any experience can occur, if the unification of my experience is the act of my 'I think'—does all this conspire to establish the priority of thought before sensibility or to deny the earlier thesis that thought is merely the 'servant' of intuition? In denying this outcome, Heidegger explains that Kant's focus had been on the element of pure thought in the unity of transcendental knowledge; it is just because thought must be shown to relate to sensory intuition that the task of logic must be broadened in a transcendental grounding. If seen in its proper context, it is apparent that Kant was deliberately working out the problem of the finitude of human reason, the essential finitude which creates the problematic and limitation of human knowledge. It is this presumption of finitude that defines Kant's problematic, the stages of his argument, the conclusions he brings forth.

The pure concepts of the understanding do not 'issue a permit' to an object to appear to us; the radical dependence of thought on sensory intuition is demonstrated by the need of thought to have an object in order for it to have something 'to talk *about*.' [113] The essential dependence of thought upon those objects which sensory intuitions report demonstrates its neediness, its indigence, its limitation and essential finitude. The "understanding is—in its finitude—the supreme faculty, i.e., finite to the highest degree. . . . It is only insofar as the pure understanding as understanding is the servant of pure intuition that it can remain the master of empirical intuition." [114] Only as there may be the presentation of objects *qua* temporal that require explanation is there any need for a-temporal concepts to explain them. The possibility of the pure form of time is thus the grounding of the possibility for the applicability of concepts to things and thereby of the possibility of concepts to attain referential meaning.

The mutual dependence of sensibility and thought reveals the essential finitude of each, just as the structural unity they comprise reveals the finitude of the transcendence they embody. This transcendence, this self-defining, enabling limitation of what can be known announces the definite possibility of knowing; it was discovered by Kant in the triune synthesis which the Transcendental Deduction aims to bring into the light. It is finally displayed in the deduction-proper.

The heart of the Transcendental Deduction, the deduction-proper, Kant entitled "The Relation of the Understanding to Objects in General, and the Possibility of Knowing Them Apriori." Its declared aim was to bring into "systematic interconnection" the three "subjective sources of knowledge upon which rests the possibility of experience in general and of knowledge of its objects—*sense, imagination,* and *apperception*." [115] Each of these is manifested empirically but is, as transcendental, only one of the three elements of the apriori cognitive synthesis from which all knowledge emanates. *Together* they comprise this triune synthesis.

In the 'preview' presentation he had considered each of these three elements separately. Here in the formal Deduction he focuses on the integral unity of the triune cognitive synthesis itself. As

Kant had explained at the outset, he has, in effect, here offered two different approaches to this same synthesis: the first, the Objective, sought to demonstrate the dependence of understanding on pure intuition, of concepts on apprehension; the second, the Subjective, began with intuition and proceeded 'up' to its relationship with the understanding.[116]

i. The Objective Deduction

Starting with transcendental apperception and the necessary unity of consciousness (as imposed by the 'I think') for the possibility of experience, Kant derived the unity of the field provided by intuition. This apperceptive unity of consciousness, as Paton has explained, "presupposes a *universal* synthesis of every given manifold by imagination. . . ."[117] The transcendental unity of imaginative synthesis is, then, "the pure form, or cognition, of all possible experience"[118] derived from sense intuition. The necessary unity of this transcendental synthesis of imagination, logically "prior to apperception," as Kant explicitly declared, "is the ground of the possibility of all knowledge, especially of experience."[119]

Thus, Kant explained, *"the unity of apperception in relation to the synthesis of imagination is the understanding"* which provides the categories of conceptualization. But the categories only provide knowledge as they operate in relationship to and by means of "intuition and its synthesis through imagination."[120] These categories, arising out of the unity of self-consciousness (apperception), provide the limitation of possible experience and enable the representations of intuition to be molded into one unified knowledge. The entire possibility of experience is thus dependent on this compounding of intuition and thought by means of imaginative synthesis.

Kant's accomplishment here, Heidegger explains, was to demonstrate the necessary dependence of the understanding upon intuition by means of the mediating imagination. Pure thought is essentially finite just because it can neither determine the to-be of an object by itself nor represent the object to itself. This means that ultimately all knowledge is dependent on the object "to come forward,"[121] to appear to us. And, after this contingent appearing within the knower's orientation to it, the object can be known only insofar as it can be 'sensibilized' and reported; only those aspects of it can be reported which sense intuition can apprehend; conceptual knowledge of the object is limited at the outset to the degree to which human sensibility can comprehensively 'take it in.'

When Kant described the necessary relationship between the categories (of pure thought) and pure intuition (i.e., time) by means of imaginative synthesis, he did not, Heidegger complains, "define with precision the structural relations involved in the unity of the unifying synthesis." [122] Yet Kant had said, "This synthetical unity (of knowledge) presupposes or includes a synthesis." [123] Heidegger emphasizes the "presupposes," ignores the "or includes," and protests this kind of ambiguity.

As seen in the preceding chapter, Heidegger had concluded that all synthesis is created by an exercise of imagination. He thus concurs with Kant's conclusion that the pure imagination is "prior to apperception [and] is the ground of the possibility of all knowledge. . . ." [124]

His conclusion is then in accord with Kant's own indications —since pure apriori intuition has been identified with time, the "pure imagination must be essentially related to time. Only in this way is pure imagination revealed as the mediator between transcendental apperception and time." [125] In the Deduction itself Kant had hardly referred to time in any explicit way. But the preeminence of time and the grounding of all possible knowledge in the realm of the temporal was made explicit: time, as the form of inner sense, Kant declared at the beginning of the Deduction, is to be regarded "throughout what follows . . . as being quite fundamental." [126]

The Objective Deduction thus focused on the essential relationship between pure imaginative synthesis as essentially temporal and the a-temporality of the pure understanding. Heidegger renders explicit what Kant presupposed throughout—the ultimate dependence of the whole structure of knowledge on the limitations of the temporal nature of pure intuition and the function of imagination to bring a-temporal concepts into relationship with it.

ii. The Subjective Deduction

The Subjective Deduction commenced with sensibility and proceeded 'up' to understanding. Its declared aim was clarification of
"the necessary connection in which understanding, by means of
the categories, stands to appearance." [127] Our perceptions are each
singular and separate; in order to synthesize them into a unified
presentation, the power of imagination is needed. So that this
unification may be ordered and may be in relation to other perceptions—instead of being a haphazard association—this imaginative synthesis requires an objective ground. From the side of the
appearances themselves, this objective ground Kant called their
"affinity," i.e., their conformity to the principles of apperception
—and this conformity permits their incorporation into cognition.
This affinity of appearances, this conformity of the things that
appear to the rules governing our awareness of appearances, "is a
necessary consequence of a synthesis in imagination which is
grounded apriori on rules." The basis of the possibility of a unified
experience is, then, the transcendental ego, the "abiding and unchanging 'I,'" [128] which imposes unity on all perceptions as they
are synthesized and rendered intelligible. Just as sense intuition,
as representation, is essentially 'reducible' to the pure form of intuition, viz., time, so all consciousness is pure apperception. The
synthesis of imagination, operating by apriori rules, organizes the
manifold of intuitional appearances and renders it intelligible by
bringing it into relation with the unity of apperception.

Thus the transcendental imagination is "the necessary connection" between sensibility and understanding. It is that "which conditions all apriori knowledge, [and] is thus one of the fundamental
faculties of the human soul." [129] Empirically, imagination functions in regard to particular objects; transcendentally, it aims at
the necessary synthetic unity of the field of appearances as such.
The transcendental imagination 'bridges' the 'gap' between the
capacity to have separate sense impressions of different specific
things at specific 'times' and the capacity to render such presentations, when unified, intelligible in terms of general concepts which
have no essential temporal reference and which emanate from

[98]

pure apperception, the capacity to pronounce an 'I think.' By rendering the particularity of sensibility and the generality of concepts amenable to each other, this 'reciprocal translating service' of transcendental imaginative synthesis is the source of the affinity of appearances to conceptual thought. It is what makes it possible for us to associate appearances in accord with prior rules.

Imagination is, therefore, the source of the possibility of experience itself. As pure imagination is concerned with appearances in pure intuition (in time), it is necessarily based on time. Thus "only through time, and the transcendental synthesis of time, is the unity of apperception the ultimate principle of the unity of the manifold in consciousness." [130]

The Objective Deduction sought to demonstrate the objective validity of categories with reference to material provided through intuition. But the Subjective Deduction, as Paton suggested, was concerned to establish the power of cognition itself.[131] As such it is basic. Heidegger criticizes Kant for not having explicitly set out the receptive nature of the finitude of knowledge which this grounding requires.

But in view of what has already been stated, it seems apparent that the Subjective Deduction, taken broadly, is fundamental to the Critical enterprise, for its task is to provide that subjective grounding of knowledge which the Copernican Revolution demands. Heidegger's basic criticism, then, to anticipate the sequel, is that Kant did not pursue it to deep enough ground; much of Heidegger's subsequent interpretation in delineating the ground of fundamental ontology can be understood as an attempt to ground the possibility, nature, and power of cognition and thus to carry forward this task that the Subjective Deduction had begun. Indeed, taken in this way, one can see much of *Being and Time* as a detailed development of this subjective justification for the possibility of human knowledge and experience in general.

At this stage, however, Heidegger sees the two Deductions as joined in setting forth the same conclusion: pure intuition, imagination, and apperception are not side-by-side aspects of the human mind but are integrally unified and mutually implicatory as an essentially internal relationship in any cognitive act. This conclusion is not only eminently reasonable but also not particularly unique.[132]

From this established unity of the 'three elements,' Heidegger proceeds to draw a conclusion in his own terms:

> the transcendental deduction has established the intrinsic possibility of the essential unity of pure knowledge. This constitutes the pure act of objectification and, by this means, first makes manifest a horizon of objectivity in general.[133]

The stated limitations within which we may encounter those objects which can be known are thus defined by both the affirmative and negative sides of their possibility—in the clarification of how, and thereby what, knowledge comes to be.

This "horizon of objectivity in general" is, then, grounded in the unity of experience. As Kant had pointed out in first discussing the apriori categories in the 'preview':

> It is only one experience in which all perceptions are represented as in thoroughgoing and orderly connections; just so there is only one space and one time in which all forms of appearances and *all relation of to-be or not-to-be occur*.[134]

This horizon of objectivity is essentially temporal; it effectively marks the reassertion of human finitude as it deprives the understanding of ultimate priority by virtue of its essential grounding "in the pure synthesis of imagination, a synthesis which is bound to time." [135] For, as Kant had said, it is "pure imagination which conditions all apriori knowledge" [136] and brings sensory reports and conceptual categories into cognitive unity. The categories, then, Heidegger points out, are *essentially* time-related by means of the mediating function of pure imaginative synthesis. Thus the principle of the "sensibilization of concepts" [137] (which is to be faced in the sequel) is grounded here.

The demonstration of the categories as essential to knowledge establishes their objectivity, their determining role in permitting objectivity in our knowledge of the perceptions which are 'brought' to them for interpretation. The categories comprise objectivity by prescribing the ways in which entities must demonstrate an affinity to them in order to become objects which we can recognize and know as such. The categories thus become, in

Heidegger's terms, the ground of the ontological characterizations with which we describe those entities as appearing objects. Their true meaning is to serve as the grounding of the ontological predicates of the specific or ontic objects that appear. From the center of the three elements, from the transcendental imaginative synthesis of sensibility and thought, the set of categories is pointed out as that which "forms the essential unity of ontological knowledge. . . ." [138] The 'origin and truth' of the categories are to be found in the fact that they set forth the modes of be-ing of objects insofar as they appear to human cognition.

Now, insofar as the Deduction is often considered the center of the Analytic and Kant seems to have solved his problem, we must ask whether Kant has succeeded in establishing the foundations of metaphysics. The matter, however, is still unfinished; Kant had seen the necessity of proceeding to the Schematism in order to elicit the principle of applicability of the categories to experience; Heidegger sees the necessity of following him in order to reach to a more rudimentary ground.

In Heidegger's examination of Kant's Analytic of Concepts, he has stressed the unity of the three elements of cognitive acts, the priority of sensibility in making knowledge possible, the ontological import of the categories with regard to the nature of the objects which are experienced, and the integrating role of imaginative synthesis in bringing sense and thought into functioning unity. The transcendental object, which Kant regarded as inseparable from sense data and logically necessary for cognition, has been identified with the 'non-thing *Nichts*' as essential ontological grounding of the functioning of finite cognition. Time has emerged into prime importance on at least two grounds: (1) as the form of inner sense and thereby of any possible experience, pure intuition in advance of any particular object prescribes a temporal horizon of objectivity for any possible experience within which concepts must function; (2) as involved in imaginative synthesis itself, the unification of sense and thought necessarily involves temporalization and temporal transcendence. Consequently, we may anticipate the further development of these themes to point out the essential temporality of all elements involved in any cognitional act. It has already been suggested that time is more than merely a pure form of sensibility; as intrinsic to imaginative synthesis, which provides the center of experience, it must somehow be the essential ground which enables us to achieve temporal concepts, in essentially temporal acts, and thus effect that synthesis whereby we can legitimately apply ontological predicates to things.

We are thus pointed ahead to the Schematism, which seeks to provide the temporal grounding of all cognition. Kant, in the Analytic of Concepts, had elucidated the nature and possibility of cognitional objectivity; as we now proceed to Kant's Analytic of Principles, we proceed to consideration of Kant's thesis concerning the ways in which that cognition comes into being.

5 · *Ground of Ontological Synthesis*

WHAT HEIDEGGER BROUGHT OUT of the Deduction is the preeminence of the transcendental imagination as the force binding the two basic elements of knowledge into integral unity. The demonstration of the necessity of the relationship between sense and thought, between the categories of the understanding and the temporal form of pure intuition, was the task of the Deduction. The internal structure of this relationship is the subject of the Schematism.

The Deduction is the second of the two chapters Kant had entitled 'Analytic of Concepts'; to move on to "The Schematism of the Pure Concepts" is to consider the first chapter of the 'Analytic of Principles,' the section in which Kant had gone beyond a discussion and justification of abstract categories to those actual operational Principles which constitute knowledge.

The chapter "The Schematism" has also been generally regarded as obscure and as 'having been the stumbling block of Kantian interpreters';[139] it has been difficult enough for some commentators to dismiss it as an architechtonic exercise. Despite complaints about obscurity, Heidegger regards it as the most carefully written and organized section of the Critique, pronounces it "perfectly clear in its construction"[140] and suggests an outline for its organization. His other criticisms notwithstanding, Ernst Cassirer has applauded "Heidegger's detailed presentation of this chapter which works out every individual feature."[141] In many ways the elucidation of these difficult pages is one of the more brilliant and penetrating parts of his entire examination.

Heidegger regards the few pages of this short chapter as "the heart"[142] of the Critique, the "basis of transcendence,"[143] the "basis of the intrinsic possibility of ontological knowledge,"[144] and as leading "to the heart of the whole problematic"[145] embodied in the Critique. This emphatic judgment concerning the central import of the Schematism is not only Heidegger's; it was also the judgment of Kant, himself, who marked it as "indispensable."[146]

Paton has offered an interesting and revealing reflection which is remarkably close to Heidegger's own ground for regarding the Schematism as central and crucial:

> If we reject his [Kant's] derivation of the categories, this chapter acquires a new and special importance; it suggests the possibility of making a fresh start, and of justifying the categories from the nature of time without any reference to the forms of judgment. The Kantian doctrine might perhaps be reformed and reestablished, if we could show that *the categories are implicit in our knowledge of time, and are principles of synthesis without which no object could be known to be an object in time.*[147]

In large part, this last sentence may be taken as a key to Heidegger's analysis of the Critique and the reconstruction it suggests of the Critical philosophy.

The Schematism was concerned with developing the *modes* of application of pure concepts to appearance by providing the "schedule" for their use in concrete situations.[148] The result is to set out the limits of their appropriate utilization.

Established by the Deduction is the thesis that apriori concepts are involved in any cognition. The subsequent problem to which the Schematism is addressed is, then, not whether but *how* apriori categories, as *forms* of thought, can relate to and define particular objects perceived in intuition. All objects are perceived under the unity of time. This unity of time emerging from the Aesthetic as the form of inner sense was amplified in the Deduction as imposed by transcendental imaginative synthesis (and, it has been suggested, itself presupposing a prior synthesis[149]). The unity of time is requisite for any experience, for the unity of your experience or mine. To be cognitively meaningful the categories must, then, be related to objects as they appear in the unity of the form of time. Consequently, for any particular object to appear in human cognition, it must be intelligible in temporal terms.

In the Schematism, then, Kant was concerned with the kinds of temporal characteristics of objects which appear, and only can appear, to human sensibility in temporal form. These temporally apprehended objects constitute the content of cognition. The Deduction's claim is that the categories *must* be applicable to these temporally framed objects; the Schematism's claim is *that* and *how* they are, in general, applicable. Only in the chapter following the Schematism, i.e., the Principles, did Kant set out to elucidate the specific categories as modified by the schematic principle of applicability—as 'schematized categories.' Finally he set out the ground of their proper utilization and the inherent limitations of this employment in the chapter "Phenomena and Noumena" (which he linked to that of the Schematism in its indispensibility[150]).

Kant began by pointing up the radical distinction between the formal universal a-temporal nature of categories and the temporal particularity of sensuous intuition: in the light of this disparity a third mediating factor is needed to bridge them and bring them into an homogeneous relationship. This bridging factor is time. It is through time that the categories organize our intuitions into coherent intelligible experience. Time, as the form of 'inner sense,' has been repeatedly identified with 'pure intuition' and the formal condition of the unification of representations. Following this, Kant argues:

> Now a transcendental determination of time is so far *homogeneous with the category, which constitutes its unity,* in that it is universal and rests upon an apriori rule. But, on the other hand, it is so far homogeneous with appearance, in that time is contained in every empirical representation of the manifold.[151]

Therefore, "the transcendental determination of time . . . as the schema of the concepts of understanding, mediates the subsumption of the appearances under the category." [152] By 'submitting' to temporalization, the application of a-temporal categories to temporal appearances becomes possible. As time is both intuitional and apriori, it has a common bond with pure thought as well as pure intuition. Through the temporal reconstruction of the categories —in their schematization—concept and intuition are brought together into functional unity.

The concept 'tree,' as such, has no content and no temporal reference. The trees I see are quite diverse in shape, color, size, and cyclical seasonal attributes. Yet I am able to recognize some botanic growth as a 'tree' even if it is strange, novel, or weird because I have a sort-of diagrammatic notion or model or pattern which, embodying the categories, corresponds to no particular tree and yet to each and every tree I must encounter at a specific place and time. It is this vague model or schema of any-tree-at-all which I represent to myself in inner sense that provides me with a criterion of essential similarity and thus enables me to connect this representation of this specific tree I am perceiving with the concept that identifies it.

This schema itself is produced by imagination; it is not the reproduction or picture of any particular tree but a general model or pattern of the sort of thing to which a tree conforms. Since imaginative synthesis only provides a unification of sense intuition, the schema is "the representation of a universal procedure of imagination in providing an image for a concept." [153] Each schema is thus a diagrammatic procedure by means of which the abstract concept and a particular percept are brought together in the temporal form in which the percept is recognized as an object of perception. "The schemata are thus nothing but apriori determinations of time in accord with rules." [154] They are pre-experiential procedures, with which these imaginative patterns or schemata are produced and provide the basis for the empirical concepts we use.

These schemata, derived from the categories, provide a fourfold plan of time determination of objects insofar as they can be represented in human experience: (a) time-series, (b) time-content, (c) time-order, and (d) time-scope. By taking the categories 'through' these kinds of time determinations, Kant developed those schematized categories or cognitive Principles which are operational in experience.*

These four species of time determination are produced by transcendental imaginative synthesis. This imaginative capacity to provide a diagrammatic representation of a concept, a model which mediates the pure concept and the particular percept, serves as the ground of cognition and is therefore transcendental; it enables concepts, *qua* schematized, to unify experiences of sensible objects by means of temporal characterizations. These patterns or models or schemata thus provide "the unity of all the manifold of intuition in inner sense, and so indirectly the unity of apperception which as a function corresponds to the receptivity of inner sense." [156]

Thus the pure concepts of the understanding and particular time-formed perceptions are cognitively unified by the schematization of the categories in temporal modes of applicability. In any empirical cognition "we use this schematism to interpret the empirically perceived time relation by the corresponding category (e.g., to apprehend regular succession as causality)." Kant's prime concern, however, was not these cognitional acts themselves but rather the essential structure or transcendental ground upon which particular cognitional acts are based. He thus sought the operational principle, the apriori mode, presumed in any experience, in which the "category, as a rule of the understanding, gives the corresponding time relations a rational basis as object of experience." [157]

Because the schemata provide the time determinations of the categories for their applicability to possible experiential objects, they restrict the use of the categories to the phenomenal world which is apprehended and represented under the form of time. As such, Kant explained, "The schema is, properly only the phenomena, or *sensible concept,* of an object in agreement with the category"; it is this schema which makes experience possible, for, as Kant had said, "a bare concept [must] be *made sensible"* in order to function in experience. [158]

Four pervasive themes of this presentation require examination.

---

* Alternatively, the pure categories may be elicited by abstracting all temporal reference from the schematized category, as the subsequent discussion indicates. [155]

Even within the few pages of Kant's chapter they are completely intertwined. To disentangle them without distortion requires that they be kept in view while focus is shifted to each in turn. So that the full force of the Schematism's accomplishment may become readily apparent, we should first review Heidegger's criticism of (i) the Kantian use of the term 'image(s)' and (ii) the subsumptive presentation of his thesis; we can then proceed to the positive interpretation of its significance in terms of (iii) the sensibilization of concepts, (iv) the temporalism which the Schematism expounds, and (v) a summary conclusion.

i. 'image(s)'

Kant's use of the term 'image' is troublesome and seems to obscure what he was trying to say. Heidegger finds the term to be confusing and misleading.

The schema was described as a "procedure of imagination in providing an image for a concept." The exposition is not aided by invoking the notion of a triangle-in-general to show that "no image could ever be adequate" [159] to its concept. We never do perceive such abstractions; we do indeed have a notion of triangularity which is not an image but a model to which any triangle conforms.

However one may evaluate the Kantian use of the term regarding empirical presentations, it is at any rate clear that "the schema of a *pure* concept of the understanding can never be reduced to any image whatsoever." [160] This is to say that the category, which receives its meaning from its schematized version for application to experience, cannot be drawn from that experience itself. As schematized it precedes any experience as prerequisite, is thereby transcendental, and cannot be 'pictured.' The schematized versions of pure concepts are rules which prescribe the manner in which we can know objects *qua* objects of perception, the manner in which the realm of objectivity-in-general is to be formed. Such rules cannot be reduced to pictures; to use language carrying such implication is to confuse the matter completely.

ii. subsumption

Kant opened by speaking of the subsumption "of an object under a concept." He then proceeded to the question: "How, then, is the *subsumption* of intuitions under pure concepts, the *application* of a category to appearance, possible?" [161]

This matter of subsumption is crucial. It tempts one to read the chapter as a lapse from the priority of intuition and the intrinsic unity of sense and thought. Kant's use of the notion of subsumption of intuitional presentation under the category, joined to his picturing of a schema as a bridge connecting concept to intuition, creates the unfortunate impression of an hypostatization of analytic distinctions into separate entities, which then stand in need of unification. This subsumptive procedure, taken seriously, subverts the essential empiricism of the Critique and the priority of the Schematism in its construction.

Kant had presented the issue as though the manifold, the unified experiential field, is just there to be perceived [162] as a collection of objects apart from which the categories remain devoid of content. The motive seems to have been the desire to endow the categories with meaning rather than to comprehend our awareness of them.

In the Kantian context, as Heidegger has insisted, the manifold can *not* just be there waiting to be rendered intelligible. The schematism of the understanding can *not* consist in the subsumption of an object under an invoked concept. The object arises, and only can arise as such, from the synthesizing unity of apperception as exercised in imaginative synthesis.[163] Kant generally regarded the schema of a pure concept as the product of the synthesis of transcendental imagination; at one point he went so far as to designate the schema as "simply the pure synthesis" itself.[164]

Heidegger is not alone in protesting this initial subsumptive presentation. In the rewritten B Deduction, Kant seemingly tried to forestall a literal reading; he there insisted that the pure category is merely an abstraction from the reference to time which the schematized category, by definition, embodies.[165]

Kemp Smith sees the meaning of the Schematism as "Creative synthesis, whereby contents are apprehended in terms of functional relations, not subsumption of particulars under universals." [166] Paton suggests that Kant's "real aim is not to show that the object falls under the pure category, but to show that it falls under the schematized category; and he cannot do this by eliminating the middle term of the syllogism." [167] In the light of the further development of the Critical philosophy, this subsumptive procedure, de Vleeschauwer points out, invites "very real criticism," for the way it "characterizes the schematism is not calculated to express the intellectual dynamism . . . which allows the pure concept to be brought close to intuition." [168]

Heidegger is thus in accord with prime critics in challenging the validity of the subsumptive presentation. He excuses Kant by suggesting that Kant usually introduced an important point by addressing his contemporaries in their most familiar mode of marking out the problem of concern. The legalistic introduction to the Deduction, Heidegger suggests, is a parallel example and one should not be taken more seriously than the other.

Heidegger refers to Kant's distinction between 'bringing under concepts' (which applies to objects) and 'reducing to concepts' (which refers to imaginative synthesis). But, he quite rightly insists, "Only in the transcendental schematism are the categories formed as categories. If the latter are the true 'fundamental concepts' then the transcendental schematism is primordial and authentic conceptualization as such." [169] Kant's real intent was to focus attention on the central issue which he was attacking, viz., the attempt to 'read' dynamic experience in terms of logical procedure; he sought to demonstrate that the possibility of basic concepts is derived from "the essential structure of pure knowledge," [170] from the inherent nature of the way in which it is possible, in advance of any particular experience, to have experience at all.

The subsumptive presentation has proved to be most unfortunate as it has contributed to the widely proclaimed obscurity of the schematic doctrine. It is not crucial and the fact that it is not points out the central import of the schematic formulation. As de Vleeschauwer has explained it, in a way Heidegger would accept:

The schematism is in reality only a certain form of the general problem . . . [which] is treated in many different ways in almost every passage of the Critical philosophy. The relationship between intelligence and experience is not a problem of a purely exterior subsumption. It is *a question of the being of the perceiving subject* rather than of a condition of perception.[171]

The Schematism brings into one perspective the several strands of Critical doctrine. As such, its import as the focus of the attempt to understand the meaning of the entire Critique comes sharply to the fore. The essential 'message' of the Schematism was pointed out in an exemplary way by Martin in a passage which may be taken as summing up Heidegger's interpretation of it:

> For Kant himself there is not first a pure category and then something added to it in the schema, but the temporal determination of the categories is something originally and inseparably given for us, which is merely analyzed. Heidegger emphasizes the importance that the problem of time acquires in this central position. . . . The decisive result for us is that the categories only have any meaning if they have a temporal modification and that this temporal modification of the categories in the schema at the same time limits the application of the categories to what can be temporally determined.[172]

This meaning is seriously distorted if one persists in regarding subsumption as having anything more than a metaphoric significance.

iii. sensibilization of concepts

"We therefore demand," Kant insisted, "that a bare concept be *made sensible,* that is, that an object corresponding to it be presented in intuition." [173] Only within the range of the perceptible can the understanding function. Before any knowledge can be achieved, Heidegger argues, this horizon of the limits of possible perception must first be determined; we must attain a comprehensive view* of the intrinsic limitations of possible knowledge. How is this to be obtained?

All knowledge is ultimately derived from intuition, from the reports of sense perceptions, which imagination unifies with inter-

* Heidegger's word is *Anblick;* Churchill translates it as 'aspect' and Richardson as 'view'; preference for either would seem dependent on context.

pretive concepts in the triune cognitive synthesis. So much the Deduction has shown. But this cognitive synthesis does not merely incorporate sense and thought into unified cognition. As developed in the Deduction, two questions were implicitly raised and left open: the manner in which transcendental imagination operates in that triune synthesis and the limitations of the possible human knowledge to which it points. Pursuit of the second inquiry helps to clarify the first.

In order to be able to cognize an object we must, first, be able to orient ourselves to it—our transcendental grounds of cognition must be such that they can assimilate what is there to be apprehended and known. In advance of any particular encounter with a particular object, they define the conditions requisite to that encounter. This anticipatory capacity of ours constitutes our transcendence.

Likewise, if an object is to be encountered, it must appear in such a way that we can recognize it; it must be amenable to our means of apprehending it: it must be perceptible. As present and perceptible, it 'offers itself' to us within the horizon, the limits of the field, of our possible experience. That horizon is defined, in advance of any particular presentation, as the Deduction showed, by being-in-time, by being within the perceptible form of pure intuition.

Finite intuition is "equivalent to sensibility" [174] and the capacity to bring concepts into relation with sensibility is the capacity to effect their sensibilization. The schematism is the process of bringing concepts into necessary relationship with the sensuous; it sensibilizes concepts so that transcendence can be operative, so that cognition can occur. The transcendental power of imaginative synthesis, in the schematism, effects this transformation of pure concepts into meaningful reference to sense intuition; it is, thus, the agency which effects the sensibilization of concepts.

Only because of this central role of imagination in cognitive synthesis are we able to encounter, become aware of, and recognize entities as objects of our knowledge. By virtue of imaginative capability to bring concepts into concert with sensory reports we objectivize the things before us which cognitive synthesis brings to our attention. To let an entity become an object for us (i.e., to be objectified) is to perform an act of representation of the unity of the unifying categories. By this process of sensibilization, the categories are rendered coherent with, and amenable to, the representations of sense intuition. In performing this function, in bringing concepts into unity with what is presented in intuition, transcendental imagination provides the fulcrum upon which the entire possibility of finite human knowledge is balanced.

What is thus expounded in the Schematism is the necessary possibility of the 'pure sensibilization' of concepts, the apriori capacity to render experience possible. A schema fuses the concept into the report of intuition; this fusion of the temporally modified or schematized category renders the concept relevant to the perceptible world and enables us to judge particular things or objects as being real for us; the object can then enter into the horizon of our possible knowledge, offer an aspect of itself to our view.

The sensibilization of concepts then "denotes the manner in which a finite being is able to make something intuitive" and known.[175] We begin to see this in the 'how' of possible appearances. In empirical concepts, a sensibilized concept, a schema, is itself a presentation of a rule by which our sense impressions are unified into totalities, viz., objects. In its nature as a rule, it prescribes in advance of any particular presentation, the range of possibility and thereby the limitations under which things may appear to us. A rule functions by prescribing the characteristics which possible entities *must have* in order to be 'inserted' into our empirical view; this sensibilization, as such, does not give us any view of the concept itself; the concept "remains concealed,"[176] and we can only gain a view of it pragmatically in terms of the way it seems to function as a regulative action, in the 'how' of its regulating. This 'how' is seen in its synthesizing function which brings forth from our partial perceptions of an object the distinguishing characteristics of the total object, of the various perceptions of it which unified are its cognition. In noting that I am seeing a house, I am seeing as a unified object what I had sequentially seen in a number of separate perceptions, e.g., it has more than the one flat side, which I see in one look. My simple statement, "I see a house," is then a report of a synthesis of separable observations from more than one vantage point; it also includes a discrimination from other past observations of buildings which are not houses as well as of other objects which are not buildings. The simple perceptive report, "I see a house," embodies a temporal synthesis of which I am not immediately aware; it distinguishes those characteristics that unify a number of observations with the concept 'house'; it also implicitly recognizes that few of these characteristics, taken alone, *must* be connected with a house (e.g., the 'whiteness' of its walls, the 'greenness' of its door-frame, the 'redness' of its roof can also apply to birch trees, pines, and maples, as walls, door-frames, and roofs can apply to barns and factories).

This process of rendering concepts sensible takes place in imaginative functioning as a schema; the "formation of a schema insofar as it is accomplished as a mode of sensibilization is called *schematism.*" [177] Beyond this schematization, this regulative functioning, the pure concept is empty and devoid of meaning, content, significance. Its only mode of attaining meaning is in its schematization, its sensibilization, its applicable adaptation to particular temporal presentations.

Concepts are rendered sensuous, amenable to sensuous intuition by the schematism and all "conceptual representation is essentially schematism";[178] all conceptualized representations are sensibilized concepts and are temporal. Because all our knowledge is conceptual it would seem to follow that in any immediate perception of an object there is already a preliminary insight, a look ahead, into the kind of a thing it is. Only by virtue of its representation as an object can the encountered entity reveal itself to us as, for example, a house; only in this way can it "present the aspect of a given house." [179] It is by virtue of this conceptual sensibilization that it is possible for the house to appear as an object qualified to be represented in cognition by apriori procedures. The schematism is necessitated by the finitude of human cognition, by its complete lack, as Kant repeatedly insisted, of intellectual intuition; human cognition thus requires the applicability of concepts, which the schematism renders, within the content of sense intuition in order to make that content intelligible.

The schematism is thus requisite to finite knowledge, which is constituted by the nature of our transcendence and which takes places as a schematism.[180] The possibility of this transcendence, of this essentially finite way by which we are able to attain knowledge, is grounded in and limited by the functioning of the transcendental schematism, which produces the possibility of bringing empirical concepts into concert with the content supplied by sensibility in intuition.

iv. temporalism

The most striking feature of the Schematism chapter is its revelation of the central role time plays in cognition. Time's function is crucial in the unification of the elements of knowledge, in bringing concepts into relation with percepts, and in establishing the possibility of a cognitive relationship generally between our capacity to attain knowledge and the things that are known to the extent that they are known.

The point, made in the Aesthetic and amplified in the Deduction, that time is the form of all our representations is here brought into full force as the universal condition of any particular experience we have. To-be in time becomes the first requisite mark of the objectivity of any object of cognition.

Only what is experiential as temporal can be known and understood.[181] Only to the extent that the categories can be redefined as time determinations can they acquire cognitive relevance. Apart from such temporal determinations they remain mere and empty logical entities; they remain as "nothing but *forms of thought* . . . the merely logical faculty . . . [with] even less meaning than the pure sensible forms [of intuition]." [182] If we were to remove every temporal consideration by de-schematizing the categories, they would remain as "merely functions of the understanding for concepts; and represent no object." [183] Thus the schematized category is central and the unschematized category is essentially derivative. The meaning of a category is acquired "only from sensibility, which realises the understanding in the very process of restricting it" [184] to the field of sensible presentations under the form of time. The schemata restrict the categories, as intellectualized generalizations which refer to the time-bound area of possible sense experience; they are but modes of 'categorizing' and classifying what is presentable in experience. Thus, as Martin pointed out, Kant's doctrine of the schematism grounded "the objective validity of the categories . . . on the objective validity of pure intuition, in particular of time." [185]

What is amenable to temporal representation is an object of possible experience; what cannot be brought into a temporal horizon is, in principle and by definition, unexperiential. Or, ontologically, as Kant suggested, the mark of temporality is the necessary mark of the possibility of the to-be of any possible being.[186] "Strictly speaking it is only true that all appearances are in time, so that strictly speaking time alone is the decisive character of being." [187] For possible human experience, to-be = to-be-*in-time*. For finite human cognition, the ontological result propounded in the Schematism is that time is the indispensable ground of the reality of the things-that-are for us.

The Deduction demonstrated the intrinsic relation of the categories (pure concepts) and time (pure intuition) by means of the synthesis of transcendental imagination. Pure intuition (time) is pre-experiential: it provides the requisite manner of having experience prior to any particular experience. This requisite mode of experience, the necessary way in which we must see objects in order to be aware of them, is the prescriptive form of time. The Aesthetic, then, set forth the problem but did not resolve it: time is not merely the pure form of intuition; it is also the form of the schema as such. Time is the form of each of the schemata; it defines their applicability to any object; it makes it possible for us to view any perceptible aspect of any thing coming into our field of experience.

Before I can become aware of any object, I require it to appear as temporal so that I am able to view it. As prime transcendental ground of my ability to apprehend it, amenability to time representation is also the prime ontological characteristic which the entity must possess in order to be an object for me, to appear to me, to enable me to establish any cognitive relationship with it. Prior to any other consideration, susceptibility to the form of time is the common factor I share with any object of which I have or can become aware.[188]

The limitations of possible human experience and thereby of the possibility of objects appearing and being represented in that experience can be categorically fixed by the bounds of the amenable-to-time. Time is the sole means by which any concept may be grounded as objectively referring to an experienced object. It is then only by a schematized concept, a concept that has been transmuted by temporal reference, that I can see an object *qua* intelligible and that an entity *can* become an object for me. Time is then, as Kant left it, within the entire realm of possible finite human knowledge, universal and pervasive; it is the prime ground of all our representations, of all phenomena appearing to-be for us, of all conceptual representations in terms of which they are known by us.

The schemata, as transcendental time determinations, present the form of time by means of the rules they formulate. In comprising this transcendental ground of my capacity for cognition of objects, in constituting my transcendence, they enable me to describe the characteristics of the being-status of the things that appear to me. They enable me to recognize ontological determinations of the objects I apprehend. As ontological, the "schematizing intuition renders distinguishable and, hence, receivable apriori the transcendental affinity of the rule of unity under the image of time." [189] Because of our prior time-forming capacity we are thus able to perceive objects as independent of ourselves, as objectively distinguishable from our subjective apprehensions of them; we are able to describe these objects as they appear to be objectively describable in terms of ontological predicates which are drawn from the transcendental grounds of the possibility of knowing them: the justification of this parallelism—of this affinity of the nature of these objects to our ways of cognizing them (to be further developed in the chapter which follows)—is rooted in the amenability to the form of time we share in common.

The transcendental schemata thus comprise the fusion of pure intuition and pure thought, of time and the categories, in advance of any particular perception. Together in this way, they make perception possible and intelligible. They permit us to anticipate with certainty the categoreal nature of any possible object that may appear to us. They thus fulfill the Kantian aim:

> Thus an application of the category to appearances becomes possible by means of the transcendental determination of time . . .

[by] contain[ing] apriori certain formal conditions of sensibility, namely those of inner sense. These conditions of sensibility constitute the universal conditions under which alone the category can be applied to any object.[190]

The transcendental schematism is, then, "no artificial theory but [one that] has its origin in the phenomena themselves."[191] In order to show this, Heidegger considers Kant's brief review of the schema of substance conceived as the "permanence of the real in time."[192] Taking at face value—for this purpose—Kant's apparent understanding of time as the sequence of nows, Heidegger carries his own conclusion forward:

> But time exists as a *now*-sequence precisely because, flowing across each *now*, it remains a *now* even while becoming another *now*. As the aspect of the permanent, it offers at the same time the image of pure change in permanence.
>
> . . .Thanks to this schematism, the notion as schematized is held in view in advance so that in this precursory view of the pure image of permanence, an [object] can manifest itself to experience as that which remains invariable through change. 'To time, itself nontransitory and abiding, there corresponds in the field of experience what is non-transitory in its existence' (i.e., in the given [thing-that-is]).[193]

The thesis, then, has been demonstrated: the transcendental schematism creates the possibility of ontological characterization by defining the objects that appear to us; by comprehending this, we see that knowledge of the transcendental conditions of our knowledge in general simultaneously gives us knowledge of legitimate ontological characterizations, viz., ontological knowledge. The categories, as abstracted from the Schematism in which they are 'encountered' as experiential functioning, are thus necessarily given in the pure form of time, which is the form of the transcendental schemata.

Time is then the universal form of any experience, of the conditions for intelligible cognition as well as mere apprehension; time is the condition of the to-be of the objects we cognize; it is the ground, the essential limit, of what is to be known and of the knowing itself. Time provides, and thereby limits, the union of sense and thought, of object and subject. Time thus provides and defines the finitude and, within that finitude, the unity of the knowing experiences we enjoy.

We can thus see that the form of time marks out, in advance of any particular percept, the horizon within which any perception must occur. Within this horizon, as an ontological condition for any appearance to appear, particular entities become objects for us. By serving as the ontological mark of any appearing object, time renders objectivity itself possible. In doing this, time further restricts my own ontological description of my self as a be-ing by compelling me to define my own to-be as limited by the not-me of the objects I recognize as such. The Schematism has thus succeeded in bringing the concept of time into focus as the ground of the possibility of experience, of my own experiencing self, as well as of the objects that denominate it.

Despite its achievement, Heidegger observes, Kant's method of getting to this point has been, to say the least, rather strange. In view of the central position which the Schematism holds, it is odd that the four kinds of possible time determinations were not developed from a systematic nature of time itself but from the categories, which were in turn presumably derived from the forms of logical judgment. Generally satisfied with Kant's presentation as far as it goes, Heidegger points out that Kant conceded that it could have been developed much further. That it was not is in itself a philosophic problem. But notwithstanding intimations of criticism and development to be examined in the sequel, Kant has, in the Schematism, broken new ground. He has here shown that the concept of time is the center of human knowledge and grounds the ontological descriptions we can offer of the objects that provide the content of that knowledge. As such, the Schematism is a crucial if "preliminary stage in a problematic of Temporality." [194]

v. conclusion

Just as de Vleeschauwer urged that the Schematism brings together various strands of Kant's formulation into one focus, so it also is unique in its own right by virtue of embodying this central synthesis. As Paton observed:

The doctrine of the schemata is not the result of formalism or of a so-called 'architectonic': it is a necessary part of his [Kant's]

argument. Indeed even if we attribute his derivation of the categories to formalism in a bad sense, we ought to recognize that in
his account of the schemata and of the Principles, Kant is break-
ing away from mere formalism. He is deriving the *categoreal
characteristics of objects* from the fact that *all objects must be
temporal;* and in this there is surely a considerable measure of
truth. The connection of the categories with the synthesis of imagination and the form of time is most important, and the least
artificial part of the Critical Philosophy. We must not allow the
difficulties of an unfamiliar and antiquated terminology to obscure
the real significance of the argument.[195]

It should now be clear just why the Schematism assumes its
crucial and central import in the interpretation of the Critique
which Heidegger is offering. Kant had, Heidegger maintains,
shown us in this brief chapter the 'essential ground and inmost
essence of what constitutes ontology.' [196] He did so by demonstrating that the transcendental power of imaginative synthesis, in
temporalizing and sensibilizing general concepts, brings them into
that unity with the particular perceptions which constitute the
unity of cognition; he did so by showing that this cognitive process relates itself to its objects: although 'in the service of intuition,' generalized concepts are necessary to our knowledge and to
the ontological characterizations we are legitimately able to attribute to the objects of our knowledge. This generality of the concepts which we must bring into cognition of the things-that-are-
for-us points us to the priority of ontology, of general metaphysics
as such.

The schematism is the primordial Kantian discovery. But, with
varying degrees of overt criticism to come, Heidegger has indicated dissatisfaction with three prime aspects of Kant's formulation: (1) the subsumptive presentation, which, if taken literally,
precludes the fundamental possibility of temporalized conceptual
sensibilization; (2) the premature concluding of the investigation
of the ways in which schemata are formed; (3) the characterization of time as a now-sequence, which has only tentatively been
alluded to. Of these three criticisms, only the question of subsumption has been discussed. But together with the other two, it points
ahead to the criticism and reconstruction that is to come.

However it may not have completed its task, the Schematism has resolved issues and yielded questions for further study. It has finally opened the ground of metaphysics—by pointing to the mode of unification of all the constituents of cognition, the elements of the subjectivity of knowledge and of the objectivity of the objects known in that knowledge. This foundation of metaphysics, of the ontological nature of the things-that-are in human experience can now be clarified once we have comprehended the central role, primordially revealed in the Schematism, of the essential temporality of the transcendental power of imaginative structuring in creating the cognitive synthesis. To that exploration, Heidegger takes us after an essential postscript: the ontological side of Kant's transcendentalism, grounded as it is in the subjectivity of the subject, must first be made fully explicit; doing so reveals the doctrine of the Schematism to be the heart of Critical transcendental philosophic thought.

6 · *The Transcendental and Ontological*

THE GROUND of human cognition, and thereby of any possible metaphysics, has been established in the transcendental schematism. It grounds all human knowledge in those forms of human temporality to which all entities must be able to conform in order to be known. We require a fifth stage of Kant's grounding of metaphysics, now, not to seek out a deeper ground but to comprehend what has already been done. The entire Kantian achievement can now be seen as a whole so that we can take "explicit possession of the ground thus won" so that we can use it for our own thinking.[197]

Kant's chapter on the Schematism, which provides this grounding of metaphysics, is introductory to the second chapter of the Analytic of Principles, the task of which is to spell out those specific cognitive principles that human understanding utilizes in the construction of its knowledge about sensory-intuition presentations. Before proceeding to the elucidation of those specific principles, Kant provided two introductory sections: first, he restricted the law of contradiction, as a sufficient criterion of truth, to analytic judgments concerned only with conceptual consistency as such; its only authority with regard to synthetic judgments was that of a necessary negative condition. Then, he set out what he called the Highest Principle of All Synthetical Judgments; as already indicated, Heidegger sees this as a comprehensive summation, as well as an autonomous restatement of the entire Critical doctrine. It focuses the import of the Copernican Revolution. It explicates the ontological implications he has drawn from the preceding stages and provides the Kantian justification of Heidegger's ontological interpretation; indeed, Heidegger later refers to this section as "the center" of the Critique.[198]

In the context of examining the Kantian laying of the foundation of metaphysics, there is no reason for Heidegger to carry his detailed examination beyond this section; all that the specific cognitive Principles can do, once their essential possibility has been established here, is to specify the ways in which ontological predicates, justified by the Highest Principle, are to be applied. In point of fact, Heidegger examined these specific Principles in a later work, published in English under the title *What Is A Thing?* That second Kant-book, in contrast to the first, which has provided the focus of this study, is written in an engagingly lucid style, requires no expository clarification, and has been continuously cited here in a supplementary way. A prime example of good philosophical analysis, its point is to insist on a careful use of the term 'thing' and to argue that the term is justifiably applicable only to an entity which appears as an object describable by the cognitive Principles Kant developed.

The function of the Highest Principle of Synthetic Judgments, which Kant presented as an introduction to the specification of the Principles, is precisely to establish their possibility and thus the possibility of ontic experiences. As such, Heidegger has argued, all of the specific cognitive Principles are based upon it.[199] Indeed, he argues that it functioned for Kant as the transcendental version of the Leibnizian Principle of Sufficient Reason and thereby as the ground of transcendence.[200] As such it has been presupposed in the principle of the Copernican Revolution and all that has been drawn from it. We can, then, understand why Heidegger has looked back on his own discussion and characterized this section of the Critique as the one in which "it reaches its deepest basis, founded by itself" and is thereby "the basic determination of the essence of human knowledge." [201]

Kant had opened his presentation by reiterating the prime importance of the question of the possibility of apriori synthetic judgments for transcendental logic. A synthetic judgment, he explained, represents an advance beyond a concept to "something altogether different," [202] to the thing which as the object of the cognition brings content into that cognition. If two different factors must be brought into unison, some 'bridge' medium must effect their synthesis:

> There is only one whole in which all our representations are contained, namely inner sense and its apriori form, time. The synthesis of representations rests on imagination; and their synthetic unity, which is required for judgment, on the unity of apperception. In these, therefore [in inner sense, imagination, and apperception], we must look for the possibility of synthetic judgments; and since all three contain the sources of apriori representations, they must also account for the possibility of *pure* synthetic judgments. For these reasons they are, indeed, indispensably necessary for any knowledge of objects, which rests entirely on the synthesis of representations.[203]

The objective reality of knowledge depends upon the object "being in some manner given." [204] But the object can only be apprehended and known in terms of the transcendentally defined capacity to do so. This transcendental *"possibility of experience is,* then, what gives objective reality" [205] to our modes of knowledge. Thus, "The highest principle of all synthetic judgments is therefore this: every object stands under the necessary conditions of synthetic unity of the manifold of intuition in a possible experience." [206]

This is to say that ontic experience is only possible when the apriori forms of intuition, imaginative synthesis, and apperceptive unity are unified with reference to a possible empirical field. Thus "the conditions of the *possibility of experience* in general are at the same time conditions of the *possibility of the objects of experience.*" [207]

Kant's Highest Principle has guided Heidegger's ontologically weighted orientation from the outset. For here is grounded the justification for attributing ontological predicates to appearing objects in terms of our transcendental capacity to cognize them. The transcendental possibility of experience determines, in advance, those characteristics of things which can appear in our experience. The limits of what can be known, and the ways in which knowledge of the known can be structured, is determined in advance by the possibilities which we, *qua* knowers, bring to a cognitive situation. The three transcendental elements of human cognition—sense, imagination, and thought—comprise a structural unity which defines the extent, nature, and limitation within which ontological predicates may be legitimately accorded; it is for this reason that Kant's focus had been on the transcendental structuring which defines "the possibility of experience." [208]

The word 'experience (*Erfahrung*)' Heidegger takes to mean the finite, passive, intuitional knowledge of the thing-that-is in our perception. The crucial word 'possibility (*Möglichkeit*),' he points out, is ambiguous. Kant did not contrast the 'possible' to the 'actual'; but the possibility of experience is crucial, logically prior, and present in what is actual. 'Possible' is the apriori delineation which determines in advance what *can be* in experience. Now, Heidegger argues, this is just what has been traditionally meant by *essentia* or *realitas;* it is precisely why the question of the possibility of things is one and the same with the question of the possibility of synthetic judgments.[209] The possibility of experience can only be understood as the defining capacity to have experience; it is our transcendence; it is the source of the defining objective reality we have within that experience. It is definable by the apriori modes of knowledge, which are simultaneously enabling and limiting.

This possibility of the kind of experience we do have provides the unification of percepts and concepts in schematic synthesis and thus founds our knowledge as objectively true. Our possibility of experience enables us to orient ourselves toward objects and to cognize them *qua* objects. We can so cognize objects just because the transcendental ground of our cognition (our transcendence), operative in the same form of time in which we perceive objects, permits us to recognize those same characteristics as they can appear to us. The compatibility of our capacity to know objects and of their characteristics in terms of which they can be known by us is the condition of the possibility of experience itself.

There are two essential limits on this possibility of experience:

a. We must be able to represent the kind of objects which do or can appear to us. This means that we are able to intuit, to be receptive of, to orient ourselves toward such objects—our capacity for receptivity and conceptual integration is such that the particular appearing entity can-be as a cognizable object for us. This precursory orientation was elucidated in the Deduction and the Schematism, which conjoin to confirm the essential temporality in terms of which all human knowledge is achieved and to which all entities must conform in order to be known as objects. Before our perceptive range was extended by microscopes, we were unable to perceive bacteria and hence were unable to extend our schematized categories to cognize them; thus we were unable to orient ourselves to an acknowledged possibility of seeing them. Since we have enlarged this sensuous capacity and can perceive them, we do so in terms of our own categoreal descriptions (e.g., magnitudes) and 'representations of necessary connections of our perception of them.'[210] To the extent that technological advances bring the be-ing of new entities into our area of cognitive awareness, we seek to understand them within the limits of the same categoreal descriptions which necessarily characterize any human cognition.

b. Finite knowledge *qua* knowledge must be true. Kant saw truth in terms of agreement between knower and known in which the known, the object, provides the standard; the object must be given within the framework of our knowing capability and be measurable in terms of our conceptual 'rulers.' What Heidegger stresses as crucial in requiring the object to be given is that it must appear within the framework of our capacity for relating to it, it must appear within the horizon of our possible experience. As such, it must be perceptible by us, it must be characterized by the ways in which we can understand it as an object independent of our knowing it. It must, therefore, have be-ing characteristics which enable it to-be in the same time in which we encounter it.

These two conditions of the possibility of experience were expressed, Heidegger argues, in Kant's crucial statement: "the conditions of the *possibility of experience* in general are at the same time conditions of the *possibility of the objects of experience.*" The crucial connective "at the same time [*zugleich*]" expresses this identity and claims that the conditions of possible experience *are* also the conditions for the object *qua* object *to-be for us*. Any thing that appears *must* appear within the horizon of this possible experience in order to be perceived as an object-appearing by us. Thus, the 'subjectivity' of our cognition is equally the condition of the objectivity of the object for us and thereby the condition of the truth of our knowledge concerning that object. The conditions of the possibility of our experience define the horizon of our experience, the possibility of all content within that experiential horizon. These transcendental conditions constitute the possibility for the things that are to appear to us.

Our capacity to form an experience that accords with what is to be experienced is essential to what Heidegger means by 'transcendence'; this capacity of transcendence may now be described as our capacity to surpass separate momentary perceptions and constitute these into a unified field of appearance, to organize and interpret those appearings in accord with our cognitive principles (schematized categories), and to synthesize these elements of our cognitive process with representations of objects that can be known in terms of this cognitive process. This capacity is not something we 'attain'; it constitutes us *qua* knowers prior to any specific cognitional act; our transcendence is truly a transcend*ing*.[211] Like a specially designed wrench which, by its nature, can 'deal' with some nuts and bolts and not with others, so our transcendence is seen in terms of our being able to 'deal' cognitively with those entities which appear as objects in terms of our own descriptive specifications by which we 'grasp' them.*

This capacity to cognize the things that meet our requirements for appearing to us as cognizable, this essential structure of our knowing, is always precursory, in advance, apriori. This capacity, as a logically necessary precondition, delineates the boundaries within which any actual cognitional act must occur. These transcendental conditions of our knowing are, by Kant's Highest

* The German word for 'concept,' *der Begriff*, stems from the verb *greifen*, which means 'to grasp.'

Principle, not only the conditions of our knowing but also of the object's possibility of being-known by us to the extent that it can be known by us. It is in this sense that transcendence is onto-logical: it defines the to-be, the characteristics of be-ing of the things-that-are (*das Sein des Seienden*), the objectivity of objects within the range of our cognitive competence. It is this capacity for transcendence, marked out by Kant in the priority of the apri-ori, that permits us to anticipate the shape of any future experi-ence.[212]

Heidegger sums this up succinctly: "that which makes the act of experience possible at the same time makes possible the content of experience, i.e., the object of experience as such."[213] The tran-scendental ground defining the kind of knowledge I am able to have, thus, in advance of any specific cognition, defines the kinds of objects I can possibly incorporate into the content of my know-ing act. Seen from the side of the known object, the ground of my knowing capability is that set of ontological descriptions which I can truthfully use in characterizing it as eligible to enter my experiential realm.

The transcendental schematism brought together into the struc-tural unity of a cognitive act the three original elements of knowl-edge—apprehension, imagination, and apperception. Because this cognitive act is focused on a thing that appears in the form of time, because the schematized categories are the ways in which I structure this time, the unity produced by the transcendental schematism may legitimately be characterized as transcendental time determination. The knowledge of these time-determining schemata, insofar as it comprises my knowledge of the ontological characteristics in terms of which I can describe the objects appear-ing to me, is then, rightfully termed ontological knowledge.[214]

The problematic of the transcendental object then arises again: *what* is really known in ontological knowledge? An essential as-pect of knowledge—its root in receptive sensory intuition—is its receptivity. The specific cognitions we have are passively receptive of what is here to be known; this area within which what is to be known must appear is produced by our ontological form-ing or creative projecting. Ontological knowledge is knowledge of the ways in which we form, we create, the horizon within which our experience takes place—the comprehensive system of the modes of be-ing which are possible for the things that are for us. What, then, is the object of this knowledge—what is the object to which the pure concepts of that knowledge refer? We are reminded that this object is not a specific thing—it is a non-thing, a *Nichts*. It is what Kant had called an 'X' which is not-a-thing, yet not 'nothing-at-all'—but a 'something in general,' an *etwas*.

The general act of representations as such must have a referential object. This object, Heidegger suggests citing Kant, is requisite for an objectively characterized field, prior to any specific cognition, in order to form the horizon within which a particular autonomous thing-that-is can be encountered in experience.[215] Empirical intuitions cannot perceive this ultimate limit of that horizon which we form and within which we must orient ourselves to any particular object. This horizon, then, must be provided in pure intuition.

As Kant had pointed out, "the principles of pure understanding can apply only to objects of the senses under the universal conditions of a possible experience, never to things in general."[216] But it is this thingness-in-general, this objectivity *qua* objectivity, that defines the possibility of the be-ing of any thing at all, to which any particular thing must conform its way of be-ing, in order for it to be for us. Heidegger seems to be taking this object of ontological knowledge, then, in the sense of ultimate defining limitation and confining ground wherein all ontic knowledge must be confined. Because of the normal tendency to translate this *Nichts* as 'nothing' there is a normal inference of mere negation. But this unknown X is not a mere lack, not a mere negativity; it is not "merely absence of being . . . [but] belongs essentially to Being as such."[217] It is not mere deficiency, not mere lacking, not mere empty negation;

> [it] is not a sign of non-presentation; it corresponds simply to a deficient presentation which does not succeed in making some thing appear as present which ought to be present were we able to apprehend it. Moreover, if one is able to *prove* that some thing is 'lacking,' it is precisely possible because the presentation does not as such exclude. And it cannot be realized in our knowledge

even under our deficient forms without already presupposing its connection with what we see as what is being withheld from our perception.[218]

Any concept includes an inherently negative factor in that it excludes other concepts from its applicable content. The entire synthesis of ontological characteristics excludes all that is not contained within it. This kind of negativity is analogous to negation only as a wall dividing one field from another 'negates' one field in reference to another; its negative command is 'go no further'; if I throw a ball against it, the ball is bounced back to me in the field encompassed as a positive affirmation of limitation. It is negation only as a sign forbidding trespassing on forbidden soil may be considered a negation.

Much of Heidegger's discussion of this 'transcendental (or, now, ontological) object' appears to be unnecessarily obscure. He almost seems to be tantalizing his reader to follow in order to unravel an engrossing mystery. What is the 'terminus' of our possible orientations to the things-that-are for us? He gives us a clue which, if taken in the light of his fully developed doctrine, gives the mystery away. This confusing limitation, this ultimate horizon cannot be empirically perceived because it is empirically presupposed. It cannot be perceptible to empirical intuition because any empirical intuition is receptivity of the object apprehended in inner sense under the form of time. But this terminus is "immediately perceptible in a pure intuition." [219] And pure intuition has been identified with time itself.

Thus it would seem that what Heidegger suggests is the identification of the transcendental object with the necessary temporality of every aspect of human experience. As schematized categories, the principles of our knowledge and their parallel ontological characterizations of the things that are for us are essentially time-bound. The essential condition and ultimate meaning of the two-sided Highest Principle would thus appear—in the light of the Schematism—to be the mutuality of being-temporal, the mutuality which we necessarily share with the objects known.

And it is ultimately time which is a 'non-thing,' which is yet a sort-of 'some-thing' and most certainly not a *nihil absolutum,* not a nothing-at-all. It is this comprehensive form of time which cannot be intuited as an object but which constitutes the structured horizon within which any thing must-be in order to-be an object for us. It is being-temporal, i.e., being cognizable by the temporalized (schematized) categories, the Principles, that defines the being and the ways of be-ing of any empirical object. It is the encompassing 'wall of time' which is the invisible yet ever-present trespass-warning marking out the boundary which Kant had discovered around the realm of all possible experience. It is the invisible yet ever-present boundary which fences in what Heidegger calls the 'horizon' within which objects and objectivity are necessarily confined. It is the invisible yet ever-present limitation which by its be-ing marks out the finitude of human cognition.

It is thus within this temporal limitation that the knowledge of ontological characterization may be identified as primal truth— the truth which human transcendence is able to attain, the truth which Kant saw as the ground of the empirical truths made possible by the transcendental schematism. It is this capacity for transcendental categories, as schematized, that yields ontological knowledge and grounds any particular empirical or ontic truths we may have. It is this capacity for transcendental categories which defines the temporal horizon within which the be-ing of the things-that-are is encountered, defined, and maintained. It is this temporal horizon, structured by our modes of describing it, that opens up the area within which the things-that-are for us come to be apprehended and known by us.

Founded, then, in our transcending capacity, ontology is the structuring of the ways in which the things that appear to us can and do appear to us; it is the way in which we structure the horizon of time which we 'project' as the area confining our experiential possibilities. Our essential finitude is itself characterized by that limitation of area within which we must confine and define our possible experience. Our finitude is confined by our projection of time; it is defined by the ways in which we structure that time, *qua* prerequisite, which we ordain as the only ways in which we can allow any entities to appear to us in order to become objects of knowledge for us.

Ontology is, then, "nothing other than the explicit disclosure of the systematic whole of pure knowledge so far as the latter forms transcendence." [220] Ontology is that system of characteristics requisite for an appearance to embody in order for it to be an appearance for us, for an entity to incorporate in order that it may be represented by us—to the extent that it may be represented by us at all—as a real, actual, or possible existent object. Ontology is that system of predicates which may legitimately be applied to objects taken as objectively real in our possible experience, objects which we may regard as such for us.

We can now see why Heidegger is able to draw the equation: "transcendental philosophy = ontology." [221] It is now apparent that the principle of the Copernican Revolution has thrust "the problem of ontology to the fore," [222] and necessitates a drastic modification of traditional metaphysics.

What now needs to be done is to 'wash down' this new orientation dug out of the Kantian Critique. We can then view it in its unity and see the full import of what has been accomplished in the analytic effort that has now been examined.

Heidegger focuses our attention on what he has dug out of the Kantian Critique—the transcendental grounding of legitimate ontological predicates, the pervasiveness of time which structures them, and the justification they provide of objectivity in human knowledge. In bringing forth these issues as *the* issues with which our own philosophic thinking must be concerned, Heidegger has completed his retrieve of Kant; he has succeeded in bringing Kant's thought and vision back to life as the starting point for a new departure in philosophic inquiry. In order to delineate the nature of this new ground upon which we must build, he now turns to explore, in its integral unity, the ground which he has now cleared.

V I

The Result of the Retrieve

FROM THE EVIDENCE which Heidegger has brought forth, we are now able to consider the conclusions to be drawn; the full revolutionary nature of Kant's philosophic achievements can now be directly examined so that we may utilize the fruit of his philosophic labors to nourish our own. The basic lesson to be taken from the analysis of the Critique may be succinctly summarized in the assertions that Kant has implicitly provided us with an identification of transcendental philosophy and general metaphysics or ontology, to use the term in Heidegger's sense, by means of the Copernican Revolution; he has shown us that temporal factors pervade all human knowledge and that the transcendental imagination provides the center of the cognitive act. In this accomplishment, Kant effectively shifted "the whole of modern thought and being into the clarity and transparency of a foundation."[1]

1 · The Basis of Interpretation

IN THE FIRST STAGE, drawn from the Aesthetic, time was designated as the form of inner sense and thereby of all representations; henceforth, 'pure intuition' and 'time,' following Kant's own indications, are taken as virtually synonomous.[2] Al-

[131]

ready at the beginning, the dependence of concepts on immediate apprehension, on intuition (which only acts "in so far as the object is given"[3]), has been seen as an aspect of an unbifurcated unified cognitive process.

The second stage, seen in the first chapter of the Analytic, carried this forward; it affirmed the radical unity of the two Kantian 'stems' of cognition—variously expressed in terms of sense and understanding, sensibility and thought, intuition and apperception, time and the categories. In seeking out the source of this unity, Heidegger has seen Kant leading us to the synthesizing power of imagination as its ground.

The Transcendental Deduction, the third stage, grounded all possible relationship between the knowing-subject and the object-known in that transcendence which arises from the 'mediating' role of imaginative synthesis. Despite any pretensions to the contrary, Kant recognized three elements—sense, imagination, and apperception—not just sensibility and the understanding, as the elemental constituents of any cognition. Taken together these three prime elements constitute the essential unity of knowledge and establish the necessity and possibility of our capacity to form knowledge. At the same time as they ground the possibility of knowledge, they decree the ontological characteristics of objects insofar as they can be known.

In the Schematism, the fourth stage, is to be found the crucial keystone of the Critique. It pronounces the centrality of the transcendental power of imaginative cognitive synthesis as the root of the temporal cognitive Principles (which, as detemporalized abstractions, are termed 'categories') in the forming of knowledge. Here we begin to see the essential equivalence of Heidegger's prime terms: 'transcendence,' 'temporality,' and 'transcendental power of imagination.'

The final stage amplified the concept of transcendence and identified its limitations as those of possible experience; in so doing, it underlined the essential parallelism of the transcendental grounds of cognition and the ontological grounds of possible objects within the horizon of that cognition; it implicitly suggested that the unification of any cognitional act and of the beings in that cognition is made possible by the mutuality of amenability to the form of time shared by knower and known.

Why has all this effort been expended? What does it all signify? What is the relevant 'message' to be drawn from the Kantian Critique? Now that Heidegger has set forth and analyzed the evidence, conclusions can be driven home. This is done in what we may take as five 'moments': an elucidation of the ground established (VI. 2); a rethinking of the pervasive significance of the transcendental imagination (VI. 3); a dual hypothesis to explain why Kant had not carried through the implications seen in his work (VI. 4); an explication of the meaning of time and temporality (VI. 5); and, a general summation (VI. 6).

Throughout, Heidegger's concern is to explicate the radical nature of Kant's departure and its revolutionary implications for metaphysical thought. For the most part, he limits himself to Kant's own discussion drawing together leading strands of the preceding analyses.

His focus is not so much on what Kant did say but on what Kant did not say and should have said in the context of the Critique. He points to certain analyses which stopped short and raised new questions which still demand answers. He seeks to discern, from the Kantian analysis itself, those philosophic directions which Kant did not take but are nevertheless indicated in, or demanded by, Kant's own thinking. He criticizes Kant quite severely—but it is plain that this criticism is, indeed, the highest praise: the revolutionary nature of Kant's Critique is so fundamental and crucial that the ground it has cleared is where we must build; the explication of what Kant had left unsaid provides the lead questions which our own philosophic thought must regard as its central concern. It is in this way that Kant still proves to be decisive for contemporary philosophy; Kant is brought back to life as crucial to today's thinking; this is the meaning of Heidegger's retrieve.

2 · The Established Ground

KANT DISCOVERED, Heidegger explains, that the possibility of ontological knowledge—knowledge of the necessary characterizations of the being-status of the things that appear to us—is grounded in transcendence, in the human capacity to connect momentary presentations by means of temporal principles into that interpretive synthesis which we term cognition. This capacity for transcendence is our capacity for experience; as such it opens up an 'area' of possible knowledge within which objects may appear and may be known.

Central to this capacity for transcendence is the transcendental power of imagination. Established as integral in both the Deduction and the Schematism, these two sections, taken together, constitute a two-step demonstration that imagination is that activity which fuses conceptually discernible sensibility and thought into one cognitive process.

Imagination is, however, not merely concerned to bring to mind past perceptions in relation to present ones. It is also able to represent "in intuition an object that is *not itself present*." [4] Imagination is thus not only reproductive or ontic; it is also productive or ontological for it provides the structure of the experiential field. As the source of the transcendental schemata, it is the productive source of possible experience and of limitations on possible objectivity in that experience. By creating the temporal structuring of all representations, the power of imaginative synthesis thus predetermines and establishes the experiential horizon, the boundaries of that area within which human cognition must be contained to be operative. As reproductive, it brings into present awareness specific or ontic memories; as productive, it delineates the ontological possibility of transcending the particularity of the present moment.

If one takes seriously the sensate source, the ultimate empirical ground, of all experiential content, it seems apparent that some active mental process which imaginatively renders present what is literally not present is crucial for any kind of coherence, order, meaning, intelligibility in experience. For, it is only by imaginative integration that we can transcend separate instant moments of perception and connect these into an ordered apprehension. In the most literal sense, one can only see what is before him in any 'now,' in the few seconds between eye-blinks. And even such a 'now' constitutes a time spread! How can we connect the content of these separate perceptions without the capacity for that imaginative maintenance of continuity we call memory (and anticipation), an imaginative connection and comparison of separable atomic instants of sense perceptions?

Kant's productive imagination, which provides the possibility of such empirical imaginative connections, Heidegger terms the 'ontological imagination' just because it sets out in advance the to-be characteristics which we are able to discern in the things that appear to us. As such, it is dependent neither upon actual appearances nor upon the actual things that do appear. It sets the 'stage' on which entities may appear as objects, as specific things, rather than as separable blurs of color patches (which would then need to be *consciously* correlated into ordered presentations). The productive or ontological imagination enables objects to come into our view by providing them with the horizon within which, the stage on which, to do so.

For example, the pure schema of substance or permanence creates the possibility of a constant presence. As Kant had observed, "The existence of what is transitory passes away in time but not time itself." [5] If time is taken as a sequence of nows, then time is 'now' at any momentary 'now.' Time is presupposed in, and as such is the transcendental meaning of, the idea of the permanent. It is prerequisite for any possible object to appear to be experienced over even a miniscule 'spread' of nows. The concept of substance is thus a way of focusing on the abiding-through-nows in the continuity of time as the possibility of any change. It is only against this 'backdrop' of homogeneous yet differentiated time, this horizon of the abiding presence of time, "that this or that 'presence of an object' can reveal itself." [6] As the presence of the flowing river 'presents itself' in the flow of any of its currents and in a log being carried by it to the sea, so this continual present 'flow' of time now presents itself in any 'now' and with the object which is 'now' appearing to me. This continuing presence of the 'flow' of time, which appears focused in any momentary 'now,' is, as the transcendental schematism showed, an essential defining structure of possible experience. This continuing 'presence of time,' as the horizon of experience, is presented by the activity of transcendental imagination.

The activity of the transcendental power of imaginative synthesis is thus logically prior to all experience and is presupposed in any ontic experience. It produces not particular or ontic images (as 'reproduction') but objectivity as such: "It is pure productive imagination, independent of experience, which first renders experience possible." [7] Just because it is presupposed in any experiential generalization, it cannot be regarded as itself a generalization from experience. Transcendental imagination sets out the structure of any ontic experience and is presupposed 'as present' in any ontic experience; as such it provides the ontological ground of the possibility of experience itself.

What then is its source? Imagination, as the center of cognitive synthesis, is itself the source of that transcendence which renders experience possible. Imaginative synthesis is then not merely one more faculty or capability alongside sense and thought but, in some sense, is their actively functioning structural unity which is the structural unity of the cognitive process. Transcendental imagination is, then, not a discernible 'entity' or 'thing' or, in the traditional terminology, a 'faculty.' It is a *dynamic* process; it forms and makes possible the radically basic unity of sensibility and understanding and is the possibility of their unity. Transcendental imagination is itself transcendence; it is the possibility of experience as the complete integrated unity of the elements that constitute the possibility of human knowledge. As such, as Kant had said, it "conditions all apriori knowledge, [and] is thus one of the fundamental faculties of the human soul." [8] This means, Heidegger points out, that it is not reducible to sense or to thought.

Transcendental imagination is the formative unity of pure intuition *qua* time and of pure apperception *qua* the source of the categories; it functions, as Kant eloquently stated it, as "a blind but indispensable function of the soul, without which we should have no knowledge whatsoever, but of which we are scarcely ever conscious." [9] Nevertheless, Kant repeatedly spoke of *three* basic sources of knowledge and discussed each in terms of both empirical and transcendental employment.[10] How could Kant speak of *three* unified 'faculties' or, more precisely, a *tri*une 'faculty' of knowledge when he also continually referred to the *two* "stems of knowledge, namely sensibility and understanding"? Is it, Heidegger asks, perhaps a way of bringing out the thought that they both spring from "a common, but to us unknown root"? [11]

Heidegger explicitly identifies this unknown common root with the transcendental power of imaginative synthesis. In doing so, he follows Kantian leads. As Smith pointed out, "This common root belongs both to sensibility and to understanding, and is passive as well as spontaneous." [12] As such it has something in common with each of these 'two stems' and would seem to be identifiable as their mediating agency. In both the A and B Deductions (despite the differences between them), imagination was presented as the source of their unification or connection. In discussing the A Deduction, Smith argued, "Only on one point is Kant clear and definite, namely, that it is to productive imagination that the *generation* of unified experience is primarily due. In it something of the fruitful and inexhaustible character of noumenal reality is traceable." [13] In his discussion of the Schematism, Smith also suggested this identification:

> Kant's description of the schema as a 'third thing,' *at once intellectual and sensuous,* seems to be in large part due to the transference to it of predicates already applied to the faculty which is supposed to be its source. The distinction between the transcendental schema and the particularised image is also given as analogous to that between the pure and empirical faculties of imagination.[14]

Kant had summarized the architectonic structure of the Critique by specifying its beginning as that "point at which the common root of our faculty of knowledge divides and throws out two stems. . . ." [15] This certainly suggests that this common root was something more than a merely suggestive metaphor; indeed, he seems to have substantiated this identification of the common root and the transcendental imagination: "The schematism . . . is a product and, as it were, a monogram of pure apriori imagination." [16]

In the textual analyses reviewed in the preceding chapter, an essential theme was the unity of cognition, the unity of that knowledge which Kant described as stemming from the combined act of sense and thought. In both the Objective and the Subjective Deductions there appeared an essential principle of linkage between sense and thought—the temporal synthesizing function of imagination as the keystone of the entire edifice. This keystone is essentially temporal and necessarily so. It does not merely serve a logical function as a middle term between a universal and a particular; it serves the cognitive function of bringing an a-temporal concept into unity with a necessarily temporally-defined sensuous apprehension.

In the implicit Kantian identification of the rational or intellectual with the a-temporal, the essential temporality of the 'mediating third' is demanded. Thus Kant identified its necessary characteristic by saying, "This mediating representation must be pure, that is void of all empirical content, and yet at the same time, while it must in one respect be *intellectual,* it must in another be *sensible.*" [17] As this 'transcendental schema' produced by the temporality of transcendental imagination, it is the keystone of the structure and the 'channel' of 'mediation' effected by imagination. Or, as Heidegger has reformulated it, the unification of the temporality of sensibility and the a-temporality of concepts is rendered in the temporal sensibilization of concepts by an act of imaginative synthesis as demonstrated in the Schematism.

In view of the centrality of imaginative synthesis in both the Deduction and the Schematism, Kant's repeated references to *two* 'stems' of knowledge is discordant and confusing, especially since he operated on the presumption of *three* 'sources' of knowledge. His programmatic statement presumed only two elements in knowledge as does the ensuing architectonic division of the 'transcendental doctrine of the elements of knowledge.' Exclusively dividing it between the Transcendental Aesthetic and the Transcendental Logic, he had left the transcendental imagination, although fundamental and central, as Heidegger puts it, architectonically "homeless." [18]

Now, in view of Kant's own architectonic emphasis, another important question is implicitly posed: Precisely what is the unique function served by the Schematism? [19]

If the Schematism merely amplifies what the Deduction had already set forth, why is it in a different section of the 'Logic'? The avowed intent of the Deduction was the justification for applying pure concepts to empirical representations; it thus aimed to show "how *subjective conditions of thought* can have *objective validity*," how the Copernican Revolution may be validated, how "the representation alone must make the object possible." [20] If the Deduction succeeded, what function is served by the Schematism? If the Schematism is *necessary*, doesn't it follow that the Deduction failed?

Such questions are valid only if the prime intent of the Schematism were epistemological. If one accepts the Deduction as the valid and successful explanation of the possibility of knowledge, the Schematism (*qua* epistemological) appears as little more than an interesting or obscure addendum to it: the focus on the temporality of its keystone, the transcendental imagination, was implicit from the Deduction in the connection with intuition and inner sense. It cannot be merely an addendum. Kant himself had pronounced it to be "indispensable." [21] Paton has suggested that it serves as a real source of the categories, and Heidegger regards it as grounding the problematic and possibility of metaphysics.[22] Why?

In the Schematism, Kant was no longer concerned with the possibility of knowledge—presumably that was settled in the Deduction, which we can assume Kant regarded as successful and valid. Significantly, the Schematism is *not* the last chapter of the Analytic of Concepts, where it would belong as a postscript to the Deduction. Rather, it is the first chapter of the Analytic of Principles, which is concerned with instructing judgment "how to apply to appearances the concepts of understanding, which contain the condition for apriori rules." [23] This second Analytic, which the Schematism begins, claims authority for the apriori specification, not merely of rules but of the "instance to which the rule is to be applied." [24] It thus appears that Kant's concern in the Schematism was with the ultimate ground structure, the metaphysics, of experience itself—the necessary structure of experience which renders and grounds the possibility of knowledge as the Deduction claimed to establish it.

The Schematism announced that it is the "schemata, not images of objects, which underlie our pure sensible concepts," [25] that time, as the form of pure intuition, is also the form "of objects as appearances," [26] that schemata, in contrast to abstract concepts, represent things in general *"as they appear."* [27] If we can say that "the schema is properly only the phenomena, or sensible concept, of an object in agreement with the category," [28] then—as the linkage between objects as they appear and concepts—we have a question about, and a reference to, the nature of what is 'given.' This is indicated by the fact that almost immediately following the Schematism, as we have seen, we are given the statement of the Highest Principle: "the conditions of the *possibility of experience* in general are at the same time conditions of the *possibility of the objects of experience,"* and thereby the objectivity of synthetic apriori judgments is grounded.[29] The objectivity of apriori synthesis is not merely a result of the possibility of knowledge. This objectivity emerges from the nature of experience within which possible knowledge is achieved, an experience whose structure is pointed to, in the Schematism, as essentially temporal and oriented toward the objects in the world as it is experienced.[30]

It is by an interpretation such as this alone, if by no other, that de Vleeschauwer's judgment is justified: "The Schematism constitutes the foundation of the harmony of these [two] faculties of knowledge *in view of the formal constitution of experience."* [31] The Schematism is, then, necessary to the Critique just because it points to the necessity of a metaphysic of experience as the ground of that knowledge which the Deduction showed to be possible. In the light of this reasoning we can see why Heidegger shared Kant's evaluation of the Schematism not as an addendum to the Deduction but as "the heart" of the Critique.[32]

If we now put together the doctrines of the Schematism and the Highest Principle, their conjunction implies that objects are somehow temporally structured just as our principles of cognition are the conceptualized modes of our knowing apprehension of them. The parallelism of the conditions for experience and the objects of that experience clearly justifies Heidegger's insistence on the ontological import of the Critique. This parallelism not only provides a doctrine of the transcendental ground of knowledge, not only provides the key to a metaphysics of experience; it also points to the ontological constitutive structure of any object *qua* object in experience. The repeated characterization of the

Critique as firmly metaphysical or ontological thus appears fully substantiated. Whatever may be said regarding the metaphysical speculation in the Third Critique,[33] it seems clear that here in the First Critique Kant presumed the necessity of an ontological undergirding of knowledge and a metaphysic of experience.

Heidegger's own mode of interpretation and development is well summarized in Schaper's comment:

> The basic Kantian insight which lurks in [the] Schematism seems to me this: though it is true that we construct, we construct not as minds, or intellects, not by being mind, but by being in time. I am not saying by 'thinking in time,' or even 'experiencing under the form of time,' which would be closer to the Kantian text, but 'being in time.' Kant never said it quite like this. But it seems to me that this is what was hidden as the 'real modes of activity' to which Kant referred, and with which he grappled in this chapter. . . . It still is, of course, only a formula for the assertion that man does not confront the given manifold, then proceed to mold it, but rather that he is *in it,* in thorough-going relation already, which on analysis then yields the time factor as bearing an unduly heavy burden.
>   . . . With this perspective, the rather commonplace insistence that human nature is *temporal* nature gains in complexity. For not only is time a human form of experience, but it is that in which man finds himself as human, and the world as 'world.' I stress 'finds himself' for that seems to me the message of [the] Schematism: not that man imposes what he is himself (to a certain extent he obviously does) but that he discovers, via the schemata as underlying the possibility of things for him, his own nature and the nature of that in which he is, his being-in-the-world.[34]

Although this passage points ahead to what is yet to come, it helps us to appreciate the significance Heidegger draws from the Schematism, the justification of the central place it occupies in the reconstruction of the Critical philosophy his work suggests, and the direction of new developments he sees proposed in Kant's Critique.

Kant had explicitly declared that the schema, implications of which have been suggested, is 'in itself always a product of the power of imagination.'[35] Imaginative capability is thus the key to the nature of our experience and the knowledge we attain in it. This capability brings interpreting concepts and the particularity of a variety or manifold of sense impressions into cognitive unity. As the schemata comprise the center of all experiences, so the synthesis of sense and thought provided by transcendental imagination is the ground of this possibility. If this transcendental capacity for experience springs from imagination, discovery of its nature and origin requires a more intensive consideration of transcendental imagination as the basis of the possibility of the synthesis of ontological characteristics which render experiential content possible. Heidegger is, then, not content to leave this fundamental imaginative capability in the realm of an unexplored unknown.

For the transcendental power of imaginative synthesis is not merely the unity of the two 'stems' of knowledge—essentially the result of the Deduction. It is itself, as the conjunction of the Schematism and the Highest Principle indicates, the source of the possibility of our experience of specific things.

Heidegger's determined exploration of this common root is, then, demanded by the fact that Kant had posed it as a fundamental yet ambiguously unresolved problematic. Heidegger's identification of this common root of sense and thought with transcendental imaginative synthesis is in accord with Kant's own allusions to it. As the root-source of our experience, it is of crucial import. Heidegger thus proposes to push the Kantian inquiry down to more basic ground, to dig deeper in order to unearth and expose to view this root of our experience which Kant had left buried in the unexplored and concealed realm of the unknown.

3 · *The Common Root*

IMAGINATION IS NOT MERELY A THIRD 'FACULTY' alongside intuition and understanding; somehow it is the unknown common root of them both. So much, at least, the inquiry has shown. What remains is to make this meaningful and demonstrate its significance. To do so, Heidegger warns us, requires the 'reduction' of both intuition and understanding to imagination.

A normal response is to shrink back from the apparently absurd. Yet, if Kant's opening thesis demanding the unity of sensibility and concepts is warranted; if cognitional content can only come from sensibility; if the two 'stems' of cognition are operative only as one unified structure; if transcendental imagination functions only as it unites sense and thought; if transcendental imagination is the source of the schemata; and if these in turn define the limits of possible experience—if the conclusions elicited from the five-stage inquiry are accepted—then Heidegger would appear to be merely pressing on to a necessary consequence.

Kant may not have wished to pursue "a dry and tedious analysis of the conditions demanded by transcendental schemata";[36] but he certainly intimated even if vaguely, the conclusion which Heidegger urges as necessary:

> It is evident, therefore, that what the schematism of understanding effects by means of the transcendental synthesis of imagination is simply the unity of all the manifold of intuition in inner sense, and so indirectly the unity of apperception which as a function corresponds to the receptivity of inner sense.[37]

Heidegger's thesis, then, is that clarification of the meaning of transcendental imagination as the common root of sense and thought requires "nothing less than reducing pure intuition and pure thought to the transcendental imagination." [38] If we bear in mind the precise definitions of the key terms,* this means that what is required is 'nothing less than reducing or tracing back the pre-experiential capacity for immediate awareness and the pre-experiential capacity for conceptual thought to the transcendental imagination, i.e., to the power or capacity to construct or constitute those forms or modes of ordered integration in terms of which ontic data may be cast.' Thus restated, the thesis does not sound so unreasonable.

Understood in this way, it is then apparent that the transcendental power of imagination is not a 'third thing' but the central

---

* The word 'reducing' is the English translation's equivalent of Heidegger's "auf die transzendentale Einbildungskraft zurückzuführen," i.e., 'to bring or trace back to. . . .' It would also be well at this point to refer back to the detailed exposition of the key terms: 'imagination (Einbildungskraft),' 'intuition (Anschauung),' and 'pure (rein)' on pp. 16–18 & 64n.

function or activity of the mind; it is this functioning that makes it possible for pure intuition and pure thought to be what they " 'really' can be" [39] in rendering experience possible. What needs to be explicated, then, is not a psychological analysis but the structure of transcendence—the way in which our capacity to structure and attain knowledge is grounded in the capacity of imaginative synthesis for forming unified cognitions.

To this end Heidegger moves to a resurvey of each of the two 'stems' in Kant's presentation, taking as a key Kant's admonition that we recognize "in understanding and sensibility two sources of representations which, while quite different, can supply objectively valid judgments of things only in *conjunction* with each other." [40]

The "in conjunction with each other" is the crucial point. In order for knowledge to be knowledge, it must represent the unity of sense and thought. Generally, Kant had spoken of the two 'stems'; when he was explicitly concerned with the relation of the intelligible and the sensible in their unified functioning structure, he referred to the imagination as a 'mediating third.'

As Kant had left the imagination—either as one of the three 'sources' of knowledge, or as a separate faculty which bridges the two 'stems'—he would seem to have left himself open to something of a 'third man' argument: what mediates between the things being mediated—between sense-and-imagination, between thought-and-imagination? Heidegger's persistence in taking seriously the essential unity of cognition as well as the Kantian intimation of imagination as the root-source of both sense and thought (and not as a 'bridging faculty') obviates the possible relevance of a 'third-man' objection. If sense and thought are not, alongside imagination, separate 'faculties' in need of conjunction; if they are rather merely functionally distinguishable facets of the functioning imagination; if imagination is the source of the temporality which is the *sine qua non* of knowledge and experience—then the structural unity of knowledge is original and primary and requires no bridging artifice.

In point of fact, the Deduction and the Schematism both implicitly presupposed this rooting of sense and thought in the transcendental power of imaginative synthesis. The unity of the cognitive act is only possible if the source of unification is prerequisite and not consequent. Of concern, then, is the discovery of the root-source or originating unity which differentiates functionally, in its modes of operation, as sensibility and thought.

Heidegger thus urges that we take the 'root' metaphor quite seriously. He sees it incumbent upon himself to demonstate how imagination, as root, must "discharge its function in such a way as to let the two stems (intuition and thought) grow out of it while lending them support and stability." [41] The task, then, is first to determine the common root of both (a) intuition and (b) thought, in the same transcendental power of imagination; and then to explore (c) the possibility of grounding, in the same way, the unification of the Kantian dichotomy of phenomenal-cognitive and noumenal-moral reason. These considerations will begin to unveil the nature of time and temporality.

a. Of Pure Intuition

Pure intuition was presented at the outset of the Critique in the Aesthetic. Heidegger has insisted that this initial presentation is only preliminary; this insistence is, of course, in full accord with Kant's own later explanation:

> In the Aesthetic I have treated this unity [of representation] as belonging merely to sensibility, simply *in order to emphasize that it precedes any concept, although as a matter of fact, it presupposes a synthesis* which does not belong to the senses but through which all concepts of space and time first become possible.[42]

A consideration of any Critical doctrine merely as presented in the Aesthetic is then essentially distortive. Because of the import of the Schematism regarding any aspect of time (pure intuition), we can then understand Heidegger's insistence that the Aesthetic be reread "only in the perspective of the transcendental schematism." [43]

As Kant had said, the *possibility* of sense intuition is not derivable from the things that are and appear to us; this possibility is presupposed in any specific exercise of sense intuition. In the Schematism, Kant showed that the temporalizing synthesis of imagination 'procedures' schemata, in terms of which we represent and understand what is given and from which we abstract the pure concepts (categories) by detemporalization.

Pure intuitions were termed by Kant 'original representations' and are "the pure forms of all sensible intuition, and so are what make apriori synthetic propositions possible."[44] They are not merely *some* modes of appearances; they are, as space and time, the *only* possible modes of any appearances. Original in a radical sense, they "contain a manifold of pure apriori intuition, but at the same time are conditions of the receptivity of our mind."[45] They thus presuppose, or set out the presuppositions of, a manifold or experiential field and are the condition, thereby, of all appearances in a unified space and a unified time. They are thus originating or formative in a basic sense: prior to any presentation, they set out "space and time as multiple totalities in themselves."[46] As such they are the requisite precursory or anticipatory condition for any possible representation.

Time is not then merely a form of intuition. It is originally unifying in that it itself gives unity of experience as the form in which experience is to be had. In an empirical intuition, which is passive receptivity, we apprehend an 'object' under this form of temporal unity. But this temporal unity issues from a subjective condition which is dictated by our own nature as the possibility of any apprehension we may have. Thus, although the apprehending act is essentially passive and receptive, its unity is imposed by us as its condition for occurring; this 'reception' of the unity of time (and of space) itself is, in a real sense, self-generating; it is a form-ing act "which gives to itself that which offers itself";[47] it is by means of the unity of time, which we impose on any presentation so that it may become a representation for us, that the representation of time, as such, enters our cognitive awareness.

Thus at the outset, pure intuition is already a unifying, an imposing of 'a place in one time' on every possible apprehended presentation. In order to have the most rudimentary notion of 'before' and 'after,' or of temporal sequence, I must already have at least a working understanding of a unifying time spread in which two separate presentations can be sequentially related. What is 'seen' in pure intuition is, in itself, a unified but by no means empty totality. "Pure intuition as originally unifying, i.e., giving unity, must *perceive* this unity." [48] This temporal unity is already present in and constituted by pure intuition; it thus constitutes the essence of pure intuition. This temporal-relating unity is essentially synthesizing in character; just because the imagination has been shown to be the synthesizing 'agency' in structuring cognition, the time-synthesizing nature of pure intuition must arise from the synthesizing imagination.

Kant had referred to the two apriori, or pure intuitions, as Heidegger points out, as "pre-formative forms." [49] As the two forms of intuition, space and time are 'pre-formative': they form, in advance of any ontic content, the 'shape,' the boundaries within which any representation in empirical apprehension must appear. Now this limitation of the 'area' in which imagination can correlate, integrate, and order the separable data of sense presentations is defined by the integrating or synthesizing capacity of imagination itself, by the extent of its capability and its modes of operating. Insofar as apriori intuition forms the limitation of the 'area' within which any presentation can appear and be represented, it seems to embody, with regard to sensibility, precisely the function of imaginative synthesis as transcendental defining of the extent of possible cognition.

If all knowledge, as Kant said, is indeed "finally subject to time"; [50] if every intuition as such contains within its presentation separable sensuous reports, which are brought together as a unified representation by the synthesis of apprehension; if each of our apprehensions is, from the outset, temporally ordered and so ordered as being 'in one time'—then our apprehensions, as such, are made possible by the presupposition of temporal synthesis embodied in the simplest perception, the presupposition of the time spread which permits me to see the house I perceive as one house 'abiding' across several separate eye-blink perceptions of it, and of my 'abiding' as well.

But this synthesis of separable presentations, this formative synthesis, this essential temporalizing prior to any ontic content, is precisely the role which Kant had displayed in the Schematism, as the time-forming function of imagination in the 'production' of the schemata. Functionally considered, the predicates are the same.

In reviewing the 'preview' of the Deduction, we saw that this synthesis of apprehension—the beginning of any cognition—already presupposes a time spread as well as the synthesis of 'reproduction in imagination,' the synthesis of memory recall with what is immediately present. Thus, even if the interpretation of the Schematism is questioned, it can be argued that Heidegger has merely made explicit what was already implicit in the opening of the Deduction: grant that the simplest apprehension must be temporal, must be under the 'form of time' (that as sequential, it must unite separable moments into one apprehending), and it must follow that this is not possible without memory recall, without the synthesis of past with present, which arises from imagination.

We can, moreover, look back at the Deduction with the Schematism in mind. It then becomes apparent that this memory recall, emanating from the activity of imaginative synthesis, already necessarily involves temporalized concepts, viz., the schemata 'produced' by imagination.

Heidegger's reduction or tracing back of pure intuition (time) to the activity of imagination is, then, in accord with Kant's own leads. Heidegger has, indeed, gone beyond Kant by carrying these leads to a more developed conclusion: insofar as imagination is necessarily involved in apprehensive reproductive syntheses (as per the Deduction) and in the formation of temporalized categories (as in the Schematism), its functioning as pure intuition sets the limits or horizon of the possibility of any representation whatsoever. The doctrine of pure intuition in the Aesthetic asserted that "every determinate magnitude of time is possible only through limitation of one single time that underlies it;" Heidegger's consequent is that imagination imposes, in advance of any possible presentation, what Kant had termed "the original representation" [51] of one time.

The problem with which we are then left is the recurring one of ontological status—just what is the transcendentally presupposed 'object' of this pure intuition? If we must be able to "perceive this unity" [52] which pure intuition imposes, what is it that is perceived? The problem is augmented by the fact that pure intuitions are " 'intuitions without things' but nevertheless they do have a content." Time is not an object of perception—only intuitional content is; but yet time cannot as such "be disavowed." As a pure intuition it is not itself intuited as such but certainly "according to the modality of an act which is originally form-giving." [53]

Kant had made it clear that pure intuition "is in itself no object, but the merely formal condition of an object (as appearance) as pure space and pure time (*ens imaginarium*). These are, indeed, something, as forms of intuition but are not themselves objects which are intuited." [54] Heidegger comments: "What is perceived in pure intuition as such is an *ens imaginarium*. Therefore, the act of pure intuition is essentially pure imagination." [55]

Now it should be apparent that Kant and Heidegger are not referring to the object of a fanciful dream or the content of a phantasy—not a unicorn, not a hallucination, not something chimerical and unreal. The *ens imaginarium,* the imaginative be-ing which is the object of pure intuition, is, as Kant said, 'indeed Some-thing,' an *Etwas* that is not a perceptible object, not some-*thing* that may be reported in a particular sensory intuition. Most crucial, it is *not* a thing which can be thought but not sensed, i.e., not an empty concept, an *ens rationis*. The object of a pure intuition is, as Heidegger has already indicated,[56] objectivity as such but not any particular object, temporality as such but not any particular time. It is, in a real sense, the *ens realissimum,* the most real, the ground, the prior possibility of the reality of any ontic thing appearing as real to us, the thing-ness of any particular thing, the 'backdrop of all time' presupposed in any particular 'now' in time. In full accord with the thesis of the Copernican Revolution, the transcendental grounds of any particular object in apprehension are logically prior to, and presupposed in, particular empirical apprehensions reported by sensory intuition. The nature of pure intuition—and the genus of the things it can report—is the ground upon and within which any particular empirical intuition, and the ontic objects reported from it by sensibility, must stand.

As Heidegger points out, the *ens imaginarium,* the imaginative be-ing, was presented by Kant in the differentiation of the concept of 'Non-thing (*Nichts*) in general,' from which Kant had suggested that the differentiations of the concept of 'Some-thing (*Etwas*) in general' be drawn.[57] The characterization of the 'Non-thing' as *ens imaginarium* is an indication of the range of the 'possible,' an "empty intuition without an object," [58] as the 'empty form' in which data must be 'shaped' in order to become referential for concepts.

What then is intuited in pure intuition? What Heidegger suggests is the form of unity itself: the form of unity which is produced by imagination (aside from any presentation) and is thus a be-ing that is not an 'object' or a thing in human experience, but yet not nothing-at-all. It is that non-thing-ness which is presupposed as the transcendental grounding of any particular thing appearing. What we can understand Heidegger to mean, in the light of the preceding discussion, is that the *ens imaginarium,* the imaginative be-ing that is the transcendental object of pure intuition and of the schematized categories brought to bear in it, is presupposed in every particular intuition and is nothing more or less than ultimate Time itself.

Kant had distinguished two functions of pure intuition: "the *form of intuition* [which] gives only a manifold, [and] the *formal intuition* [which] gives the unity of representation." [59] The prime focus in the Aesthetic was on the first; its necessary connection with imagination appeared in the 'preview' of the Deduction. As 'formal intuition,' the source of unified representation, pure intuition must be grounded in transcendental imagination if Heidegger's argument for the source of unification is to hold. As pointed out in the preceding pages, this imaginative source of intuitional unification is seen in full force in the Schematism and is reinforced by rereading the Deduction in its light.

To 'reduce' intuition to imagination seems initially plausible just because of the close relationship between the two in Kant's own discussion. Having explicated transcendental imagination as the source of pure intuition, as grounding the capacity to integrate separable representations in terms of the imaginative (and unperceivable) be-ing of time, Heidegger is now able to refer to pure imagination as "transcendental intuition," [60] as the capacity for forming the representation of the form of time as such.

b. Of Pure Thought

At first blush the prospect of reducing theoretical reason to imagination strikes one, as Heidegger himself recognizes, as sheer absurdity. And this reaction is reinforced by Kant's description of imagination as apriori but nevertheless 'always sensible' [61] together with his evaluation of it as a 'lower' faculty. It appears less preposterous, however, if the precise meanings of 'imagination' and the transcendental context of the entire enquiry are kept in mind.

Sensibility has already been shown to be the source of all conceptualization. [62] As essentially sensible, my human finitude is dependent upon objects coming into my perceptive range for sensory intuitions; these intuitions do not create, but report, the objects entering their perceptual field.

The transcendental power of imagination is, as Kant had insisted, sensible—but not exclusively so; it is also the source of concept sensibilization; it is, as Heidegger says, "the condition of the possibilities of all the faculties." [63] Consequently, it is somewhat meaningless to talk of either intuition or reason as 'higher' or 'lower'; they are but distinguishable aspects of the genus of representation in general.

Repeatedly Heidegger has insisted on this central theme—the integral unity of sensibility and conceptualization. In both the Deduction and the Schematism, Kant had shown the categories to be merely analytic distinctions of pure synthesis, which is always dependent upon apprehension and the unity of apperception for any meaning. And Kant himself grounded this unity in the "pure (productive) synthesis of imagination, [which] prior to apperception, is the ground of the possibility of all knowledge, especially of experience." [64]

Heidegger fully accepts Kant's characterization of thought as "the *faculty of rules*." [65] A faculty of rules holds out before us those unities (or categories) which guide and limit, prior to any presentation, any representational act. As regulative, they comprise a unity which defines, before the object appears, the possibility and characteristics requisite for it to do so. They predict the kinds of particular apprehensions which may be correlated with others, what kinds of objects can be germane to that with which the concept is concerned. If I am seeking an example of the idea of a typewriter, it is pointless to direct my attention to a fox-terrier.

Pure understanding pre-forms the horizon of possible experience. It does so by my 'I think'; but my 'I think' always requires a specific object; it always refers to a specific concept as its object: I think X or Y or Z. The 'I think (X)' thus reveals my self, my ego, which brings the categories of the unifying understanding into a position whereby the essentially regulative function can be exercised.

Pure understanding is, then, representational, formative, anticipatory, and spontaneous; it functions, as shown by the transcendental schematism, the "schematism of our understanding," [66] as an imaginative procedure by means of which pure concepts can be related, in pure synthesis, *to the possibility* of having any referential meaning.

The system of transcendental schemata then forms "a transcendental product of imagination." [67] Schemata are not produced by the understanding but are employed by it. This pure schematism is produced, as we have seen, by the transcendental power of imagination which, in the transcendental schematism, constitutes the foundation of the understanding itself. Thus, despite any seemingly different origin, an act of the understanding is constituted by thinking unities—thinking modes of possible unification of the particular presentations of sensibility. As such, it is a free[68] formation of a way in which such presentations as may occur would be integrated. As pre-experiential creator of those integrating modes that it will use in order to interpret data as meaningful, it is, Heidegger argues, "a spontaneously formative act of representation, a fundamental act of the transcendental imagination." [69] It is spontaneous, in contrast to the receptivity of sensibility, because it does not merely report what is presented but, in the most literal sense, 'pre-scribes' what may be, and how it may be, represented.

As Kant had presented it, imagination was an identifiable 'bridge' between intuition and the understanding; it was able to 'mediate' between them by virtue of having something in common with each. But merely to suggest, as Kant had, that imagination has, in addition to the receptivity of intuition, the spontaneity of thought, still leaves it as a 'third thing' mediating two separate 'faculties.' Heidegger's essential argument is that the relationship is *not triadic but triune:* intuition and thought are not separate 'things'; they are merely discernible aspects of one cognitive process. As such, the Kantian formulation is grossly inadequate and cannot be taken as such.

Although Kant had demonstrated the relation of both intuition and thought to imagination, he did not identify them. If imagination can, indeed, bring intuition and thought into concert, it is necessary that each of the two 'stems' have something of the other. Now, Heidegger argues, this closer relationship of the two 'stems' has already been demonstrated: pure intuition, as pure and pre-experiential, has this free spontaneity of thought just because it 'proclaims,' in advance of any particular empirical encounter, the temporal form which a report of that encounter must take in intuition so that it can be represented. It has this free spontaneity just because it operates under no external compulsion and enjoys freedom within the limits which it imposes on itself. Its transcendental receptivity is prior to any ontic reception. It is thus pure spontaneous receptivity and, as such, comes out of the transcendental imagination.

If pure thought is to be reducible to the same imaginative ground, it must be essentially comprised by the same two characteristics: the free spontaneity of pure thought has, as pure imagination, been shown to belong to pure intuition as well; it now remains to show that pure thought also includes the receptivity of pure intuition.

Kant's polarization of sensibility as receptivity and thought as spontaneity, Heidegger argues, came from an overemphasis on his separate treatment of each. By specifically eliciting the point, we should readily be able to see that pure thought necessarily has the essentially receptive character attributed to intuition and, thereby, an essentially intuitive character.

The unity of the categories precludes mere random organization of sensory reports. Employment of the categories depends upon what is apprehended; categories function merely as rules for forming a meaningful unity of the imaginative presentation of the apprehending synthesis: they are no more than "rules of connection (synthesis) which compel as they connect." A category is *pre*-cursive, in advance of, prior to, any presentation; its unificatory function is referential to possible apprehensions reportable in intuition. As such, it is a rule for the correlation of sense data and it functions only in the actual "receptive act which lets it rule." It is thus nothing more than an idea which as "the representation of rules can itself represent only in the mode of receptivity." [70] If thought is the mode of interpreting the meaning of what is given or received; if it is the mode of finding significant possibilities and prescribing order to what is receivable—then it is dependent on the capacity for receptivity for any content at all. If, as we were told at the outset, 'thought is always in the service of intuition,' it finds itself invoked, functioning, explicated, only in the given as it is represented *qua* given. It is then essentially involved in the intuitive apprehending of any object just because it already, in any cognition, represents the rule(s) as characterizing the object that is seen as the given.

Pure thought is then intuitive. Its spontaneity is essentially receptive. It can arise only from the transcendental power of imaginative synthesis "in order that it can be what it is." [71] The transcendental power of imagination sketches out or projects, prior to any representation, the entirety of the range of possible object-characterizations before it, in order to form the horizon within which the knowing self knows. This imaginative possibility of the systematic unity of our knowledge is necessary in order that the understanding is able to function in terms of actual presentations intuitively received. The scope of understanding is thus limited by the realm of cognitional possibility, the horizon circumscribing the area of possible experience. This horizon is formed by imaginative functioning; the exercise of the categorical unificatory rules of thought can be applied only within it to those things that are sensed as having be-ing within it.

If we keep the precise meanings of 'intuition' and 'imagination' in mind, Heidegger appears to be doing nothing more here than insisting on what might be termed an explicit and uncompromising empiricist reading of Kant: if thought is restricted in its valid employment to presentations in our immediate awareness of an object, it is not something which goes 'to work,' so to speak, on this representation; it is invoked and activated in the moment and act of awareness, in the immediacy of the perception.[72] It 'participates in' our perception of what is presented. It becomes aware of the characterizations it imposes, not by contemplating which possible characterizations to apply to the object, but by projecting them onto and eliciting them from the object as the act of apprehension reports the object in the presentation of it. An act of perception is in itself a synthesizing act and already involves not only the mere 'appearing' but also the characteristics which I take that 'appearing' to incarnate and represent.

Thus, in the actual perception of the country house before me, I do *not sequentially* (1) perceive color patches, (2) relate them to each other so as to form the house-object against a landscape background, and (3) then cast about for a concept to apply by association with past perception and search among my concepts for an appropriate one. I see the house *qua* a house in the immediate apprehending act and I see it in terms of the conceptual similarities and differences and memory references which it—the house-object—evokes. In the perceiving, the house stands out for me from its background with all the meaning I see it as offering. In the fullest sense Heidegger's point is that the act of empirical cognition is an integrated and structured fusion, *at the outset,* of components that are only analytically discernible.

Thought is receptive as it takes into itself the representations of what is before it. It is intuitive—or perceptual or apprehending—and thereby passive insofar as it depends upon the given for the representation in terms of which the object *qua* a thing-that-is is perceived. Thought is only meaningful when it is referential, when it 'reads into' the object those conceptual characterizations which it simultaneously 'reads from' it.

In the Kant-Heidegger sense this intuitive apprehension must be carefully distinguished from the merely 'imaginary' or hallucinatory. Although it can best be illustrated in terms of physical perceptual objects, such illustration must be distinguished from the principle illustrated: for Heidegger, as for Kant, apprehension is not restricted to sense perception. Just as 'immediate (intuitive awareness) knowledge' can apply to principles as well as to things, so we can also intuit (immediately apprehend), become immediately aware of, the pure forms of space and time. We become aware of them, as of the categories, as pure schemata. By providing the center of the structure of our cognitional experience, these schemata incorporate all elements essential to that experience and, in the operational unity of the structure of the cognitional act, they define and indicate the contributing nature of each of its constituent elements.

The receptivity of intuition thus functions as the restraint on the spontaneity of thought. Likewise, the spontaneity of thought permits intuition to provide the 'form' through which it 'receives' what is there to be 'received,' what is given, or, to use a phrase Heidegger frequently employs, what is 'offered.'

Intuition and thought are thus essentially reciprocal; they function together only in the systematically integrated cognitive act. The nature and capability of this act determines what and how things can be brought into human knowledge and just how each of these two elements functions in union with the other. Kant is thus justified in having said, "Human reason . . . regards all our knowledge as belonging to a possible system." [73] This systematic unitary structure of cognition is the combining of intuition and thought—each of which has a degree of spontaneity and of receptive necessity; this systematic structuring is the activity of the transcendental imagination and is exercised in the schematism, which is the name for that system of temporal procedures that imagination embodies and integrates in rendering the possibility of knowledge.

The transcendental power of imagination is thus the ground of the unity—and thereby of the distinction—of intuition and thought. Each appears as merely a differentiated function of that imaginative capacity to rise above, go beyond, or transcend momentary sense perceptions; by connecting them, interpreting them, eliciting meaning *from* them, imaginative synthesis creates the possibility of the continuity of the subject as well as of the object from one momentary presentation to another. As such it is the source not only of the unity expressed in a cognitive act but of the possibility of any cognitive content in it.

For anything to be within cognition, what is first requisite is the capability of the knowing-subject and the object-known to become accessible to each other. This capacity of imaginative integration—the subject's knowledge of his own self and of the object as something distinct from his self—is the ground and source of the possibility of knowledge. It is also the source of the to-be of the subject as such—for it is only within the apprehending realm made accessible by transcendental imagination that one is able to become aware of the unifying cognizing self that he himself is.

This transcendence—this capacity to become aware of the objects perceived together with the perceiving 'I'—rests on the schematic unification and analytic differentiation of intuition and thought. Thus the schematic unificatory concepts or rules are the ways in which the transcendental imagination creates the possibility of experience itself.

It is this creativity of transcendental imaginative synthesis that points out transcendence—its need, capability, and inherent limitations—which 'makes possible the essence' of human finitude. This same transcendence Heidegger can now explicitly describe "as the essence of the finite self." [74] It is this imaginative capacity to achieve transcendental modes of knowing that makes it possible for me to be having an integrated knowledge, a continuing achievement that makes me aware of my own reality, of my own be-ing as the knower. Thus the 'essence of the self'—mine or yours —is no longer to be described merely in terms of 'subjectivity.' The 'subjectivity of the subject' is 'revealed' in the nature of transcendence, an act of be-ing which is present in any and every particular act. The self, *qua* knower, is not discovered as a 'thing' but as the dynamic demarcating and invoking of the cognitively possible. Its transcending is an enabling act of knowing to-be. In the ontic cognizing which our transcending permits, we are able to discover our own to-be, our own mode of act-ing, our own be-ing, which we name with the label 'self.' The self then is not so much a subject as it is an act-ing, a way of be-ing in, at least, a cognitive relationship to other be-ings and things.

This 'essence of the human finite self' is thus rooted in the act of the transcendental imagination, manifested as the schematism, which imagination produces as the mode in which our cognizing occurs. It is in the functioning of transcendental imaginative synthesis that the discernible elements of intuition and thought are identified; it is as functional aspects of the cognitive synthesis which 'produces' finite human knowledge, that they are found as elements in our knowledge.

Imagination is no longer, as Kant had left it, a mysterious power hidden in the depths of the human soul. It manifests itself as the ultimately basic source of the possibility of a systematic and structured mode of our be-ing, of our possibility to be, at least in cognitive terms, a true unified be-ing, a true self.

c. And Practical Reason

Kant's deliberate exclusion of the imagination from the moral doctrine[75] now emerges as a serious problem. If Heidegger's reasoning holds, the essence of selfhood, as developed in the First Critique, is manifested in the temporalizing schematism rooted in the transcendental imagination. The only 'self,' however, which is presented there is the phenomenal self appearing to inner sense. The true moral self, *qua* a-temporal and embodying the essence of selfhood under the idea of freedom, was outside of phenomenal appearance, outside of the temporal, in the realm of the ultimately and truly real and intelligible.[76] The dual restriction—of cause-and-effect necessity to the phenomenal world of appearance, and of the 'true self' to noumenal reality—was Kant's method of denying the competence of what we might today call a determinist psychology to reduce moral choice to sequential causation and thus abolish the reality of moral choice. By postulating this absolute dichotomy, this unbridgeable gulf, he sought to ensure the possibility of both science and morality; safely sequestered from each other, each was accorded complete sovereignty over its own legitimate province and the security of each was to be guaranteed by permitting neither to encroach on the other's domain.

Yet Heidegger has, on the basis of Kant's justification of cognition in the phenomenal world, insisted on the temporalization of the cognizing self. Is there any way of reconciling his interpretation with an essential motive of Kant's entire system? If some such reconciliation cannot be effected, his interpretation must be regarded either as an open assault on those foundations of the Critical philosophy upon which he sought to build a new structure or as wholly illegitimate within a Kantian context. For, aside from ignoring Kant's animating motivation (which yielded the spirit if not always the letter of his work), how can we accept Heidegger's insistence on the integral unity of the cognitive act if he himself bows before the Kantian bifurcation of the whole man into cognitive and moral selves? If there is to be an exclusive division at the heart of the one self, subordinate dichotomies seem less crucial. If my self is not ultimately one self, I face on a 'total' level what Heidegger has discussed on a cognitive one: how do I unify my two distinct halves which comprise the whole one being I take myself to be?

The crucial problem of the Kantian morality is thus posed. Let us grant (at least for the sake of argument) that Kant's formulation of the nature of a moral act is correct; we still have before us the problem of its possible relation to the temporal world in which all moral dilemmas appear, in which they must be resolved, and to which the moral law itself must be applied in order to attain meaning.

There is presumed throughout Kant's discussion—by virtue of the principle that 'ought' implies 'can'—the principle of applicability: moral decisions of the moral will do relate to specific acts and situations. Indeed, Kant had expressly justified the separation of the conditions of cognition from those of obligation as grounding the possibility of applicability.[77] Yet the 'mechanics' of *how* this noumenal moral will is to be applied in the phenomenal realm, inhabited by the empirical self, is again left in the realm of the unknown.

Kant's moral system, as he had left it, thus posed two distinct but closely related problems. First is the problem of applicability —yet no analogue to the cognitive schematism was suggested for pure practical reason; indeed, he expressly denied that "any schema can be supplied for the purpose of applying [the moral law] *in concreto.*"[78] The second problem is that of how to bring into unity the cognitive temporal and the moral a-temporal aspects of the selfsame self. For Kant's formulation presumed an uncrossable gulf between that self appearing to me, as experiencing subject, under the form of time, and my own true "Ego as this may be constituted in itself."[79] He never really explained just how the cognitive and moral become integrated into one being, how these are but two related aspects of the selfsame one self that each person considers himself to be. In order to comprehend that actual self for whom Kant's practical reason was intended, such integration is crucial. For it is a temporal being, not an a-temporal intellectual formula, that experiences moral dilemmas, formulates moral judgments, and undertakes morally motivated acts.

Kant had defined 'to be free' as being "independent of determination by causes in the sensible world," [80] and as crucial to the possibility of morality. He identified freedom with that reason which "as pure spontaneity . . . is elevated even above *understanding*." [81] In cognition, the traditional formal logic was accorded only the negative function of guarding against error.[82] It was to be superseded by transcendental logic which concerned itself with the apriori relationship between concepts and content, and it was here that the transcendental imagination was proposed as the requisite connecting agency. Yet Kant, restricting a purely conceptual logic in cognition to negative regulative utility, looked to its legitimate use in its 'practical employment,' in the practical determinations of the moral will in "everything that is possible through freedom." [83] His elucidation of morality is consistent with his distinction between the formal and transcendental uses of logic, but he neglected to carry this forward in order to relate moral concepts to moral situations; he neglected either to formulate or to see the necessity for formulating a transcendental logic or systematic mode of procedure for relating the pure concept of the moral law to the specific temporal moral situations which it is called upon to resolve; in contrast to the analysis of cognition, he failed to see the need for a systematic logical procedure for filling moral concepts with content.

The ground and criterion of the Categorical Imperative itself was that formal principle of noncontradiction.[84] Its prototype seems to have been the necessary universality, not of the laws of nature repeatedly invoked as analogous, but of the laws governing the use of the syllogism, the laws of the traditional logic. Both are claimed to embody that universality which Kant made the essential mark of a moral judgment; but the laws of nature do so in an essentially descriptive and predictive way while the syllogistic laws are rules that are essentially prescriptive in function.

Like the rules of the syllogism, the Categorical Imperative does not describe how we *do* act (or reason) but how we *should;* it does not tell us what specific acts to undertake (or specific arguments to invoke) but how we shall distinguish moral acts (or valid arguments) from those which are not; the form of the Categorical Imperative, as the form of a valid syllogism, is meaningful only as we match any specific content we bring to it; but it does not tell us how to resolve a conflict between alternate value claims (or alternate prime premises).

And why should I bother? Why should I be moral? Why should I be logical? The ultimate motive for testing either moral judgments or presumable logical arguments against the standard of the moral law or of the laws of the syllogism, Kant would have to ground in the same source, "the general concept of a rational being as such." [85] This ultimate motivation presupposes a basic respect for rationality as such, a basic respect for ourselves, which we see as embodying a nature essentially rational in character; this "Rational nature separates itself out from all other things by the fact that it sets itself an end . . . [which is to be] conceived only negatively—that is, as an end against which we should never act." [86] To conclude that the Kantian morality, as Kant had left it, goes no further than pronouncing a negative criterion of what is *not* moral is to suggest that its parallelism to its inspiration in the traditional conceptual logic is complete.

For pure concepts to have content, as Kant had seen in cognitive terms, requires the necessity of a method systematically prescribing the way by which to bring concept and content together into a unity comprising them both. In cognition this act of unification, as Heidegger has demonstrated, was effected in the schematism by the transcendental imagination. The moral law ostensibly required no such synthesizing agency just because sensibility is concerned with the actual, not the possible,[87] and consequently is beyond its pale; moral rationality is somehow not to be concerned with actualization or temporalization of the possible.

But the parallelism which has been suggested—between the pure moral law of practical reason and the pure concepts of the understanding—also suggests carrying it forth. Just as a formally correct conceptual argument is empty until given content, so a pure categorical moral commandment remains empty until confronted with a particular situation demanding resolution. When seen in terms of possible employment or application, both the pure concept and the pure moral law are essentially futural in meaning—both are abstract criteria for measuring specific possible instances, which may appear, against their requirements. In both cases they point ahead to the kind of thing or situation which could be validly cited as an instance of meaning and reference. If pure concepts need to be joined to specific percepts, pure moral law would seem to stand in a similar need to be joined to specific situations. If one requires temporalization, the other does also.

The problem Kant presented is thus a twofold one, or, perhaps more precisely, a two-sided singular problem; for the temporalization of the pure moral law and the unity of the acting cognitional and moral being would appear to be mutually implicatory. In considering this problematic, Heidegger focuses on the unity of the self. It is, however, suggested that his argument, if successful, also points out the direction for resolving the Kantian legacy of the question of temporalization as well.

Kant had grounded the essence of selfhood in a somehow timeless moral ego. Heidegger, in working out the reconstruction of the Kantian epistemology which we have been examining, has grounded the essence of selfhood in the time-bound transcendence manifested in the schematism by the transcendental imagination. As if the developing gulf between them were not already broad enough, Heidegger will augment it through his subsequent temporalization of the transcendental imagination itself (see VI.5.a). This subsequent argument is implicitly presupposed here; for this reason it is urged that a final verdict on Heidegger's truly ingenious argumentation here be held in abeyance.

Crucial to the Kantian morality, as well as to the entire Critical philosophy as its central dualism, is the distinction between 'persons' and 'things.' The cognitive categories were designed to comprehend 'things'; the moral inquiry was concerned with the 'moral ego,' which Kant had clearly identified with the word 'person' and the concept of 'personality' in what he called a 'kingdom of ends.' [88] Heidegger's point of departure is precisely this identification of the concept 'person' with that of the 'moral ego' which is at the center of Kant's work.

According to Kant, a person is a being with an absolute (end-in-itself) value and not merely an instrumental one; a person is characterized essentially as rational and having legitimate account-ability or responsibility for his acts, a being whose reason is the governor of his will. A person is a rational being with a will who is capable of making choices (as issuing from the presupposition of the reality of moral freedom), who can subordinate his will to prescriptive self-imposed law in the form of duty or moral obliga-tion. This free self-imposition is itself an act of will; it renders the distinction between what is conceived as a desire for happiness and freely accepted obligations, the fulfillment of which are seen to make him worthy of such happiness as he is able to attain.

A 'thing,' on the other hand, is precisely that; it is an object that is merely present or a tool that can be used as a means, an instrument, to goals we seek to attain. It becomes, in the Kantian formulation, the subject of hypothetical, as contrasted with moral categorical, imperatives. The thing makes no decision, manifests no reasoning or will or self-consciousness, and, when used as a tool, is subject to the will of the person using it as prescribed by the mechanical rules by which he is able to use it. A thing reacts to external causes in a manner wholly predictable by mechanical rules; a person responds to external pressures in accord with his own mode of interpreting their significance to himself and is not wholly explicable in terms of external mechanical rules. But me-chanical rules define that relevant aspect of the thing-world to which, say, a hammer, nail, wall, and body-of-the-person all be-long. For what purpose does a person use a hammer—to drive a picture nail into the wall? to assault the picture's critic? This is the person's own moral decision, which 'mechanics' alone cannot discuss. It is, Kant would have said, a moral decision, a person's internal decision which, as his act of will, is an original center of causation and can *somehow* manifest itself by entering the phe-nomenal mechanistic thing-world of necessary structuring and sequential order in order to manipulate it as he wills to do so.

It was to 'save' this area of self-causative rational will from the necessity of causal sequential order, which he saw as intrinsic to the structured world of the now-succession, that Kant created that gulf between things and persons, locating each in somehow separated realms of distinct sovereignties.

But, Heidegger notes, central to this Kantian portrait of what it means to be a person is our capacity to have *"respect* for the moral law as in itself a sufficient incentive of the will." [89] It is this 'respect,' this willingness to place oneself under a moral commandment, this capacity to make a distinction between what I want to do and what I feel myself obligated to do, that enabled Kant to distinguish man not only from things but from animals as well. The word 'respect,' Kant stated, "is the only becoming expression";[90] respect for the moral law is an intellectually based apriori feeling that, he emphasized, is not merely the incentive to morality but "is morality itself." [91] For the comportment of respect toward the moral law enables one to voluntarily place oneself under its demands and thus characterizes a moral person as such. It is here that we begin to see all that is meant in the idea of a person: "the idea of the moral law, with the respect which is inseparable from it . . . [is] personality itself";[92] it is in this sense that the "idea of personality awakens respect." [93]

Just as we do not freely place ourselves under the authority of another unless that authority is respected, so the respect for the moral law is what induces us to respond freely to its demands and accept its authority over us. In placing myself, by a completely free act of self-determination, under someone else's authority, I am limiting myself—but, in so doing, further defining and realizing the capacities of my self. In placing myself under the authority of an educational institution and of the teachers and students within it, I limit my choice of activities but am able to derive the value incumbent on teaching and studying within it. In placing myself under a military commander, I restrict my possible activities but participate more effectively, say, in a war I favor than I could do all alone. In placing myself under the moral law, I find new opportunity to focus my attentions and actions in a certain direction, achieve a sense of ordered unity in the course of my acts. By restricting my responses to myriad desires pulling in all directions, I thus attain a liberation in the sense of positive freedom, freedom-for, opportunity to-do. I thus develop, define, and realize my own individual self-identity and its chosen capacities as I bring greater coherence, order, and intelligibility into my actions and my relations with others.

Kant had regarded this 'respect' as a feeling; but, Heidegger points out, every meaningful feeling is intentional; it is a feeling-for some particular entity or kind. The respect of which Kant spoke is thus really respect-for the moral law. As such, it was deemed requisite for the possibility of a moral act. But, if this is so, it cannot serve, as Kant thought, as the ground of the moral law itself. My respect-for the moral law does not create the moral law; my feeling of respect-for it presupposes it. My respect-for it only affects me as I permit it to do so. To the degree that I augment my respect-for the moral law, I augment the definition of my own self and more fully realize, and become aware of, myself as a deliberating choosing being. As Heidegger puts it, "That for which the respect is respect, the moral law, the reason as free gives to itself. Respect for the law is respect for oneself as that self which does not let itself be determined by self-conceit. . . ." [94] The respect for my own self, which emerges from my respect for the moral law and my free self-determination to place myself under its authority, is requisite for Kant's Categorical Imperative to respect and treat myself or any other person as an end and not merely as a means.

My determination of myself to accept the authority of the moral law, my moral self-determination, means that I am finding myself as a rational being; because this self-limitation, by virtue of the moral law, is freely imposed, I also realize myself thereby as a free being in this basic act of my free decision. Because acceptance of the authority of the moral law of practical reason presupposes that its authority must be freely assumed, my free submission to its dictates manifests my own self to me as rational, as free, as responsible for what I do; in acting on my respect for the moral law, I thus find and begin to realize my own self. Respect-for the moral law is thus a 'mode of the being-as-self of my ego'; it is the root of my responsibility for my own to-be, my own be-ing as a rational, free, choosing, acting person. It is the foundation of my personal living authenticity as such.

My respect for the moral law is not the ground of the moral law; it is the ground of my responsiveness to it, of the development of myself that I am deriving from my free decision to act in accordance with its requirements. This respect-for the moral law has thus been transformed from a mere feeling into the requisite capacity to place myself under it. Were I not able to respect it, how could I, in an act of freedom, accept its authority over me? This respect-for the moral law has thus been transformed into a "transcendental, fundamental structure of the transcendence of the moral self."[95] This respect-for the moral law thus emerges as the apriori ground of my capacity to make moral judgments, conceived as universal, concerning particular situational presentations, and manifested in particular responsive acts.

My self-submissiveness to the dictates of the moral law is analogous to the 'receptivity' of intuition in the cognitional act; the free self-imposition of its authority over my desires is analogous to the spontaneity of pure thought. As in the union of intuition and thought I attain cognition, so in the fusion of self-submissiveness and free self-imposition I attain the unity of my acting self and my dignity as a moral person. This self-awareness of my own self as a person requires these two seemingly discordant capacities. As Kant's problem in cognition was the 'how' of the unification of the disparity of perceptual presentations and conceptual thought, so here in the moral realm of practical reason the same kind of problem is posed.

Indeed, Heidegger's critique of Kant's moral theory provokes the observation that, as Kant had left it, moral reason could not become operative—just because he did not elucidate the necessary exercise of moral imaginative reasoning. For universalization of a possible moral maxim in thought requires, as many of Kant's own examples show, that the Kantian test of morality rests on imagination, that imaginative universalization provides the possibility of moral decision and is a necessary condition for it.

Practical reason then is analogous to cognitional reason. Heidegger suggests that it finds its unity in the same transcendental power of imagination which he saw as the keystone of Kant's epistemological doctrine. Neither the choosing, acting self nor the moral law as such is apprehended in the respect-for, which is the ground of their unification. Merely the respect-for the moral law does not, of itself, show the moral law to us—nor does it show us the possibilities for choice and action which the self discriminates in a moral act. We discover our respect-for the moral law in an act of self-imposed duty; that act of self-imposed duty points to the ground of its possibility in just the same way in which an ontic act of cognition presupposes its transcendental ground. The act, freely performed 'because duty requires it,' points to the submission to that duty, to the fact that it was accepted in the face of conflicting desires; the free self-imposition points to the moral law itself as that which is submitted to, and to the being of the freely submitting self. Their union is effected by imaginative synthesis, by a synthesis which essentially temporalizes the moral law in terms of the moral being facing a temporal situation and making a temporal decision.

Heidegger's consideration of practical reason underlines his continual emphasis on the essential finitude of human beings; here he puts it on a radically basic level. Human finitude is not marked, in this context, merely by the Kantian insistence on our inability to foresee the future effectiveness or ramifications of a particular act. I am not an omnipotent being who is able to dismiss temporal limitations on my will and do everything I want to do or feel obligated to do. I am not an omniscient being who knows how to select the perfect means to a perfect end. I am not a perfect being who has completely integrated his conflicting desires and obligations. As an essentially limited being, I must focus on the alternative choices for action which I see any situation presenting to me; to the extent that I submit myself to the universality of the moral law as I interpret that law to myself, I focus not on transforming that situation into a means to an end (the effectiveness or ramifications of which I cannot with any accuracy foretell), but on what does the situation, as I see it, require of me: what *should* I do?

And in this self-imposition of the *should,* Heidegger implicitly suggests, the nature of human finitude manifests itself on a truly radical level. It manifests itself in our *need* for finitude, our need for the self-limitation which the moral law provides in order to find the self and to define one's self as a free person in the ordered self-fulfillment that the self-limitation permits.

What is thus demonstrated, then, is not merely the thesis that we are already finite; in order to become moral persons, in order to develop the characteristic of personality, in order to become true individuals, we need to intensify that inherent finitude. The need for orienting ourselves to the demands of a universalizing moral law, our need to respect its authority over our random wishes, our free self-imposition of it upon our selves, our free submission to its requirements, all conspire to permit us to realize that individuality of the self and to develop our capacities to grow into and enhance an individual personality.

We are thus pointed to the transcendental question, how is morality as self-submission to the self-imposed moral law possible? Heidegger has traced this ground back to the self; in *Being and Time* he does, indeed, seek to provide an existential basis of the possibility of morality in the experience of guilt, in the capacity to be guilty and thus invoke the notion of moral conscience, the notion of the *should,* which arises in its possibility from the capacity for self-judgment and awareness of the *should-not.* We are then pointed to the centrality of temporality in any moral judgment, which requires the capacity not only to be guilty, to invoke the mantle of moral obligation, but also to act with resoluteness in accord with the demand of conscience I impose upon myself. Indeed, it is in this anticipatory resoluteness that we first discover our essential temporality. It is this free selfhood, whose freedom is transcendence, which grounds the possibility of moral self-consciousness and makes possible the discovery of the moral 'I' in the relationship to the 'Thou.' For I discover my own selfhood in this "call of conscience . . . [which] in its basis and its essence is *in each case mine."* [96]

The parallelism between the moral and the cognitional is thus, as Heidegger has suggested, fairly complete. In a cognitional act I bring the particularity of the report of sensibility and the universality of the pure concept into the schematic unity of an 'I know that   '; in the moral act I bring the particularity of the act I am considering, or the moral dilemma which I face, by a similar imaginative universalization, into concert with the imaginative particularization of the universal maxim I accept as binding, into the unity of the 'I decide that I should do that   .' I join the two into an autonomous moral judgment by which I consider myself bound. I thus join together my interpretation of the meaning of the situation, as I define its moral dilemma, in terms of an imperative prescribing its resolution which I regard as universally binding. By bringing into one perspective the particularity of the situation and the universality of the demand of the moral law, I conclude simultaneously from the situation itself both the problem it poses and the solution it demands. It becomes a real moral situation only as I can simultaneously 'read into' it what I 'read from' it, as I see it as demanding the interpretive resolution I bring to it.

In thus defining the 'is' and the 'ought' which I see in the situation before me, I am further bringing into synthesis the factuality produced by cognitive synthesis with the prescriptive canon of practical reason. In doing this, I am not merely seeing or observing the situation. I am also determining what I should do about the situation as I understand it. In so doing, I am manifesting the self that I am and more fully realizing and comprehending the possibilities of my own selfhood.

Heidegger's insistence on the unity of the self has necessitated a common grounding of practical reason and the understanding. Despite the violence done to many Kant interpretations, the necessity for the unified ground was seen by Kant himself; in the Second Critique he had said:

> But if pure reason of itself can be and really is practical, as the consciousness of the moral law shows it to be, *it is only one and the same reason* which judges apriori by principles whether for theoretical or for practical purposes.[97]

What Heidegger has done in welding the unity of moral and cognitive reason, then, is no more than to face the task of working out this unity, which Kant had discerned as necessary and left as a problematic. Heidegger's temporalization of the moral will, in its reduction to imaginative synthesis, in its grounding in guilt and anticipatory resoluteness, does, indeed, run counter to innumerable Kantian texts. But even Kant had somehow discerned this necessity; even Kant had seen that somehow temporalist categories are crucial to the moral law; for he had explicitly grounded the postulate of immortality on "the practically necessary condition of *a duration adequate* to the perfect fulfilment of the moral law." [98]

If Heidegger's argumentation is at all successful, the ground of morality as of cognition then lies in this same capacity to go from the particular presentation to its representation, infusing it with meaning, significance, intelligibility. Both the cognitional and the moral acts are defined together within the temporal horizon of the living individual. In each case, and in both together, human finitude is defined by the need for, the recognition of, and the acceptance of the restriction of what-is-*possible,* what can be known, what can be required. Both rest on a transcendental structure which permits us to describe what is before us in objective terms. Both emanate from, and are rendered possible, in a temporal horizon by the transcendental power of imaginative synthesis; the transcendental imagination has been transformed from a somewhat mysterious 'third factor' of cognition into the formative center of the capacity for each human being to be a free cognizing, choosing, acting person.

In the exercise of cognition, as of practical moral reason, we have receptivity and spontaneity, the limitation of necessity and the necessity of freedom. It is in this unity of the finite, cognizing, choosing, acting self—not in a bifurcation of somehow related a-temporal moral and temporal cognitional entities—that Heidegger sees the source of the unified selfhood characterized by the notion of 'person.'

Receptivity and spontaneity, necessity and freedom, time and thought, as sensibility and understanding, do not merely go hand in hand. They are merely discernible aspects of an integrated self whose being is an activity and whose differentiated unity is made possible by its synthesizing imaginative functioning. In any of these dualistic distinctions, which are nothing more than analytic tools, we can say that "in themselves, the two are originally one." [99] The possibility of morality and of knowledge, of the employment of knowledge in action and the cognition of that action, both arise from and illuminate the structure of this one unified self, an autonomous person, whose essential nature in any aspect of his be-ing is to be pervasively temporal.

4 · *Allegation of Retreat*

SOME DEFINITE THESES have been brought out of the preceding examination: the finite essence of human knowledge, the limited role of the understanding in the formation of that knowledge, and the root position of imagination in bringing forth the structural unity of intuition and thought. The central role of imaginative synthesis was demonstrated as the theme of the Deduction. By means of the Schematism, the independence of the categories was shown to be a mere artifice; for, once seen as schematized, "the pure categories, being concepts of the synthesis of the manifold of *intuition in general,* must also be, in a sense, concepts of the synthesis of the manifold of pure intuition." [100] Thus, a point of focus has been the key statement of the Highest Principle: "the conditions of the possibility of experience in general are at the same time conditions of the possibility of the objects of experience." [101] These conditions are to be found in the central temporal imaginative synthesis.

The transcendental power of imagination has been shown to be the foundation of the possibility of knowledge and experience. Yet Kant did not pursue an investigation of its nature. As Kant had left it, this foundation of knowledge is an indeterminate unknown. The only source-ground to which Kant had pointed is the imagination; but it remained for him "a blind but indispensable function of the soul, without which we should have no knowledge whatsoever, but of which we are scarcely conscious." [102] It remained, in the end, an unexplored, uninvestigated, "unknown root" [103] of cognitive possibility.

It might well be argued that exploration of this unknown root was no part of his problem; that given the dualistic distinction between sense and thought, the Kantian problematic was the contribution of each of these to that objectivity in the knowledge we can and do have; that insofar as any problem must be limited by definition in order to be fruitfully explored, there was a justification for Kant to limit his beginning at that point where the two 'stems' of knowledge were seen to emerge. But, it could be countered, such a beginning which merely takes these two 'stems' for granted, without seeking out the nature of a common origin, commences with a bifurcation which cannot really be overcome.

Heidegger's question of unification and his concern with the unity of experience are focused by this dualistic description of the nature of human cognition. He has made explicit what Kant had already dimly seen—the need that this duality poses for some sort of mediating third. This mediation, performed in Kant's original formulation by the common root of the two 'stems,' was invoked when needed to bring the two elements into cohesion but was itself left uninvestigated in the realm of the unknown.

But, Heidegger points out, this common root was known to Kant to be unknown; it was, then, something of which he was not completely ignorant. To be aware of his own ignorance of it, he had to be aware of its presence. Why, then, did he not pursue an investigation of the nature of this source—which he found necessary in order to unify his two elements of knowledge? Heidegger's charge is that Kant had led us to the edge of the unknown and before this unknown Kant recoiled. He pursued it no further. From this precipice of discovery he retreated in what followed. And in the B Edition he abjured his own discovery and abandoned his great new insight into the nature of human knowledge.

It is certainly clear that there were changes of doctrine and emphasis, as well as of exposition, in the B Edition. Generally speaking, they seem to have been motivated by seeking to defend the new Critical standpoint against unexpectedly bitter attack. In the face of charges of subjective idealism and skepticism, of being a German Berkeley and a Prussian Hume,[104] Kant tried to clarify what he had to say. A number of changes—major and minor— were made in preparing the B Edition; some were attempts to improve the clarity of exposition; others were substitutions which appear to be more or less at odds, in doctrine or in emphasis, with the A Edition sections they replaced. Rather than rewriting the entire work, it appears that for the most part only those sections were revised which seemed to attract the focus of misunderstanding and attack. In Kant's reformulation of these prime points, de Vleeschauwer has suggested that there was an implicit change in the problem of the Critique itself from the "question of objectivity . . . [to] the problem of the limitation of reason to phenomena."[105]

From the viewpoint of Heidegger's interest, the doctrinal substantive changes are to be found in the removal of two prime elements which Kant owed to the psychology of his day, the Subjective Deduction and the centrality of imagination; they were replaced "by a more logical factor." [106] The significance of "possible experience as an operative medium" [107] was diminished as was the importance of the Deduction itself, now effectively limited to the demonstration of the categories as "the conditions of the empirical use of reason." [108] The priority of time gave way to something of a coequality with, if not a preeminence of, space, which in the B Edition comes to look much "more like a condition of all experience." [109]

Apparently, "Kant had made it his duty in rewriting his work of 1787 to prune away the traces" [110] of the psychology of Johann Nikolaus Tetens, described by Randall as "the greatest of the psychologists of the *Aufklärung* . . . [who] pushed beyond the limits of both rationalism and empiricism . . . [and] supplies most of the structure of the mind with which Kant worked." [111]

With a degree of justification Paton has remarked that "Kant is right in saying that it [the B Deduction] does not add anything which was not implicit in the first edition." [112] Heidegger would agree that this statement is correct as far as it goes. The problem is not one of addition but of a deletion which radically alters the character of the entire work, a deletion whose import is possibly presaged by the reverential praise accorded to Aristotle's logic in the B Preface.

Why did Kant really shift doctrinal ground in the B Edition? What impelled Kant's thought to change direction instead of to carry forth the explorations which the A Edition presented? What is the real nature of the crucial change which, in Heidegger's view, merits the charge of self-apostasy? Heidegger suggests two hypotheses in explanation, one biographical and the other doctrinal.

The crux of the First Critique was the problem of the objectivity of human knowledge in the light of the Copernican Revolution. In the belief that this work had provided a solution for his problem, despite attacks from critics, Kant turned his primary attention to working out the apriori objective grounding of morality, for which the First Critique was to have paved the way. Four years after the First Critique appeared, he published the *Groundwork of the Metaphysic of Morals;* this was designed as prefatory to the *Critique of Practical Reason,* whose publication followed it by three years. Significantly, the publication of this Second Critique was apparently delayed as the manuscript had already been completed when the First Critique was hastily revised for republication at the publisher's request.[113]

This simple consideration of chronology immediately places the B Edition in a different projective context. It seems fair to conclude that the B Edition of the First Critique was revised under the influence of the time-consuming work and thought which had gone into the development of the moral doctrine. The A Edition was, in part, designed to clear the ground for the reestablishment of morality and moral freedom; the B Edition, prepared immediately after the completion of the two moral works, may reasonably be expected to reflect the thinking that went into the development of the moral doctrine (quite aside from the motive of mitigating the attacks upon it). This, in effect, is what Heidegger claims to be the case and is one of the prime reasons for the very sharp cleavage he finds in the philosophic doctrines of the two editions.

Kant's preoccupation in the elucidation of objectivity in moral judgment was, Heidegger suggests, opposition to the "superficial and palliative empiricism"[114] of the period. Consequently, Kant focused on sharpening the distinction between the apriori and the empirical. Personality, the moral ego, "the essence of the subjectivity of the subject" was thus identified with reason and with thought.[115] Human finitude was then located, not in sensibility, not in the necessity of perceptual appearances, but in reason itself. Imagination—tied by Kant to sensibility—is then of little direct import. Morality is derived—in an additional step to the reenthronement of pure reason—from nothing specifically human but from a rationality-in-general of which the human is only one postulated example. Morality is derived from rationality as such, is held universally valid 'for any rational being,' and the moral will is identified as practical reason. The A Edition took its ground in *human* finitude; the B Edition, apparently taking its cue from the moral doctrine, enlarged the problem to that of finitude-in-general.

Heidegger sees this doctrinal shift most prominently displayed in the Deduction. First there is a substitution for the last paragraph of its introductory segment; second, a substitution of an entirely new deduction-proper.

The paragraph deleted from the introductory segment is that which builds on the theme: "the three original sources . . . of the possibility of all experience . . . [are] sense, imagination and apperception." [116] These three sources were there regarded as ultimate and irreducible to any other mental power. In the B Edition three new paragraphs were substituted: the first two discussed the shortcomings of Locke and Hume as examples of a pre-Critical empiricism; the third explained the meaning of 'category' as a concept under which an empirical intuition is subsumed as the subject of predication.

The substance of the doctrinal change in the new Deduction Heidegger summarizes by saying that the imagination has been "thrust aside and transformed." [117] Instead of its characterization and function as the source of synthesis, as an indispensable 'faculty of the soul,' it emerges from the B Deduction as a mere function of the understanding.

In the A Edition imagination was the source of the construction and interpretation of what sense perception reported: in interpreting this given, sense and thought were united by an imaginative projection from immediate awareness. One might visualize it as a capital letter Y with the stem yielding forth the two differentiated branches, sense and understanding, which only have meaning, i.e., produce knowledge, at the one point from which the three differentiated functions draw out separately; in terms of such an illustration, the point at which the three join is where the 'focus lens' of cognition is located.

In the B Edition, however, imagination, even as an analytic distinction, seems to have disappeared; imagination is seen merely as a functioning distinction within the understanding. Visualize the capital letter T with the horizontal bar representing the pure concepts of the understanding, which are channeled by a sort-of gravitational conceptual law entitled imagination, down to an application at the sense-base of the vertical. All synthesis in the B Deduction seems to derive not from an organizing, projective imagination but from the understanding's mode of restricting itself in order to apply to empirical sense perceptions. In place of the integral unity of the triune ground of possible knowledge, Kant gave 'full command' in the B Edition to the understanding.

Strangely enough, although imagination was virtually eliminated as a mediating medium in the newly written Deduction, the Schematism, where the imagination achieves its most centrally important role, was left completely unmolested in the B Edition. Retained intact, it was nevertheless in a new conceptual context. Read after the new B Deduction, it seems to have been reduced to "the synthetic influence of the understanding upon inner sense." [118] Imagination no longer brings sense and thought together. In the B Deduction imagination is regarded as synthesizing only in reference to sensibility, and as such it is contrasted to the intellectual synthesis, "which is carried out by the understanding alone, without the aid of the imagination." [119]

In the A Deduction the pure productive imaginative synthesis was categorically placed "prior to apperception [and] is the ground of the possibility of all knowledge." [120] In the B Deduction imaginative synthesis, as transcendental, becomes a mere 'title' of the understanding. Except as empirical, imagination has no real function remaining; although it may function in experience, it serves no function in explaining the transcendental ground of the possibility of experience. In the B Deduction the two stems of knowledge, brought into unison by the transcendental imaginative power, are reduced to two sources of knowledge—sense and thought—without any ostensible mode of connective bond.

How then can they be brought together? Without imaginative synthesis as an autonomous, binding third source of knowledge, the consequence is that "the possibility of comprehending the unity of pure sensibility and pure thought in finite human reason is lost." [121] If concepts are not abstracted from temporal perception (the essence of the Schematism in terms of the A Deduction) but are imposed upon temporal perception (which seems to be its meaning as following the B Deduction), then it would seem that concepts are not, even in principle, necessarily referential to empirical data, to particular temporal experiences of ontic things.

If this reading is valid, then Heidegger's insistence on the A Edition is an insistence on the empirical originality of the Kantian *Critique* and a protest against the B Edition's 'reversion' to rationalism. For with the B Edition a new rationalism has, indeed, preempted the Critical philosophy: as de Vleeschauwer points out, it is now claimed that the categories are the necessary conditions of sensible intuition, or in other words, "perceptions themselves are constituted only by the categories." [122]

Yet Kant had originally maintained, "the chief question is always simply this: what and how much can the understanding and reason know apart from all experience? not—how is the faculty of thought itself possible?" [123] Heidegger's investigation shows that although the objectivity of possible objects was examined in the Objective Deduction, the Deduction itself is justified on its subjective side, which set the limits to the 'what and how much . . . apart from all sense experience.' If the preceding discussion has any validity, its focused result is that the grounding of all knowledge, transcendental and empirical, is in imaginative synthesis, in the imaginative unification of sense and thought, percept and concept. The transcendental power of imaginative synthesis is then the center not only of the possibility of awareness of objects that appear as they appear but of the possibility of any appearing at all, and any receptivity of that appearing.

Why, then, did Kant 'retreat' from the primacy of imagination? Was it merely because of the rationalistic development of the ethic? Was it, we may ask, merely a restatement, or a clarification, in the face of unexpectedly vehement opposition? Or, as Heidegger suggests, did he perhaps see that the foundation-laying of metaphysics necessarily pointed to a ground more basic than sense and thought?

Even though it may not have been part of Kant's purpose to examine the transcendental imagination, we cannot dismiss it: for, as Kant first showed us, it necessarily forms, Heidegger reminds us, "the unity and ob-jectivity of transcendence," [124] the Kantian prerequisite to the possibility of knowledge itself. Rather than examining the nature and functioning of the transcendental imagination, he seems merely to have accepted the psychology of his time and thus worked with an inadequate and somewhat superficial insight into the essence of the transcendental grounds of knowledge, his avowed concern.

To go beyond sense and thought to a deeper ground leads, as

we have seen, to the "transcendental revelation of the essence of the subjectivity of the subject," a problem Kant had recognized.[125] Kant was thus "aware of the possibility and necessity of a more primordial laying of the foundation, but it formed no part of his immediate purpose." [126] Such a further investigation bears upon the possibility of our knowledge in the most profound manner. It is the real meaning not only of the Schematism, which he explicitly declined to pursue, but also of the Subjective Deduction, which he did not carry through. From this perspective one can see the significance of Heidegger's own study as precisely this: carrying forth the Subjective Deduction and the Schematism—a task which Kant did not pursue to firm enough ground; (broadly conceived, the First Division of *Being and Time* can be seen as working out and grounding the Subjective Deduction and the Second Division can be seen as developing the essential theme of the Schematism in the nature of temporal experience and thus grounding it and the theory of cognition, which it itself grounds).

Why, then, didn't Kant pursue these inquiries? Heidegger suggests, because "the subjectivity of the subject, 'the subjective deduction,' leads us into obscurity." [127] In Kant's Critique, pure reason was transformed into transcendental imagination. Kant by his own "radical interrogation . . . saw the unknown; he had to draw back." [128] The result of the First Critique, seeking to reestablish the possibility of metaphysics, 'led to an abyss; the unknown—the transcendental imagination frightened him.' [129] This fear of the unknown, and presumably unknowable, ground of all knowledge to which the A analysis pointed, coupled with the fact that in the development of the formalist morality the priority of the non-sensory rational came to the fore, explains, Heidegger suggests, the nature of Kant's development in the transition from the A to the B Editions. Yet, the fact that Kant retreated from the directions revealed in the A Edition and in the B sought to detour around the 'abyss of the unknown and prerational imagination' should not detract from an appreciation of what he had truly accomplished:

> The 'strangeness' and obscurity of the transcendental imagination as it appears in its capacity as the established ground in the first attempt to lay the foundation, on the one hand, and the luminous power of pure reason on the other, combine to obscure anew that

prospect of the primordial essence of the transcendental imagination which, as it were, opened up only for an instant.[130]

Kant had achieved this new insight: the content of our knowledge is completely dependent upon the mode of our knowing, the postulation of experiential reality is dependent upon the defining limits of our capacity for the kind of experience posited, to-be for us is to-be-perceiv*able,* taking the 'perceivable' as combining or uniting sense-and-thought in what has been pointed out as 'sensibilized reason,' viz., the temporalized, intuition-related concepts expounded in the Schematism. Kant's entire approach to this insight came from the imaginative synthesis toward which the A Edition had worked its way; having achieved this preliminary insight, it became clear that the foundation of all experience, the "what and how much the understanding and reason know apart from all experience" is determined not by reason itself or by sense experience itself but by a mysterious and unexplicated synthesis of imaginative capacity. From this discovery he drew back to try more traditional or purely rational paths. But just because Kant did not explore his new discovery is no reason for us to decline to do so also. We are deeply indebted to him for taking us this far. We may regret that he chose not to push further on. But his choice is not binding on us.

However one may evaluate the particulars of Heidegger's explanation of Kant's 'recoil' from the implications of the A Edition, it seems clear that one must give priority to one of the two editions as a point of departure. As Heidegger suggests, this should not be done on the basis of which we 'like' better, or which is more 'empirical'—both versions stress the *pre*-empirical, the transcendental—but which better defines the philosophical problems for us. Either edition can be justified, on varying grounds, for being more 'logical' or 'psychological' or 'empirical' than the other.

Aside from Heidegger's own reasons for his explicit preference for the A Edition, there are other considerations which suggest, in terms relevant to his philosophic concerns, confirmation of the priority he gives to it. De Vleeschauwer has suggested two:

[a.] [As the Second Edition leaves it] the opposition between the sensible and the intellectual was neither overcome nor reabsorbed, so that the constructing subject finds itself divided against itself

and the union of the two constituents in the intellectual spontaneity scarcely rises above the level of a kind of pre-established
harmony with little explanatory value. . . . Only a harmoniza-
tion, still too external to explain anything, or the unity of the
thinking activity invading the matter, remains possible. Indeed
both alternatives are to be found side by side in our texts but are
never united into a homogeneous and perfectly intelligible doctrine.[131]

[b.] It is absolutely impossible to condemn the first edition [by
ignoring it]. . . . I would not even affirm in an absolute sense
that the second edition is better than the first; but in any case it is
hardly intelligible without the development in the first edition.[132]

It may be argued that, in view of Kant's apparent intention to
rid the B Edition of 'psychological considerations' (such as the
Subjective Deduction), the B Edition is more clearly an epistemological treatise emphasizing the role of conceptual thought in
knowing. But this ground of preference invites the appropriate
comment:

The first edition is rich in suggestion, some of it incautious, which
the desperate and somewhat disappointed author of the second
edition sought to tighten up. . . . [But we should not] make the
distinction between the psychological approach and the epistemological one as sharply as it is made by Kant's critics. It seems to
me a frequently arbitrary one, smacking of the faculty psychology
which often hampers Kant's own exposition.[133]

The A Edition, despite internal problems, seems to be generally
a more coherent work, less open to internal doctrinal conflicts
between reworked and original unretouched segments. In any
event, regardless of how much weight be given to Heidegger's
explanation of the change of doctrine in the B, whether or not we
might feel that at least equal weight ought to be given to the very
human motive of seeking to come to terms with one's critics—the
fact is that Heidegger justifiably focuses on the A Edition just
because of his interest in the priority of temporality as pervasive
in human experience; this priority is far more clearly unmitigated
in the A Edition. In terms of a point of departure for a 'retrieve,'
if not for a deeper understanding of Kant's own philosophical
development, we can, for this reason alone, at least appreciate the
ground of Heidegger's preference.

As Heidegger sees it, then, the B Edition abandoned the original ground of the finitude of human reason in favor of a generalized finitude of rationality as such. As a consequence it effectively abandoned its problematic of objectivity and substituted that of the phenomenal limitation of reason. Insofar as concepts, in the B Edition, are not genetically tied to temporality but are, therefore, imposed on objects (as, in a loose analogy, a Platonic Idea may be said to be 'temporalized' for purposes of seeing the genus of its physical imitation), they contain here no *necessary* reference to perceptual experience. The B Edition has then disrupted the key insight of the A, the temporal dynamic from which 'pure concepts' are abstracted.

Just as all finite human thought is within a temporal horizon, the rational grounds of our knowledge and our metaphysical thought can only be found by us in the only rationality we ourselves know, in terms of human thought—and not in a thought-in-general which is nonexperiential. Human concern about metaphysics is, Kant urged, a feature of 'human nature.' If we ourselves are the source of the possibility of our knowledge, the whole possibility of our metaphysical thinking must be grounded in ourselves. We can only start not from an abstract reason-in-general but from human reason, not from a generalized abstraction of rational beings in general but from the rational beings we are, from man, from man's own peculiar kind of finitude.

The direction of further philosophic development which emerges from the interpretation of the A Edition is posed as a philosophic problem by the change of direction in the B Edition. By its turning away, the B raised a crucial question concerning the implicit but abandoned thesis which the revolutionary outlook of the A Edition all but enunciated: "Is the transcendental imagination as the established ground solid enough to determine primordially, i.e., in its unity and its totality, the finite essence of the subjectivity of the human subject?"[134] To face this question, to offer an affirmative response to it, as the full result of this analysis, we can now proceed.

5 · *Time and Temporality*

WE ARE NOW ABLE to see to where this Kantian investigation leads; we can now face explicitly the underlying concern which animates Heidegger's interrogation. Why has he insisted on extricating the transcendental imagination from an ambiguous status and positioning it in the center of the stage? Why has he been concerned, in view of his metaphysical interest, to reconstruct Kant's theory of knowledge? These seemingly peripheral considerations are germane just because they lead directly to the Heideggerian thesis concerning the priority and nature of the temporal.

The rooting of all cognition, as of all morality, in the transcendental power of imaginative synthesis was expedited by the complete priority accorded to the Schematism as its systematic grounding. The system of the schemata, prior to the distinguishable aspects of sense and thought, is itself produced by imagination and provides for the sensibilization of concepts. In these precise steps Heidegger has, in effect, developed the identification of 'human pure reason' as, what he can now refer to as "pure sensible reason," [135] manifested in the activity of transcendental imaginative synthesis.

Pure sensibility, the capacity to 'receive' sense data as pure intuition and inner sense, has been consistently identified as 'time.' 'Pure sensible reason,' therefore, is essentially temporal in character. On the face of it, this appears completely counter to Kant's insistence on the a-temporality of reason and the characterization of the pure ego, the source of the 'I think,' as somehow beyond time, as a-temporal. Is there any meaning in Kant's a-temporality of the ego? If so, how can it be meaningfully retained?

These questions take us to the core issue, the differentiation between Kant's and Heidegger's conceptions of time; it makes explicit the Kantian ground of Heidegger's temporalism, the direction of criticism and the suggested reconstruction; it thereby provides the transition from Heidegger's Kant to Heidegger himself. The fruit of the retrieve, the new ground opened up, emerges into light; we see that Heidegger's temporalism, extricated from the Critique, does indeed serve as a systematic as well as a "historical prolegomena" [136] to the more amplified formulation resulting from the existential analytic which is the burden of the First Division of *Being and Time*.

a. Temporality of Imagination

The transcendental power of imaginative synthesis is, of course, Heidegger's fulcrum. He has demonstrated that, as the 'root' of the two 'stems,' it is the source of thought, of sensory intuition, and, thereby, of time itself. His task is now to show the manner in which time is grounded in transcendental imagination.

The basic characteristic of time which Kant utilized is that of a continuity of now-sequences. As such a continuing 'flow' of now-points, time is, he said, "in constant flux." [137] But how can such a 'flow' be intuitively perceived? Intuition is essentially receptive— it reports what is given to it as singulars; it is receptive of particular apprehensions.

If intuition were merely receptive of temporality as something of a frame within which to 'place' the given object, it would only be able to apprehend a particular now; but this is impossible. A particular now *qua* now can only be distinguished as a point in a sequential succession. A now already is an 'extension,' a 'time spread' as the Synthesis of Apprehension demonstrated; it is not a mere point. It is a continuity extending into the immediate-as-just-passing and the immediate-as-just-arriving. Apart from the continuing movement of the junction between past and future, the notion 'now' is meaningless. To distinguish any particular momentary now requires a Janus-like outlook: simultaneously I must look ahead and behind; simultaneously I must take in both future and past.

If, then, pure intuition is the source of the form of time—or is itself intuition of time—it is not merely receptive of 'this-here' now, i.e., what is present in 'this' instantaneous presentation; it must 'bind' the presentation of a few seconds or minutes ago with the content of the present instant and its anticipation of the next. In some sense, intuition must form the sequential succession in which objects appear to it; but this is, in fact, a continuing act of imaginative reconstruction. Insofar as intuition itself forms this time-succession, it is imaginatively creative or identical with the power of imaginative synthesis.

The three sources of experience—sense, imagination, and thought—Kant had presented in terms of the triune synthesis at the base of cognition; each of these is essentially oriented to one of the three modes of time; just as each aspect of the triune synthesis must be present in any actual cognition, so must each of the three aspects of time be present in any temporal presentation. This, Heidegger explains, is in concert with Kant's own discussion of the forms produced by the imagination as presentation, reproduction, and anticipation.[138] Each aspect of the triune cognitive synthesis has a necessary temporal orientation. Pure intuition, he argues, is only able to form the now-sequence if it is in itself the presentative, reproductive, and anticipative power of imaginative synthesis. His thesis is that

> Time as pure intuition is neither only what is intuited in the pure act of intuition nor this act itself deprived of its 'object.' Time as pure intuition is *in one* the formative act of intuiting and what is intuited therein. Such is the complete concept of time.[139]

Time is not, then, *merely* a sort-of 'enclosure' within which imaginative synthesis operates. The characterization of time as a continuity of now-succession, from which Kant never seemed to depart, cannot, even in the framework of Kantian transcendentalism, be regarded as basic. The ground here, as always, is the essential concern of transcendental philosophy, the ground of enabling possibility. Heidegger means to show that the transcendental source of time itself is the transcendental power of imagination "as that which lets time as the *now*-sequence spring forth . . . [it is as its origin] primordial time."[140] The temporal horizon within which experience happens, as the temporality of the happening itself, is formed by imagination.

Transcendental imagination—which the entire preceding examination has been engaged to bring to stage-center—is inherently temporal in character. That this follows from what has already been established is to become evident. The discussion of the

Deduction demonstrated the unity of knowledge as derivative from its only possible source—triune cognitive synthesis; by demonstrating the essentially temporal character of each aspect of this synthesis, Heidegger's running contention—that it is rooted in imagination—receives final confirmation as a necessary conclusion. The lesson of the Schematism—that time is the source of the unification of knowledge—further grounds its possibility in imagination. If knowledge is only expressible in temporalist terms, if the transcendental temporalizing imagination grounds the possibility of knowledge, then the conclusion is apparent: the transcendental capacity for imaginative synthesis "is primordial time." [141]

The cognitive synthesis is triune not merely because three elements are the necessary sources of knowledge but, more fundamentally, because of the triune nature of time itself. The cognitive synthesis is essentially triune, and there are three aspects of the knowledge-producing synthesis just because *all* knowledge is temporal and time itself is triune in character. Implicit throughout the Critique, it was suggested in the Aesthetic, adumbrated in the Deduction, established in the Schematism, and substantiated in the Highest Principle. Heidegger's delineation of the nature of time in human experience thus serves to help ground the essential thrust of Kantian epistemology.

Although Kant's own discussion in the Deduction is noteworthy for its lack of explicit temporal reference, he had stated at its outset:

> All our knowledge is thus finally subject to time, the formal condition of inner sense. . . . This is a general observation which, throughout what follows, must be borne in mind as being quite fundamental.[142]

Heidegger's explication of the essential temporality in each stage of the triune synthesis makes this abundantly clear. Each aspect of the synthesis in its empirical employment corresponds to a specific kind of temporal orientation in the transcendental synthesis which grounds it; the transcendental synthesis, produced by imagination, the explicated thesis argues, creates the possibility of the temporal discriminations of 'past,' 'present,' 'future.' The temporality of each of the three elements of the triune cognitive synthesis can be demonstrated in turn:

i. Synthesis of Apprehension in Intuition

Every apprehension is of a field or manifold unified as being-present. We can, however, hold together a set of impressions by distinguishing the now of what is present from what is no longer or not yet present. In the 'running through and holding together,' intuitive representation of the immediately given is thereby itself synthesizing. In empirical use it immediately takes up into unified perception what is given—the intuitive representation takes up the content of a now, and in its succession the contents of a succession of nows.

This capacity is grounded in the transcendental apprehensive synthesis of intuition, which makes it possible for us to discriminate this now from other nows in a now-sequence. As transcendental, it is thus the capacity to render a present-in-general; as apprehension, it is presentative and transcendentally grounds any ontic present now that is experienced; it is then a synthesis that is itself "time-forming." [143] This apprehending synthesis Kant had identified as the action of imagination "immediately directed upon the perceptions." [144] If this transcendental now-forming synthesis is merely an imaginative act, then imagination itself, even in the temporal stance of the immediate now, necessarily has a temporal character.

This apprehending synthesis of the now-presentation was clearly labeled "in intuition." But pure intuition is not only the intuition of time; it is the form of time. Thus there is clear Kantian ground for Heidegger's repeated insistence that this apprehending synthesis does not take place within time; it forms time by maintaining the continuity of immediately present nows.

ii. Synthesis of Reproduction in Imagination

This aspect of the triune synthesis is the only one which Kant explicitly identified with imagination and with temporality. In order to have knowledge, we must be able to unify the present now-perception with those which 'have been' but are no longer immediately present. The capacity for doing this transcendentally precedes any particular awareness of memory recall. As the apriori ground for any recollection, transcendental imagination is thus time-forming. It creates the possibility of distinguishing present-now from past-now and brings them both as disparate simultaneously to awareness in inner sense. As transcendental, it does not, as does the empirical imagination, bring back the memory of a once perceived object; rather it is the capacity for such ontic recall. It makes it possible. It creates the horizon of a possible past by bringing it into the present, by constituting the area of that-which-*is*-as-having-been.* For experientially it is not accurate to say, "there was a past," which is an inference, but "there is a past which is somehow present," which is a report of primary experience.

This requisite of bringing the past into the present, this requisite for memory recall for the possibility of knowledge, Kant made abundantly clear. The act of imagination in making possible this recall and joining it with the present is what makes temporal distinctions as such possible. As Kant had said, "The synthesis of apprehension is thus inseparably bound up with the synthesis of reproduction." [145]

The point is then made. The unity of past and present constitutes, in the Kantian statement, two elements of pure synthesis; the former is intuitive as an act of imagination; the latter is imaginative in its own right. Kant had thus demonstrated that the transcendental power of imagination is, in fact, time-forming.

In close harmony with the Kantian statement, Heidegger has merely made quite explicit the principle common to two of the three aspects of time. The task remaining is no longer that of establishing a principle; it is establishing its universality.

iii. Synthesis of Recognition in Concepts

This third mode of synthesis is apperceptive; the third mode of time is futurity. Can they be brought together? If the identification of cognitive synthesis and time is to be complete, if pure

---

* Heidegger's reference to the experiential past is in terms of *Gewesenheit*—what is-as-having-been; as contrasted with the notion of 'before' or 'preceding' that is no longer, *Vergangenheit,* which, in accord with tradition, Kant usually seems to have used.

imaginative synthesis is in and of itself time-forming and the only source of time, then this third aspect of the pure triune synthesis must correspond to the third aspect of time, viz., futurity.

This, it is readily granted, is more difficult. Kant had explicitly, repeatedly, consistently denied any temporal quality to "pure thought, the ego of pure apperception . . . the 'I think' and reason in general." [146] The issue is of crucial import on at least two counts: (a) the empiricist insistence on the subordination of the categories of understanding to the content of intuition, i.e., 'thought in the service of intuition,' the reduction of pure thought to its rooting in pure imagination as 'primordial time,' and the sensibilization of thought all join to necessitate the temporalization of pure thought itself; (b) the centrality of the futural in Heideggerian temporalism makes the establishment of the transcendental ground of futurity, in terms of the Kantian exegesis, decisive. If this were to fail, the implicatory import of much of the preceding interpretation is to be questioned, as are claims concerning both the derivation of Heidegger's conception of time from the Critique and his temporal analysis as grounding it.

Kant began his own discussion of the conceptual aspect of cognitive synthesis by noting its prerequisite necessity to the other two: "If we were not conscious that what we think is the same as what we thought before, all reproduction in the series of representations would be useless." [147] Without a concept to unify a present apprehension with one that is recollected, there would be no principle for selection of past representations as relevant to the present one. A concept establishes a discriminating identity between present and selected past representations. A concept which brings about the unification of past apprehensions with the present apprehension is universal and "serves as a rule," [148] a principle of unity or identity.

In both the apprehending and the recollecting aspects of cognitive synthesis, concepts provide that principle whereby the synthesis is oriented, in advance of any particular presentation, to the possibility of cognizing what appears as an object in its context, environment, or field. [149] Thus the concept is a mode of unification of sensory experience; it is the mode of integrating myriad sense experiences in terms of universally necessary principles of order, which thereby render them intelligible and amenable to cognizing interpretation.

As developed in the Schematism, such a universal ordering principle must, *qua* universal, function in terms of the one pervasive principle of order in all human awareness, the form of time, of inner sense in which every apprehension, idea, or notion must appear in order to be represented in a comprehensive perspective.

The concept as 'recognition' thus reconnoiters, explores, scouts out the grounds of possible identification of representation. Apperception, *qua* understanding, provides the rules by means of which appearances are brought together into concert—in the time of human thought. It investigates appearances in order to detect some rule or principle of unifying order, within the temporal context which universally describes human mental activity, which these appearances suggest.[150] Only within those methods of unification spelled out by these rules of identity may objects as such be encountered. By defining the ways of possible identification within which apprehension and memory recall can function, this capacity for 'recognition in a concept' provides the transcendental possibility of any empirical 'recognition' by means of a concept. This capacity to apprehend presentations in terms of a conceptual framework enables us to identify what it is that we apprehend as a particular kind of thing. Without this anticipatory transcendental capacity, it would be impossible for me to look for, say, my friend's new house, to know that it is what I sought when I come upon it, and to relate it to my memory of his last one (so I know it is new) or any other houses I've seen (so I know it is a house, not a barn).

Transcendental 'recognition in a concept' does not seek out ontic objects in propounding the pure concepts, the categories, or rules which limit the possibilities of identification. It defines the kind of conceptual framework in terms of which I can apprehend presentations-as-objects, the horizon or context within which those objects can be brought together as such. It projects the conceptual range defining my possible apprehensions, the apprehensions which I may order into a unified field or manifold.

As such a transcendental capacity, recognitional or apperceptive synthesis projects the limitations, the essential general characteristics, the basic forms of any possible future I may conceivably come to know. It defines what *can be* in my experience, the range of future possibility from which an actual present now can emerge. It constitutes the horizon of my possible future experience.

This conceptualizing aspect of the triune cognitive synthesis is then truly time-forming. It sets out the range within which the context or horizon defines the limits of possible experience for me; it determines the limits within which identification of present perceived objects with recall of similarity of previous perceptions can be maintained. It provides the categories in terms of which I *will be* structuring any future experience. It designates the kinds of questions to which I can legitimately seek answers. It predicts, at the very least, what *kinds* of things can*not* enter my experiential domain and, therefore, will not do so. Kant's attribution of the three aspects of empirical synthesis to the empirical imagination urges this same conclusion.[151] If the projecting of such time-forms can be empirical, then its transcendental ground, the provision for the horizon within which it can be exercised, must, as an anticipatory act of pre-formation, be an act of pure or transcendental imagination.

Although this future-forming act of conceptual construction is the last of the three arrived at—because Kant's presentation of each aspect of synthesis began from empirical utilization—the future-forming function is not really third. It is first and foremost just because it is "the one which governs the other two." [152] It anticipates them, sets out a field of characteristics of possible objects, thereby a possible world of objects. Within this experiential possibility the other two aspects of the triune synthesis are able to function.

Despite the 'anti-intellectualism' of much of Heidegger's repute, despite his attack on Kant's rationalistic tendencies, despite his persistently empirical interpretation of Kant, Heidegger roots this priority of futurity precisely in that aspect of imaginative synthesis which is conceptual and apperceptive. Emerging then from the Kantian formulation is the necessary priority of futurity, in contrast to Kant's own priority of the present.[153] This future-forming priority of conceptualization as forming the horizon of possible experience, is thus tied, in contrast to Kant's traditional priority of the actual,[154] to a parallel priority of the possible—manifested in the functioning of understanding as it brings into apprehension awareness of those possibilities which serve to define the present situation.[155]

But again, this is to say that there will be a future is an inference and does not report primary experience. The future *is not* merely the not-yet-but-will-be. The future *is qua* what-can-be; the future is now *qua* experiential possibilities.[156] In full fidelity to primary experience, and in the full sense of the German word for 'future,' *Zukunft,* it is that which I *am seeing* as now coming toward me, as now presenting me with options and anticipations and expectations. As the present presentation of genuine possibilities, it is present in any now and is crucial to my understanding and my constituting of any now, of any discernible present. It presents the possibilities in terms of which I select and bring to present awareness the relevant what-is-as-having-been. It presents the conceptual horizon, the defining horizon of possibility, in terms of which my present is formed. It is thus crucial to constituting my primary experience.

The world, then, in which I live and know and act is not constituted solely by my actual momentary presentations of which I am *now* aware. My world includes my past and the whole of history of which I am aware. It includes that whole realm of the possibilities that I regard, even preconceptually, as real, as genuine. It includes them *both* in any *now.* In any present moment they enter into my awareness, my interpretation of that awareness, and the significance I derive from it. This interpretive cognitive awareness is framed by the concepts defining its possibility to-be and is guided, in the light of relevant memory recall, by those specific kinds of future possibilities toward which I see it 'pointed' and which provide the criteria of 'relevance' for experiential integration.

In the face of the initial seeming absurdity of the 'reduction' of thought to imagination, despite the seeming lack of temporal reference in concepts, despite Kant's own focus on the momentary now, it is now evident, as Heidegger suggests, that Kant's analysis of the conceptualizing element of the triune synthesis "reveals the most primordial essence of time, that is, that it temporalizes itself primarily out of the future."[157] It temporalizes itself by anticipatory thinking out of the range of possibility which it sets before itself.

The completely temporal character of imaginative synthesis has been shown in each of its three functional aspects. We can now appreciate the thesis that "transcendental imagination is primordial time." [158] The question raised, at the end of the last section, by Kant's 'retreat' from the centrality of imagination, can now be explicitly answered:

> The transcendental imagination, therefore, is capable of forming and sustaining the unity and primordial totality of the specific finitude of the human subject which . . . has been presented as pure, sensible reason. [159]

Before proceeding, however, we should be clear as to just what Heidegger has accomplished by his repeated emphasis on the crucial import of imaginative synthesis.

The pervasiveness and priority of time considerations in Kant's Critique is certainly apparent. Yet Kant's understanding of time, and its meaning as he employed it, was essentially the traditional notion as derived from Aristotle. Time was taken as a now-sequence delineated by the distinction of 'before' and 'after.' *

But a before-and-after delineation is essentially tenseless. It refers to the sequential order of things (or events) in time, positing their unalterable 'location' along the 'line' of a chronological ordering conceived in an essentially spatial metaphor. The truth or falsity of a statement based on this unalterable chronological placing remains unalterably true or false—'Roosevelt died before Churchill'—regardless of when it was uttered. Such a tenseless order seeks to date things in relation to each other, not to their discovery by human inquiry or apprehension. It claims reference to the known, not the knower (except as it implicitly posits the now in which the event 'would be' or 'would have been seen' as present by a perceiving subject—but doing so refers to the alternative). Useful as such an object-oriented mode of dating may be, it

---

* It is well to note Aristotle's classic statement: "For what is bounded by the 'now' is thought to be in time—we may assume this . . . when we do perceive a 'before' and an 'after,' then we say that there is time. For time is just this—number of motion in respect of 'before' and 'after.' . . . The 'now' measures time, insofar as time involves the 'before and after.' " [160]

is not truly empirical in the sense that it claims to speak of events and not of the primary experience which makes them known; focusing ostensibly on the objectivity of events, it ignores them *qua* experienc*ed*.

This traditional way of perceiving the nature of time, as a series of nows delineated by before-and-after discrimination, cannot be fundamental insofar as it ignores an empirical priority on the experiencing subject. As Heidegger points out, even Aristotle may have seen that it cannot be basic, that time depends on the apprehending 'subject': "But if nothing other than the soul or the soul's mind were naturally equipped for numbering, then if there were no soul, time would be impossible." [161]

Lovejoy stated the problem of the now-sequence tradition quite neatly:

> Time as ordinarily conceived is sundered into separate moments which are perpetually passing away. The past is forever dead and gone, the future is non-existent and uncertain, and the *present* seems, *at most, a bare knife-edge of existence* separating these two unrealities.[162]

Heidegger insists that we do not and we cannot intuit time, perceive the things that appear in time, be aware of temporality, in this way. As a knife-edge of being separating a non-existent future from a non-existent past, this traditional view of time sees time, and reality within time, as the fleeting momentary actual, a somehow continuing succession of nows defined by non-being on both sides. This atomicity of now-points necessitates Augustine's question (with which this study began): how can we even say that 'the present *is*'? It yielded Descartes' worry (in the third Meditation) of how we get from one moment to the next. It has resulted in little more insight into the nature of time or of our experience of time than emerged from the somewhat fruitless discussions of the 'specious present' which arise from it.

This curious knife-edge of the fleeting now may well have been a motivating cause for Kant's curiously Platonic insistence on the a-temporal noumenal nature of the human self. Merely as the knower of events in time, if not the full source of temporal ordering itself, the self cannot be reduced to such transient momentary existence, the knife-edge of the now-succession. Within the terms of this conception of time with which he worked, it seems that Kant, in order to save the reality of the self which was requisite for knowledge as well as morality, had little choice but to borrow from Plato and locate the real self in an intelligible world of timeless noumenal reality. The result can be seen in the essential paradox: a declared aim of the Critique is the grounding of morality;[163] yet, because this knife-edge notion of time cannot sustain an enduring experiencing and deciding self, Kant was forced to ground morality—which in a normative perspective is essentially temporal and future-oriented—in a somehow timeless self.

If we are to take time, or the temporality of our human mode of be-ing, seriously, then this traditional picture of time—as a sequence of nows somehow arising out of non-existence onto the knife-edge of true actual being and passing into non-existence again—must be abandoned. For an empiricism that places a premium on the immediacy of any experience, the before-and-after can only be an explanatory construction that is wholly derivative from the experiential continuum of future-present-past experienc-*ing* of the individual human knower. What I now perceive as future—the rolling stone will stop when it reaches the bottom of the incline—progressively, in my apprehension, becomes present and then past; the truth of an interim-tensed statement thus changes in the relation to the *when* of its utterance; and any statement accurately describing my own experienc*ing* must be loyal to the shifting tensing of that experiencing.

Kant's crucial distinction, then, between 'persons' and 'things' is crucial not only for morality but also for the time in which cognition is experienced as happening. As Dewey has wisely observed:

> an important part of the problem of time is that what is true of the human individual does not seem to be true of physical individuals. . . . Time, in physical science, has been simply a measure of motion in space. Now this apparently complete unlikeness in kind between the human and the physical individual is a part of the problem of time.[164]

From the viewpoint of the experiencing human subject—for Kant as for Heidegger, the source of any time determination—

the very different orientation of temporal perspective of the human knower must take precedence: the 'subjective' perspective of future-present-past. What I am seeing now is what is-present; what I recall having seen 'before now' is 'what-*is*-as-having-been' for me previously, or 'what-I-now-recall-as-having-seen.' [165] In view of the subjectivity of time in Kant's work, its rooting in and restriction to the knowing of a knowing subject, the point is well taken by Heidegger that Kant's handling of the concept of time is strangely traditional: it is strangely discordant with its subjective source and its inherent restriction to the subjective perspective of the experiencing subject.

We could even say that it is essentially pre-Critical. The explanatory construction of the before-and-after now-sequence, on the prime thesis of Critical transcendentalism, can only result from the temporalizing of concepts within the framework of sensory experience as received by intuition. This temporalization must proceed from apprehension in inner sense, the sequence of experienc*ing*—not a speculative causal explanation of why I experienced what I experienced in the order experienced.

This experienc*ing,* as the 'out-look' of my subjectivity—especially in the light of Heidegger's amplification of the meaning of the triune cognitive synthesis—is of what-*is*-as-having-been, of what-*is*-being-present, and of what-*is*-being-anticipated. Only as I deliberately try to render a particular kind of sequence of apprehendings intelligible do I recast their content, by an explanatory construction, into the object-oriented before-and-after serial order. I wonder as to why my perception of the storm cloud becomes 'past' when the then-anticipated rain becomes 'present'; but this again involves conceptual thought about nature so that I may know whether or not to anticipate rain when I next see a storm cloud in a future-present.

The before-and-after of events is of events in time; but 'in time' can mean no less or more than having a being-status in my inner sense. And, to-be in inner sense is determined by the sequence not of the things represented but of the chronology of my apprehendings of them in intuition. These apprehendings become representations in inner sense by means of imaginative synthesis. If Heidegger's thesis concerning the correlation of imaginative synthesis and temporality—to which we can now proceed—is maintained, the priority of future-past-present discrimination before that of unalterable serial order is, in this context at least, firmly established.

Our awareness of ontic temporal distinctions is dependent on ontic content in knowledge. Thus our awareness of time distinctions is grounded in the temporalizing aspect of the imaginative synthesis which renders this knowledge possible. When we abandon the priority of external before-and-after sequential order and turn to the temporality of the cognitive synthesis, which permits us to know time and the things in time, we can first begin to comprehend the integral unity of the three modes of time.

For—and this is Heidegger's prime point—just as the three aspects of imaginative synthesis were shown to be structurally unified, so the three aspects of temporality are also. Temporal experience is not an addition of separate 'past' + 'present' + 'future.' Time is one, and only because time is one can we speak of different 'times' as 'parts' of 'one time.' The modal distinctions in time, as in cognitive synthesis, are primarily analytic conveniences that are pragmatically justifiable; they are not primarily descriptive or ontological. As imaginative synthesis is one triune synthesis, the time formed is one triune time.

Heidegger is certainly not unique in his insistence on the mutually implicatory unity of past-present-future, on the integral unity of temporality and temporal existence. Dewey spoke of "the union of past and future with the present manifest in every awareness of meanings." [166] James expressed it quite vividly in his observation that

> Past and future . . . conceptually separated by the cut to which we give the name of present . . . are to some extent, however, brief, co-present with each other throughout experience. The literally present moment is a purely verbal supposition, not a position; the only present ever realized concretely being the 'passing moment' in which the dying rearward of time and its dawning future forever mix their lights. Say 'now' and it *was* even while you say it. [167]

Whitehead, in terms akin to Heidegger's, wrote, "What we perceive as present is the vivid fringe of memory tinged with anticipation. . . . The past and future meet and mingle in the ill-defined present." [168] Human temporality, as Heidegger repeatedly insists, "does not consist of unrelated phases, but forms a dynamic system of references in which one form implies the other." [169] Anticipation and memory are necessarily and integrally involved in any actual present.

My present is, at least, limited by prior possibility. For what is actual first must be possible. My present is, at least, an earlier future-possibility. It is that in which I apprehend the future range opening before me; it is here in the present focus of apperceptive-apprehending that the 'where-from-here?' must be discerned. I can only see what I can-do with an object from the possibilities spelled out by those concepts in terms of which I do see it as present to me now. I am helped to discern these inherent possibilities of an object by recalling what I have done with it in a previous present, which is 'reproduced' by imaginative recall. In my present apprehending I thus bring together in the present that aspect of my memory of what-has-been which the possibility-defining conceptual structure I use determines as relevant. I reread this present representation in terms of the same concept-structure as it lets me see, in the object, the new possibilities it can yet develop. I know that I can drive a screw into wood cumbersomely, if at all, by using a hammer instead of a screwdriver—just because I compare previous moments when I tried each; but I consider these alternative means only because I first see the screw as 'offering' the possibility of being driven into the wood. If I have a choice of tools, I seize the screwdriver instantaneously only because I have done this often and the concept-structure for comparing these two instruments for a selected purpose is so 'second nature' that I 'see' this past together with this limitation on future use *in any* screw, hammer, or screwdriver; I 'read into' each as I 'read from' them.

The 'past' then is not something dead. It is not a 'now that is no longer,' not a 'dead past' as a sort-of tomb in which to bury all those presents which no longer are; it is available for present use in terms of possibilities I select for guidance of action. [170] The 'past' is, perhaps, forgotten but somehow available to me, ready to be recalled to service if, when, and as needed. It is the present reality of that-which-has-been (the *Gewesenheit*), which *is* available for memory recall. It is, as Kant's triune synthesis reveals, crucial to the possibility of any present cognition.

How and when is such 'pastness' brought back? As Kant had shown, it is brought back in terms of concepts; concepts as schematized fill out an idea in terms of possible future representations seen as related to the present one. Only in terms of such concepts, which define finite possibilities, do present and past apprehendings function. If my present cognition is necessarily oriented in terms of anticipation of what may be expected, hoped for, feared; if it relates to a problem I face which demands some resolution; if my present cognition is not an idle passive reception of disinterested and unfocused perception but is, in any sense, interpretive or action-oriented—then my present cognition is thereby future-oriented. The future, then, has a certain priority in my understanding of any present, of what is now anticipated or can be reasonably expected. In a real sense, then, as inherent in present cognition, "the future is *not later* than having-been, and having-been is *not earlier* than the Present." [171] As operative in any actual cognitive act, the three aspects of time are structurally one—as the three aspects of imaginative synthesis constitute one cognitive synthesis.

What I discern when I consider that hammer and screw driver comes from a unified experience. I do not see them as color-patch presentations; I see them in my act of imaginative apperceptive apprehending, in the light of the concept-structure by which I identify them with certain possible acts I can undertake with them in the light of invoked past experiences I have had with them. I see them *qua* hammer and *qua* screwdriver, not as indifferent or neutral things but as specific tools in my experiential context. As James would probably have suggested, I see each of them, and both together, as a nexus of possible relations.

The triune nature of temporal experience as it constitutes the present perception is, one might say, focused on revealing the presentation to me in its depth—as three differently angled spotlights focus on an actress on stage, permitting me to see her as a three-dimensional being and not as a photograph. They are three different ways of lighting up the object; in 'taking it in,' I necessarily bring the three 'lights' to bear as one and do not imme-

diately discern how the object might look in an analytic reconsideration under each separately. The 'light' of the future takes
full precedence as defining the possibilities in terms of which I see
the object appearing to me at all.

The intrinsic relationship of future and past to any present
apprehending is, as we have seen, not unique to Heidegger although what he does in its development certainly is. But the full
priority of futurity emphatically seems to be his own.* Heidegger
has shown this priority of futurity to have been buried in Kant's
work and to have been a real discovery of Kant's, even if Kant,
like Columbus, was unaware of just what it was that he had discovered.

This discovery is embodied in the triune cognitive synthesis:
presented in the Preliminary Remark of the Deduction, its possibility was established in the Schematism and grounded as ontological prescription in the Highest Principle of Synthetic
Judgments. It grounds Kant's dissatisfaction with the universal
competence of formal logic and the primacy he attributed to a
temporalizing transcendental logic, his system of relating thought
to things.

Only when we recognize the integral triune nature of temporal
experience and the triune temporal form of any cognition, Heidegger suggests, can we comprehend the real significance of what
Kant had done. But to comprehend this, we must be aware of
what Kant had *not* done. Kant had not succeeded in seeing that
the Copernican Revolution necessitated a repudiation of the
primacy of time *qua* now-sequence. If one accepts the subjective
ground of time together with a now-sequence definition of time,
as one instance, one is hard pressed to account for datability and
irreversibility. The difficulty with datability arises from the fact
that the concept 'now' does not inherently offer any principle by
which to distinguish one now from another; they can be distinguished only in terms of the events from whose constructed
order the now-sequence is derived. More pressing at this juncture:

---

* However, it seems to have been suggested by Plotinus: "[Contingent things
such as are amenable to being apprehended by sense experience] are in continuous process of acquisition; eliminate futurity, therefore, and at once they lose
their being." [172]

if one takes time as merely a sequence of nows, Heidegger points out, "it is incomprehensible in itself why this sequence should not present itself in the reverse direction." [173] To see this sequence as derivative from the priority of futurity, to see it as dependent on the related priority of possibility in human experience, does, however, promise to preclude this crucial ambiguity. But grounding such priority more firmly requires that we go beyond epistemology, as we shall, to an explication of a more fundamental ontology.

What is germane here is the fact that Kant has drawn us back to the essential conditions of primary experience and made us realize that it is permeated by temporal considerations. Any experiential present inherently involves not a mere however-defined actual now but an anticipatory future and an invoked past. This invoked past provides the utility of knowledge, but the anticipatory future provides the key to the possibility of the content that is seen as present and the significance we can elicit from it or project into it.

Whatever meaning we read into or derive from what is present to us is rendered by the time-spread in which it is encountered. In a word, then, what Heidegger has extricated from Kant is the twofold thesis: that the temporality of any given present is, in Wyschograd's happy phrase, "a field rather than a point," [174] a field that is essentially dynamic and, equally crucial, a field that is actively maintained by me, the knower, that is my way of know*ing*. Time, then is not an invariable line of infinitely divisible points but a moving field of focus, a field which is dominated by the limited but open range of that to which it may next turn. This is to say that the nature of time delineates the nature of how I can know—set forth in the rooting of cognition in the transcendental imagination—*and* the nature of the knower, an inquiry to which we next turn.

It is to this kind of temporality that Heidegger has been moving. It is this that he sees as the real meaning of the conceptual priority in the Kantian structure of cognitional experience. He sees this temporality, this priority of futurity, in the temporal synthesis, in the priority he has extricated from Kant's Copernican Revolution—the priority of the power of imaginative synthesis, which roots the whole man, the man of action, of moral decision, as well as the man who is capable of cognition.

Thereby Heidegger has implicitly suggested a way in which to ground the Kantian morality without invoking a speculative or hypothetical metaphysic. As the concept of Concern, in the fundamental ontology to be developed, shows, imaginative synthesis is dominated by purposive considerations, ends-in-view, courses of proposed action, problems to be solved, situations to be resolved. If any investigation is, indeed, some sort of interrogation, any cognitive synthesis is not merely a passive assimilation of presentations; it is an active quest for answers. If knowledge is to be, in any sense, creative or instrumental, it requires a temporal synthesis which, in the light of possible futures, examines the relevant past in constituting the face of present representations. This consideration alone lends considerable justification to Heidegger's own focus on the primacy of futurity as well as to his insistence on the primacy of imaginative cognitive synthesis as its ground.

b. Temporality of the Self

If time is the moving field of experiential focus; if the temporalizing framework of the subject's experiential capacity provides the 'form' of those objects which do appear as the content of cognitional experience—then time is an essential mode of be-ing of the experiencing subject and is thereby not a 'thing.'

Time is then rooted in the temporalizing structure of the subject; as such, the nature of time has immediate implications concerning the nature of the time-forming self and of the time that is itself formed. If we take seriously Kant's grounding of time in the nature of the cognitive self, it is reasonable to anticipate some kind of mutuality between the structure of the self which produces time and the nature of the time that is produced.

Heidegger's interpretive principle throughout has been an insistence on taking Kantian theses seriously. Having achieved an identification of time qua pure intuition and imaginative synthesizing capacity, he is now able to turn to the relationship between time and the self. What he has to say seems to be implicit throughout the Critique. His conclusion is that time is the form not only of the objects of experience but of the experiencing self as well; that the essential subjectivity of time is the ground not only of objectivity but also of the free transcendence of the subject: 'The more subjective time is, the more primordial and broader is the delimitation of the subject.'[175] The more subjective time is, the less dependent upon outside determination is the time-forming horizon within which knowledge can occur. The more subjective time is, the less constrained am I by anything other than limitations which are self-imposed. Time, then, emerges as the capacity for affecting one's own self. Obscure as this conclusion initially seems to be, Heidegger has done nothing more startling here than to draw out the implications of that subjectivity of time with which Kant's own statement of his transcendentalism had begun.

Three Kantian texts provide the foundation of this discussion. First is an addition in the B Edition of the Aesthetic, an addition which Heidegger regards as an improvement in that it makes an implication quite explicit:

> Now that which, as representation, can be antecedent to any and every act of thinking anything, is intuition; and if it contains nothing but relations, it is the form of intuition. Since this form does not represent anything save in so far as something is posited in the mind, *it can be nothing but* [*nichts als*] *the mode in which the mind is affected through its own activity* (namely, through this positing of [their] representation), and *so is affected by itself;* in other words, it [*time*] *is nothing but* [*nichts anderes*] an inner sense in respect of the form of that sense.[176]

Again, in initially presenting the categories Kant had pointed out that insofar as time (1) 'contains a field or manifold of pure apriori intuition,' and (2) constitutes a necessary condition for our receptivity of the reports of sensibility, it follows that time must *"always affect* the *concepts* of these objects" as they are represented in temporal form in our minds.[177] Finally, in the Schematism, he argued that insofar as we are able to intuit a presentative field as one unified field, this can only be "due to *my generating time itself* in the apprehension of intuition."[178]

Time is not then merely the horizon within which *things* must appear to us; this thesis could have been elicited from a pre-Critical metaphysic which postulated temporal realism as an essential characteristic of the physical world. If time were taken as an ultimate or absolute category of the structure of nature-in-itself, or if the physical world were conceived to be 'in time' as some sort of absolute repository, the priority of temporal horizon could conceivably be taken from the world of independent objects. Whatever might be said about such a view, it certainly was not Kant's —because it transgresses the principle of the Copernican Revolution in presuming the cognitional possibility of speculative metaphysics, because it could only offer inductive generalization and not the necessary universality guaranteed by apriori subjectivity as the pervasive form of all inner sense.

Kant's radical thesis is the rooting of temporal necessity not in entities-in-themselves but in our capacity for knowledge of them as experiential objects. As the form of inner sense, Kantian time is the first and necessary condition for our perception of any thing at all; it is *not* derived from the world of things; it is the universal form which we *pre*scribe as requisite for us to become aware of and understand that world of things.

For Kant our idea of time is not a conclusion about the world but about our knowledge of the world and about ourselves as cognizing beings. If the temporal horizon must be projected by us in order for us to know anything at all within it, it tells us little about the world except insofar as we are able to experience it. But rooting this temporal horizon in inner sense tells us a good deal about the nature of the beings we are. It tells us that time-projecting—the capacity and its necessity—is an essential constituent of the structure of the kinds of selves we are. It tells us that this capacity, which is the root of any apprehending at all—including apprehending of our own be-ing and thereby our own self-consciousness—is thereby crucially fundamental to our own selfhood.

As such, this capacity to form and project time onto the 'objects' of apprehension is not merely one more 'faculty' alongside others. It is not in the mind alongside sensibility; as the rooting of intuition in imagination suggested, it is the forming of intuition itself. It is not in the mind in addition to apperception; as rooting pure thought in imagination suggested, as the priority of sensory intuition before thought showed, as the function of 'thought in the service of intuition' indicated, time is presupposed by and included in every exercise of thinking and thereby is the form-ing of thought itself.

Time is, as Kant maintained, "nothing but the mode in which

[203]

the mind is affected through its own activity." [179] Time is the necessary universally enabling condition for our apprehending objects outside of ourselves; it is the enabling condition which we project as a 'form' and which permits us to represent those objects, to think about and interpret them, to have ideas of and about them, and thus to have the life of our inner sense affected by our awareness and knowledge of them. Insofar as time is *the* universal projecting in terms of which these representations of objects are brought 'into' our minds, it constitutes the universal structure of the way in which we enable ourselves to become aware of these objects, to cognize them, to be internally affected by our representations of them. Insofar as each new representation or thought is a new 'event' in the life of my mind, and itself represents a change in the content of my mind, each new representation and thought thereby affects my mind merely by virtue of entering 'into' it. In my projection of time, I open myself up to the reception of reports, which are taken into inner sense and thereby affect the life of my inner sense.

Thus, 'time-forming,' as Heidegger capsules it, is the way in which the self affects itself. As transcendental, this capacity which I have to form time, and to project it as the condition for the appearances that appear, is the ground capacity, the root of the entire transcendental 'apparatus,' which functions to make knowledge possible. As the foundation of this possibility to affect myself by enabling myself to receive sensory reports and attain knowledge about them, it is, transcendentally, a pre-empirical or pure capacity for 'self-affecting.' [180]

Perhaps a spatial metaphor would provide a clarificatory illustration. We might think of the temporal horizon as the path of a boomerang.* Originating from the subject, it is thrown forth (pro-jected), circumvents an area, and returns to its source. From within this enclosed area, then, objects are 'captured' and 'brought back' to the subject in a cognitional act as representations. Insofar as the formation of the temporal horizon has been shown to be

---

* The illustration is particularly appropriate because the German root-word for 'project,' *entwerfen*, means 'to sketch out a project' with the literal meaning being 'to throw off (or away) from' oneself in the sense suggested by the hyphenated 'pro-ject.'

prerequisite to the possibility of any cognition at all, the 'throwing' of the 'boomerang of time' in order to form an area of temporality for possible cognition is an act by the knower-subject which makes it possible for him to be affected by, to affect himself by, new representations, new ideas about objects, in that circumscribed area he has made his own. Similarly, to hear a melody means the projection of an 'area' of time in which sounds already heard, being heard, and being anticipated, are kept together in one appreciative act.

Time-projecting, as the formation of a temporal field, is thus an enabling act for the knower to be affected by the cognitive experience of what is to be found within that field. As instrumental to that possibility, it is an act by the knower-subject to be affected, to have new experience. Insofar as this act is requisite to that possibility of being-affected and is undertaken for this (even preconceptually understood) end-in-view, it is the essential enabling act whereby the knower affects himself by virtue of the experience whose possibility he has thereby created.

The metaphor of the 'self-conscious magnet' may also be brought forward as helpful; it structures the field about it, and, by this invisible projected structuring, it is able to 'recognize' and 'receive' impressions of compatible or responsive objects in that field. Similarly the mind structures the field about it in terms of schematized (temporalized) categories; by this act it enables itself to be affected by those aspects of the entities about it which respond to the kind of 'magnetic' structuring it has put forth. As the operator of a generating station is able to see the generator itself, as well as other objects, i.e., affect his mind with these perceptual awarenesses, by the light produced by that generator he has turned on, so our ability to have awarenesses, cognize them as 'internal' ideas, and consider them as such is first made possible by my 'generating the time' in the 'light' of which I am able to see the objects of which I am aware and thus affect myself in the knowing of them.

Any new idea affects my mental history even if as nothing more than a new fact or 'event' in my mental history; any new perception is, in addition to being a new fact in my perceptual awareness, thereby a new idea affecting the self I am. Such a new idea affects my mental history, affects my own self—through the means of its possibility. We can, then, perhaps see why Heidegger sums up the Kantian thesis by describing time as the prime mode of affecting my own self, as the mode of 'self-affecting.'

This is to say that time "forms the essential structure" [181] of my subjectivity wherein my capacity for knowledge is grounded. Thus, "Time is implicated in the internal possibility" of any object, any representation of any object or of my own awareness of my own be-ing. Time, then, "is that finite intuition which sustains and makes possible the pure concepts . . . as that which is essentially at the service of intuition." [182] As the ground of our capacity to attain ordered knowledge, it is the structure of our transcendence. It does not merely ground cognition; it is the source of the possibility to have any experience at all including the cognitive experience, which was the focus of Kant's concern.

This capacity to have a unified experience is essentially involved in what we mean by 'selfhood.' Time, therefore, as the structure of our capacity to receive, unify, order, and interpret separable sense reports, to integrate these into a coherent experience, to enable us to investigate and resolve difficulties, to undertake actions, is the ground of the possibility of our selfhood.

Because I can only become aware of myself insofar as I 'am affected through my own activity', [183] the time-forming nature of my mind is an activity whereby I engage in the requisite enabling act of 'self-affecting' and activating the self I am. By this enabling active capacity, I form the means by which I can have experience and discover my own self in the experiencing. My transcendental capacity to do this can be described, in Heidegger's capsuled term, as 'pure self-affecting.' It is the transcendental requisite for the experiential capacity I exercise; it permits my transcendental cognitional structure to become operative, and thereby enables particular awarenesses and ideas to enter my consciousness. As such, this transcendental time-forming act of pure self-affecting, 'forms my finite selfhood in such a way that I can become a self-conscious being, an operating self.' [184]

Time-forming is, then, this capacity to create the conditions for experience in enabling me to be affected by the acts of the self; as such, it is "the transcendental ground-structure of the finite self as such." If my self becomes aware of itself, and develops itself *qua* a self, a self-conscious center of experience, in the process of cognition—which reveals me to myself in the act of cognizing—this time-projecting capacity, which enables this cognitional process to occur, is what "first constitutes the mental character of the mind as a finite self." [185]

One does not first find one's self alongside objects and then try to establish some kind of cognitive relationship to them. Apart from our immediate involvement with the world of objects about us, in our developing awareness of them, as Paton said in regard to Kant, "the self could neither exist as a thinking being nor be aware of its own existence." [186] This essential be-ing with other beings is requisite to our knowledge of them and of ourselves, just because we only know ourselves as we experience ourselves experiencing what is in our experiential field to be experienced. Therefore, the self, structured by time, affects itself by constituting the possibility of becoming aware of objects in temporal terms and is thereby essentially a being-in-the-world as a continuing act of temporalization.

As the ground of my capacity for knowledge, for the experiencing in which I find my own self as its functioning center, time is not found 'in the mind' merely as intuition; time is involved in every thought I have and is thus integral to apperception as well. As imaginative synthesis, it is the functioning possibility of awareness and reflection of my recognition of objects and of my self in recognizing and coming to know them. Time is thus the enabling act of self-affecting; it constitutes the essential structure of my be-ing; it thus constitutes the basis of the possibility of selfhood and "first enables the mind to be what it is." [187] It is thus the mode by which the self creates its experience and thereby creates itself.

Time is thus the ground of the perceiving, comprehending 'I.' As any thought presupposes the 'I think' of self-consciousness, time is the basis of the transcendental ego, the 'pure self.' Heidegger is certainly aware of the fact that this is unmitigated Kantian heresy. His temporalization of the self is argued on three distinct grounds: (1) it was first proposed in the rooting of the moral self of practical reason in the temporalizing imagination; (2) it has just been argued in seeking out the fuller meaning of 'time as the form of inner sense' as the pure self-affecting capacity; (3) it is now argued from what is to be understood by pure apperception, Kant's 'third element' in transcendental imaginative synthesis:

> The pure finite self has in itself a temporal character. Therefore, if the ego, i.e., pure reason, is essentially temporal, the fundamental determination which Kant provides for transcendental apperception must first become intelligible through this temporal character.

The conclusion is unmistakably clear: "Time and the 'I think' are no longer opposed to one another as unlike and incompatible; they are the same." [188] How is this possible on Kantian grounds?

One of Kant's pioneering achievements, Heidegger suggests, is that he subjected time and the 'I think,' each taken separately, to a transcendental investigation. What resulted, without Kant's awareness of it, was his identification of the two. The predicates he used for each—'abiding,' 'unchanging,' 'permanent'—are the same.[189] Whether this was intended or merely coincidental is not the issue. What is at issue is that Kant's use of these terms facilitates, if it doesn't really demand, the denial that either the ego or time is *in time*. But this does not mean that the ego is a-temporal.

These predicates, in view of the Paralogisms,[190] cannot refer to the ego as some sort of mental substance. They can only signify that the self can form a horizon of possible experience insofar as it sees itself as more or less permanent through the changes in the experiences it gives to itself. The predication of some sort of enduring through change is a transcendental requisite for the possibility of an experiencing finite self—just because it enables the self to be a continuing center of experience. Only as such can a finite self engage itself in "forming time." [191]

As an 'I think,' the ego is essentially temporal insofar as it is capable of 'binding' time; insofar as it postulates its own enduring through change, it is, as a finite temporal self, 'abiding and unchanging' in the transcendental sense of necessarily presupposing itself for the possibility of its experiencing. For, presupposed in the ordering of a multitude of impressions into one coherent experience, in the welding of disparate experiences into the

[208]

one experience of a unitary 'I think,' is the awareness of a relative kind of permanence or enduring.

As Heidegger amplifies this point:

> Kant grasps the phenomenal content of the 'I' correctly in the expression 'I think,' or—if one also pays heed to including the 'practical person' when one speaks of 'intelligence'—in the expression 'I take action.' . . . The "I" is [not a 'logical subject' but] rather the subject of logical behaviour, of binding together. 'I think' means 'I bind together.' All binding together is an '*I* bind together.' . . . The *subjectum* is therefore 'consciousness in itself,' not a representation but rather the 'form' of representation. That is to say, the "I think" is not something represented, but the formal structure of representing as such, and this formal structure alone makes it possible for anything to have been represented.[192]

The self, then, is not a thing but an activity; it is not *in time* precisely because it projects time; it is the source of temporality in its experiential field. It is the ground of the time it projects and it maintains itself as the relatively-abiding center of its experience under the form of time it 'offers' to the objects about it. It makes time possible.

When these same predicates are applied to time, they do, indeed, signify that "time is not 'in time.'"[193] But they indicate something more. As the projecting of the structure of the experiential field and thereby the 'creator' of the modes of its experiencing, as creating the possibility of being affected by experiencing, time *qua* pure self-affecting lets the now-sequence arise. This now-sequence, which is assumed in everyday unreflective activity, issues from the time-forming of the self as a means to its experiencing. This now-sequence is thus not primary but derivative; it arises from the subjective ground of my capacity to create the possibility of experience by creating a time field, which I give myself as its enabling condition.

As a consequence, in denying a temporal character to the ego of pure apperception, Kant had merely stated that it was not itself subject to the form of time. The transcendental ego, then, is 'not in time' just because "it is time itself and . . . only as such in its very essence is it possible at all."[194] Thus, sensibility as such, which is intuitional, and conceptual reason "are not only homogeneous,

they belong together . . . [as that] which makes possible the finitude of human subjectivity in its totality." [195]

If human reason as such is temporal *qua* manifesting time as
the ground of its own being, what does this say about such rational
laws of logic which we take to be non-temporal or trans-temporal?
In the same sense as pure apperception, the logical laws, such as
the law of contradiction, are time-less only because they are 'categories' applicable to all phases of thinking regardless of specific
content and because they postulate the conditions of application
of any principle in terms of which we identify and relate two
sensory appearances. Such laws of reasoning may be considered
as an aspect of the self-imputation of 'permanence' through time
which the self projects in order to make its own temporalization
possible; this time-less-ness of logical laws, be it noted, is only possible on the basis of the implications of the subjective ground of
time. Kant had denied their relevance to temporality just because
he retained the now-sequence, which does not correlate in the
serial order it designates with the time of pure intuition which is
the first manifestation of the nature of subjectively grounded
temporality.

What then may we consider 'original' or 'ultimate' time to be?
Can we take it to a ground more basic than the self-affecting enabling capability? Here Heidegger stops: "It would be contrary
to sense to try to effect an essential determination of primordial
time itself with the aid of what is derived from it." [196] So far—but
no further! This is the final limit of the present exploration; he
does not permit himself to inquire beyond this point.

Indeed, in *Being and Time* he examines the general conception
of time that has been developed more extensively in its ramifications as transcendental grounding of 'everydayness,' in the 'category' of Concern that makes it possible, and in relation to history. He also clarifies the distinction, which remains somewhat
ambiguous in this Kantian retrieve: the distinction between temporality—as the transcendental capacity for structuring a temporal
field, time—as the derivative mode of reckoning with it in terms
of clocks and calendars, and world-time—as the 'objective' intentional referent of *our* time and temporality. But in scope he does
not go beyond what has been accomplished here.

These last few pages have tried to elucidate and clarify a rather obscure and difficult doctrine, which yet has a ring of truth. What Heidegger appears to be doing is restating and developing something suggested by Plotinus and Augustine without either the pre-Critical metaphysic or the luxuriant use of poetic metaphor.* And it is in large part this attempt at conceptual rigor which accounts for the legendary difficulty of much of Heidegger's prose. To say that time is the essence of what we mean by a functioning, living self is something of a poetic statement until 'reduced' to abstract conceptual language; but linguistic 'reduction' (or articulation) usually involves the use of language more readily adapted to expressing abstract conceptual distinctions than concrete dynamic identities. To describe time as the form of the self which, in its dynamic be-ing, makes it what it is as the center of an experiential field takes us into the linguistic stumbling-block of the subject-object dichotomy which Heidegger seeks to avoid. To analyze distinguishable elements of what is seen as essentially a unity without distorting that internal unity, is not readily conducive to eloquent clarity; for, precisely what Heidegger has been concerned to do is express, in conceptual terms, a philosophic understanding of the self-unifying nature of time as the fount of human be-ing. To express this kind of intrinsic and enabling identity without pointing to a 'thing' or 'substance' necessitates an attempt to rise above the language which seems better suited to discussing entities than acts or events; he, then, calls upon us to free ourselves from the ordinary kind of thinking which our noun-oriented language induces. For, in large part, Heidegger has been trying to say that the self is not a thing or an entity but a kind-of reflexive

---

* By substituting 'self' for 'soul' and ignoring Plotinus' speculative metaphysic, the following passages may help elucidate what Heidegger has been trying to say:

Time, then, is contained in differentiation of life. . . . Time, however, is not to be conceived outside of Soul. . . . It is a thing seen upon Soul, inherent, coeval to it. . . . The Soul-Act (which is the Essence of Time) . . . the origin of Time, clearly, is to be traced to the first stir of the Soul's tendency towards the production of the sensible Universe. . . . Is Time, then, within ourselves as well? Time is in every Soul . . . present in like form in all. . . . And this is why Time can never be broken apart.[197]

event, a 'subject' whose be-ing *qua* subject always necessitates the essential circularity of both the active and passive forms of any action verb simultaneously.[198]

The essence of Heidegger's conception of time, which may have been inspired by Plotinus but has been extricated from Kant, can perhaps be summed up in this thesis: temporality is not something which we can add to human existence; it is integral to human existing and to the acts, cognitions, and decisions which are elements of that existing and comprise its constituting 'moments.' That time is integral to human cognition was clearly suggested by the central place Kant assigned to it. Heidegger has clearly built out from here.

A man is essentially temporal. The essential temporality of his experience is the 'form' of his be-ing, the ground of any experience he may possibly have; it defines his finitude and the capabilities which arise within it; in advance of any ontic experience, it defines the kind of experience it can be in terms of the temporally imaginative synthesis of the constituents of that experience. It constitutes the structure of each individual experiencing as a field in which the three aspects of temporal out-look are brought together into a dynamic unity as a focus on the situation of concern. This structural unity of primordial triune time is then the fundamental reality of our capacity to-be.

Throughout, Heidegger has been concerned to establish explicitly those fundamental transcendental grounds which the to-be of our experience presupposes. For it is on these grounds that our particular individual selves are able to be and to become what they are. As Dewey suggested, there is an "intrinsic connection of time with individuality. . . ." Heidegger would join him in the "unescapable conclusion . . . [that] human individuality can be understood only in terms of time as [its] fundamental reality."[199]

For clarification of the nature of time as this fundamental reality and presupposition of every human experience, Heidegger sought the key. He extricated it from the priority of imaginative synthesis as the central theme in the chief work of "the first and only person who has gone any stretch of the way toward investigating the dimension of temporality."[200]

6 · *The Meaning of the Retrieve*

WITH THE COMPLETION of the Kantian retrieve, we are in a position to review what has been accomplished in order to see what it portends. We can now approach the bridge that takes us from Heidegger's interpretation of Kant to his own philosophic proposals and his development of a temporal ontology.

Heidegger's Kantian examination ends with the Schematism and the Highest Principle, presented by Kant as introductory to elucidation of the specific Principles of knowledge. Heidegger has no need here to examine each of these cognitive Principles; they are the specific temporalized definitions of the specific categories and Heidegger's concern has been with their grounding, not their specification. The examination of this specification is the business of Heidegger's second Kant-book, which is something of a postscript to the first one. Translated into English as *What Is A Thing?*, it demonstrates that Kant's cognitive Principles *qua* temporalized categories function together in any ontic description of any particular thing. Concerned with modes of describing the objects appearing in cognitive experience rather than with the subjective grounds of that experience (which is the theme of the first Kant-book and in a sense of *Being and Time*), he is able to use the traditional philosophic language with eloquence, clarity, and commendable style. But the essential point not to be overlooked is that these categoreal descriptions of objects are projections of our ways of knowing them; by virtue of the Highest Principle (which plays a prime role in the second Kant-book) these emerge as merely *our* modes of describing the things-that-are for us; thus their justification depends upon the grounding of objectivity in our modes of subjective knowledge-formation, a problematic proposed by the Copernican Revolution, the problematic which has been at the center of our discussion.

From the outset of the present examination and in accord with Kant's own declared aim, Heidegger has seen the Critique as attempting to lay the foundation of metaphysics in the light of the Copernican Revolution. Kant had established the fact that metaphysics, as traditionally understood, is speculative, not cognitive. What has emerged and is to be explored in the sequel is that metaphysics, as meaningful for us, is grounded in the ontological characterizations which we bring to any object we encounter. Because of the import of the problem of objectivity raised by the Copernican Revolution, Heidegger has focused his attention on the grounds for objectively characterizing the objects that appear to us. As these characterizations involve the ascription of being-status to these objects, he has been concerned with the kind and source of those ontological characterizations we may rightfully impute to objects as determined by the cognitional modes in which we come to know them. Thus, as Martin suggested, "Heidegger confines himself to the interpretation of the being of appearances and the being of the knowing subject, but this very limitation shows the far-reaching importance of the purely ontological approach." [201]

Heidegger has thus accepted Kant's limitation of the whole of possible experience by its subjective grounding.[202] Both of them are concerned to seek out the grounds of objective cognition within the framework provided by the transcendental enabling-and-limiting conditions of human knowledge. Both seem satisfied that this is not a new subjective idealism but an empirical realism; both presume the be-ing of that which appears to us. As Heidegger has put it, the appearance *is* of the entity as it appears to human cognitional capabilities, the "Appearance takes place in and with [the thing-that-is] itself." [203]

Kant had focused, as Heidegger has seen it, on the ground of the ontological determination of the objects which appear in human knowledge. It is from this knowledge that we have obtained our knowledge of the transcendental conditions of that knowledge and of our own be-ing as well. To talk about the nature of an object, or its being-status, to talk about ourselves as truly be-ing, to discuss either or both meaningfully, we first have to determine just what it is that we mean by the infinitive verb 'to be' itself. This understanding is, in principle, prior to any meaningful assertion that something 'is' or has an affirmative being-status. This is the *Seinsfrage,* the question of the meaning of be-ing as such. In human thought this question is related to the nature of man's mode of knowing, man's mode of be-ing, to the characteristics of the ways in which human finitude is manifested in any act of knowledge—just because man's finitude, and its own categoreal limitations, is the essential mode of be-ing we have.

In facing the problem of objectivity provoked by the Copernican Revolution, Kant had tried to determine the range of the possibility and degree of unity in our knowledge of the things we encounter. In formulating his solution, he postulated a dually segmented mind (intuition and pure concepts) and two strata of the real (phenomena and noumena). Heidegger's reconstruction has consistently protested these bifurcations and has sought to transmute the Kantian dichotomies into a unified ground. In place of Kant's two strata of the real, Heidegger's aim has been the unification of man with the world as it appears to him, the unification of his structure in order to account for the coherence of human experience; in place of the two independent sources of knowledge within the human subject, Heidegger has reconstructed the trancendental imagination as a unified cognitional process, the functioning of which can be analytically discriminated into Kant's two 'stems' of cognition. In pursuing this end, he has remained faithful to the Kantian problematic and has insisted on 'pulling' all possible human experience out of any supersensible realm into the Kantian subjective ground of experience.

This synthesizing power of imagination has been shown to be integral to the three modes of cognitive synthesis as their unifying agency and enabling ground. As such it is the source of the possibility of any cognitional act, of the experiencing and acting self, and thereby of experience itself and of the objectivity of the objects in that experience. Triune in nature, imagination corresponds and gives expression to the unity-and-differentiation of the nature of temporality; it thus emerges as the grounding of time itself. This essential relation of time, imagination, and cognitive unity is neatly summed up:

> Primordial time makes transcendental imagination, which in itself is essentially spontaneous receptivity and receptive spontaneity, possible. Only in this unity can pure sensibility as spontaneous receptivity and pure apperception as receptive spontaneity belong together and form the essential unity of pure reason.[204]

By rooting sensibility and thought—intuition and understanding—in transcendental imagination as the ground of our knowledge, by comprehending this transcendental imagination as the essential temporalizing and temporal mode of unifying the constituents of experience, he has rooted human experience—its possibility and finitude—in the transcendental time determination exercised in imaginative synthesis. It is thus in terms of temporal characteristics that we are enabled to cognize objects and ascribe ontological characteristics to them. Our knowledge of these essential objective characterizations of objects that appear, our ontological knowledge, is thus rooted in that mode of manifesting time, expressed in the triune cognitive synthesis, which characterizes our mode of knowing. Time is thus the prime constituent of every transcendental condition of knowledge, as Kant's Analytic demonstrated; it is the necessary 'ingredient' of any valid ontological characterization of the objects we come to know; as such it is integral to any comprehension of intelligibility and, thereby, to any meaningful concept or a meaningful relating of concepts.

Heidegger's reasoning has explicated the central role in which Kant had cast time and has drawn together the temporalistic 'threads' which run through the Critique. Whatever else may be taken from the Critique, a central thesis is the necessity of recognizing the complete priority of time and temporality in human cognition and its content. For Kant the ontological status of time was that of being 'transcendentally ideal' and 'empirically real.' Time was thus taken by Kant as the ultimate mark of reality *in human experience*. In order for an appearance to deserve designation as an object, it must be capable of being reported by sensory intuition; it must be amenable to the forms of temporality. Heidegger's explicit ontological priority of time thus appears to be in accord with the essential Kantian thesis; as Martin states it:

> Space and time, for Kant as for the ancients, are ontological characters, and Kant's thesis . . . is a continuation of an old argument. . . . Strictly speaking it is only true that all appearances are in time, so that strictly speaking *time alone is the decisive character of being*. . . . Everything real is in time and may also be in space. . . . Everything that is in time is actual, and only that which is in time is actual; time is the criterion of actuality.[205]

The problem of the Copernican Revolution, the problem of objectivity, is resolved by Heidegger in terms of the ontological priority of time, which emerges from the elucidation of the Highest Principle in conjunction with the Schematism: the complete compatibility of the temporal field in which the knower functions as a cognizing being and in which objects appear *qua* representations to be known.

Kant had not explicitly developed the subjective nature of time beyond its designation as the form of inner sense manifested as pure intuition. In working out the clues Kant had offered—the source of all cognitional content in sensory experience as formed by the temporality of intuition and the unifying function of imagination as the common root of sensibility and thought—Heidegger has developed the capacity for imaginative synthesis as the unifying source of experience by means of the temporalizing synthesizing of the elements of knowledge which it exercises. Insofar as we become self-aware through the cognitional acts we perform, insofar as these cognitional acts are made possible by the synthesizing temporal imagination, this imaginative power is requisite not only for 'external' knowledge but also for our knowledge of our own selves.

Insofar as the temporalizing activity of imagination makes this self-knowledge possible and thereby expresses or manifests the self, Heidegger argues that the human self is essentially a time-forming activity. The self emerges as 'primordial time,' which manifests itself in the terms of temporalization provided by imaginative synthesis. Time as such is thus manifested as the basic nature of the self in the projection of imaginative temporality. The self thus 'temporalizes time itself' [206] in the imaginative cognitive synthesis which produces knowledge. Time thus is the form of the self; as such, the capacity to project temporality upon a cognitive field is the ultimate transcendental ground of the possibility of ontic knowledge and of the transcendental cognitive structure, elucidated in the Critique, which produces it. As the ground of the entire possibility of knowledge, the time-forming capacity of the self constitutes the possibility of 'bringing' information, knowledge, and ideas 'into' the self and thus affecting it as its own experience. The capacity for imaginative temporal synthesis is thus the capacity for experiencing and being affected by that experiencing.

[217]

The self creates its experience for itself—by projecting the temporal horizon within which it is able to have experience, thereby enabling objects to enter into its experience, and by integrating into a unified experience whatever appears in that temporal horizon by means of interpretive concepts. Thus, the content of experience is basically a 'happening' within a temporal horizon, an essentially dynamic continuity in accord with the most inner nature of the temporalizing self.

Experience itself is, then, really an essentially dynamic and ongoing process, a continuum of experiencing in which the self discovers its own to-be in the experiencing it enables itself to enjoy. The self is thus akin to a 'time-magnet' that is the center of the time field it forms by 'radiating' temporality; this field is its 'world' of possible knowledge and experience; it creates and sustains this field *in* which it finds itself as it comes to know the things-that-are which also inhabit that area of its 'radiating' projecting of time determination from its core of temporality.

What Heidegger has then done is to develop the Kantian notion of inner sense as the essential requisite for any cognitional content. Its full meaning necessitates recognition of it as the ultimate ground for the possibility of experience, as the basic characteristic of the experiencing self with the consequent of its complete temporalization. If we are to take Kant's subjective grounding of time seriously as the requisite for meaningful experience, we can only conclude that time is the form of the self as such. For whatever else we may mean by selfhood, we do mean this capacity to have a temporally integrated experience, to have a unified, coherent experience in time; and time, as Kant had insisted, can be nothing more or less than the subjective condition for any experience we have.

To any objection to this identification of time as the form of selfhood, Heidegger would ask for an alternative way of unifying the three Kantian 'sources' of knowledge—sense, imagination, and thought, or the two 'stems' of knowledge—sense and thought—without sacrificing either Kant's transcendentalism or the original empirical cognitional prerequisite of sensory experience provided by pure intuition or inner sense.

Kant had characterized time as a now-sequence but did not work out the nature of time itself. As primary, its discordance with Kant's subjective grounding of time has been elucidated. Heidegger has shown that the now-sequence is just as derivative from subjective temporality—expressed in the triplicity of future-past-present—as is space; it serves the same function of objectivization, and this functional similarity can account, I might add, for the essentially spatial vocabulary in terms of which everyday clock-time is usually expressed (as Bergson, for one, protested but failed to explain).

It is, Heidegger suggests, just because Kant had not worked out a conception of time more basic than the now-sequence that the Schematism, as he left and declined to pursue it, remains fragmentary and thereby obscure and mystifying. The Schematism is the center of Kant's attempt to bring sensibility and thought into concert. It embodies his insight that these two dissimilar cognitive constituents can function together only by being made homogeneous *qua* temporal. He had pronounced the necessity for doing this, pointed out the direction of needed development, and promptly abandoned the task. Yet, as Heidegger has pointed out, it is here that the fundamental thesis of the Critique is to be found.

Kant had pointed out the direction in which a grounding of legitimate metaphysics must proceed: by comprehension of the way in which our capacity for knowledge can produce a coherent experience of entities appearing as objects to us and of our selves as well. But this, in turn, requires a deeper investigation into the synthesizing function of time, the theme of the Schematism, and the working out of the Subjective Deduction, in which the subjectivity of the subject and its mode of manifesting itself can be explicitly brought to light.[207]

Taken together, both tasks frame Heidegger's exploration. In large part Heidegger's work, both here and in *Being and Time,* can be understood as an attempt to carry forth this work which Kant had begun but neglected to carry down to deep enough ground. Both the Schematism and the Subjective Deduction lead, as Heidegger has shown, to the primacy of the transcendental power of imaginative synthesis, which is identifiable as 'original time' or original temporality. In large part, then, Heidegger's work is essentially an attempt at reconstruction of the Critical philosophy. For the insight of the Copernican Revolution requires a fully developed Subjective Deduction to ground the problem of objectivity and the possibility of knowledge; the Schematism requires explication of the centrality of the temporality in experience, the nature of its being formed, and thereby the grounding of cognitional possibility and the cognizing self. Both together point to the temporal nature of unifying imaginative synthesis; as mutually implicatory, both must be developed as one.

In carrying forward this twofold task, Heidegger has found the essential characterization of human experience, and of what can appear in that experience, to be rooted in the Kantian thesis which identified time as inner sense. Exploration and development of this thesis, in fullest seriousness, is an essential philosophic task which Kant has bequeathed to us. For time has been shown to be the ultimate subjective ground—defining the limits of any kind of experience we may have, characterizing any content or understanding of that experience, and the form of the experiencing self; further developed, the concept of time provides the means of unifying Kant's separate moral and cognitive selves into the unitary selfhood of any actual be-ing. In carrying out these two undeveloped theses of Kant's analytic, Heidegger has demonstrated the meaning of temporality as the intrinsic possibility of our own be-ing as experiencing subjects and of any kind of experience we might have, of time as the ultimately pervasive form in which the things-that-are as objects for us can be apprehended and understood.

If we are concerned with attaining a fuller comprehension of the nature of the be-ing characteristics of the objects we encounter or of our own be-ing for ourselves, Heidegger's thesis is that a further step is requisite. Implicitly he urges that we proceed from Kant's examination of the requisites for something to be in our experience, as our point of departure, to what has become the consequent problematic, the meaning of the infinitive verb 'to-be' itself as it is manifested in our modes of human experience.

The basic question, then, is this: 'what does it really mean to say that something has be-ing, that something is, that something has the capability to-be?' The pursuit of this question takes us from Kant to Heidegger, from epistemology and metaphysics to ontology; it takes us to an ontology that is rooted in the subjective structure of human knowing and be-ing; in full recognition of the revolutionary import of the Critical edifice, it takes us from the Copernican Revolution, and by its light, to 'fundamental ontology.' It is then a short step from Heidegger's Kant to Heidegger himself.

VII

Kant and Fundamental Ontology

KANT'S AVOWED INTENT was the discovery of the ground for rigorous metaphysics in the light of the Copernican Revolution. He pursued his goal by exploring the nature of human knowledge and the presuppositions found in it. The characteristics necessarily possessed by an object in order for it to be within human experience were identified as those apriori constituents defining the possibility, extent, and inherent operational limitations of human cognition itself. These transcendental grounds of human knowledge thus comprise the modes of be-ing of any object insofar as it can be known. As such, they constitute the ontological determinations of any object within human experience.

Because time is central to human cognition, Kant thus effectively shifted the locus of ontology from the nature of things to the nature of time and temporality as the center of the be-ing of man, who experiences things. As such, time emerged as "the fundamental ontological character of the objective reality of appearances,"[1] which are, in the Critical perspective, the objects constituting the content of our knowledge.

He thus limited metaphysical inquiry to the temporal and grounded it in the nature of the human knower, in the human capacity for and mode of knowing. In this sense the Critique set out the necessary structure of 'any future metaphysics'; for this reason he described the Critique as providing "the *metaphysics* of metaphysics," [2] for which the theory of knowledge was to serve as foundational. It is in this very Kantian sense that Heidegger regards the Critique as the propaedeutic to his own thought. From the interpretation of Kant and the lessons it provides, from what has been established and what has been left open, Heidegger proceeds to work out his own answers to the questions Kant has raised.

I · *The Legacy from Kant*

IF OUR KNOWLEDGE of objects is indeed knowledge, if the nature of these objects as known is grounded in our modes of knowing them, then we require the coordination of the conditions of knowing and be-ing. But Kant had said very little about the be-ing of the human knower. Just as he had presumed the two 'stems' as emerging from a common root, so he also took for granted man's capacity to project his subjective transcendental categories onto the things-to-be-known as ontological predicates.

But how is man able to do this? What is the nature of man's to-be that permits this kind of ontological projecting? Kant's inquiry focused on grounding the characterizations of things-that-are for us; but whenever his inquiry seemed to point beyond the necessity of this human grounding to its nature and its own possibility, he seemed to stop short as if deflected by an invisible obstacle. We are, then, Heidegger urges, now impelled to reopen this question: what *is* the nature of man that enables him to project ontological predicates, create and comprehend ontological distinctions? What is the essential nature of the to-be of finite human beings, of the peculiar human mode of be-ing?

Man is not merely a cognizing entity: man not only knows; he also chooses, acts, and hopes. In each of these characteristic modes of being human, Heidegger points out, the Kantian thesis presupposes human finitude as an essential aspect of his being: in moral choice as well as in cognition the philosophic problem arises from man's essential limitations, from the peculiar human way of being finite. What is to be understood from the fact that every mode of our be-ing is that of being-within-limitation? Any meaningful metaphysic must start from our essentially finite nature, from the nature of the being who is asking metaphysical questions.

The fundamental ontological inquiry is, then, the systematic investigation of what is involved in essential human finitude; its result should give us insight into what is meant, implied, and presupposed by us in the notion of the to-be as such. Because comprehending our human mode of be-ing, from which all questions about being-status arise, is fundamental to any meaningful metaphysical inquiry, this investigation to which Heidegger invites us is entitled 'fundamental ontology.'

As Kant's entire framework of thought was this essential finitude of man and the problems it poses, it constitutes his essential insight; the presumption of essential finitude provides the context within which each of his inquiries and arguments was developed and attained its meaning. Preoccupation with the implications of finitude defined the problem of morality as well as of knowledge. The study of the essential structure of human finitude thus emerges as a task imposed by the outcome of the Critique. It calls for a new metaphysic of finite human nature which explicates the structure of the possibility for human finitude to-be, to be what it is, to become what it can be. From the retrieve of Kant, Heidegger thus urges us on to a retrieve of the problem which Kant had raised in its most basic dimension, the problem of just what it means for us, as finite human beings, to be the kind of beings we are. In facing this new problematic, we face, in effect, the opportunity to ground the Critique itself; more fully developed in *Being and Time,* this Kantian road to Heidegger's major work sees this task as one of the philosophic functions it serves.

Kant had grounded human cognition in imaginative synthesis and, in the B Edition, 'retreated' from this outcome. Heidegger's thesis of 'recoil' (described by Spiegelberg as "the most important aspect" of his book[3]) must, Heidegger insists, also "belong to the result." For it manifests Kant's own 'forgetfulness' of the problem which animated his concern.*

* Heidegger suggests that those who came after Kant followed in these same footsteps by completely forgetting this ground of essential finitude which had originally defined Kant's problem. From this systematized 'forgetting' of human

Kant's *Critique of Pure Reason* did not ground ontology in reason but in the human imagination, in the "subjectivity of the subject." [4] But 'to question one's way into the subjectivity of the subject, leads us into an unexplored darkness.' [5] It is from this darkness, this obscurity, that Kant had 'recoiled.' The Subjective Deduction and the Schematism, which promised clarification of the nature of the human to-be, were cut short just because, Heidegger suggests, Kant had implicitly realized that he was cutting away the ground upon which the Critique had been set. He had manifestly come to the abyss of metaphysics. [6]

Kant's 'recoil,' then, Heidegger sees as revealing the prime import of Kant's basic discovery, the subjective grounding of ontological knowledge: the essence of metaphysics is to be found, not in things-in-themselves, not in a timeless rationality as such, but in the essential imaginative unity of the subjective conditions of human cognition. Just as Kant had suggested that science is based not on contingent passive observations but on a systematic interrogation of nature, so, Heidegger urges, the new foundation of a Critical metaphysics can only arise from a systematic interrogation of man. But a systematic interrogation requires a direction, an understanding of how to conduct it, and some insight into why it need be undertaken: why is it necessary to bring man into the grounding of metaphysics?

Although Kant's focus had been on general metaphysics or ontology, on the nature of the to-be in human experience, his motive was to expedite his anticipated fulfillment of special metaphysics. Kant had summed up the entire range of those metaphysically ultimate and motivating concerns in three basic questions. "All the interests of my reason, speculative as well as practical," Kant declared, "combine in the three following questions:

1. What can I know?
2. What ought I to do?
3. What may I hope?" [7]

---

finitude and the sensory source of cognitional content arose the Hegelian identification of logic and metaphysics—prompted by the 'rationalist' forgetting of the B Edition. To understand what Kant had set out to do, then, we must turn away from the development of Absolute Idealism and return to its 'misread' source, the Critical Idealism of the A Edition.

As Kant himself indicated, these three questions are all reducible to a comprehensive fourth question, "What is man?" [8] Together they were taken by him to characterize man as a 'citizen of the world' and not merely as a member of the phenomenal order.

Be it well noted that each of the first three questions is posed in terms of futurity, possibility, and finitude. The first question, "What *can* I know?" provides the theme of the First Critique, looks to the future, and confesses the defining priority of finite possibility: an omniscient being would not ask such a question and an omnipotent being would find it unintelligible. Likewise, to ask about duty or obligation is to ask about the future and to confess a lack of moral completion and fulfillment. To ask about hope is, again, a confession of lack of omnipotence and knowledge and in both regards "reveals a privation." [9]

The fourth and comprehensive question thus seeks the 'essence of man' in terms of reasonable and thereby limited anticipation. This anticipation is determinable in terms of those genuine possibilities which are presented by a finite future and an awareness of rational concern for the 'lacks' which comprise essential finitude.

Each of these questions, singly and together, explicates the finitude inherent in the essence of what it is to be human and each underlines our characteristic concern about this essential finitude which defines one to himself. These questions, Heidegger suggests, clearly demonstrate that self-awareness of one's essential finitude provokes the Kantian query about human reason; they indicate that in our own "rationality this finitude is at stake," [10] that the nature of this finitude and my questions about its limits are always presupposed in whatever I think and do.

The fact that "all the interests of my reason" are combined in these questions demonstrates the central place which the 'category' of 'Concern' * holds in the constituent structure of my thinking. These 'interests' of intellectual concern define the essential motiva-

* I have followed Churchill in rendering Heidegger's *Sorge* as 'Concern,' despite its usual translation as 'Care,' because the latter seems more ambiguous and removed from the essentially problematic sense implicit in Heidegger's usage. It should be taken in a transcendental-ontological sense and distinguished from the 'concern' of his *besorgen*, which is ontic in meaning as in the query 'what is it that you are concerned about now?' [11]

tion of the Critical edifice and thus define the context in which its doctrines and arguments function and attain their meaning.

The first question, which expressed rational concern about the possible attainable extent of my knowledge, provided the theme of the First Critique. It is not strange, then, that Heidegger has developed the priority of the futural aspect of temporality precisely from here. Despite his open disagreement with Kant's explicit time-description and regardless of whether one accepts all of his reasoning from the Kantian texts, Heidegger's derivation of the priority of futurity is in accord with the prime concern exhibited in the Critique itself: concern for the essential possible limit of the kind of knowledge which I, as a finite human being, will ever be able to achieve and, thereby, concern with the necessary limit of 'all future metaphysics.'

It would then seem that an abrupt dismissal of Heidegger's derivation of the priority of futurity from Kant carries the suggestion that Kant's doctrinal 'reply' to his own question is an irrelevant reply, that what he offered as the fruit of his labor has no relevance to his own inquiry and that, far from possibly being 'wrong' on some points, he did not even know what kind of question he was asking, did not know what his own interrogation was all about. Such a dismissal constitutes in itself a rather serious charge, a charge which should specify the question(s) to which Kant had, in effect, replied; it is a charge serious enough to require explicit justification on its own before Heidegger's interpretation of the implications of Kantian time, in accord with the animating spirit of Kant's intent, is cavalierly brushed aside.

Heidegger has developed the Kantian 'combination of all rational interests' as the existential 'category' of 'Concern'; it emerges as the prime characterization of the modes of be-ing of finite man, as the prime ontological delineation of what is involved in any human act, in being a unified person.* It is developed as the source

---

* 'Concern' is developed as the central 'category' of human existence, i.e., an 'existential' in the language of *Being and Time,* which elucidates and develops it in detail. We have already seen, in the temporalization of practical reason, how such an 'existential' (i.e. 'respect') functions in Heidegger's thought. The cognitive analogue of the existential of Concern is the apriori transcendental structure of human cognition: just as the transcendental synthesis is the foundation of any empirical cognition, so the transcendental 'existential' of Concern is the apriori

of the three aspects of imaginative synthesis and the three aspects of temporal unity. It is to be developed in an 'existential analytic,' an analysis of the modes of be-ing of the whole man, the analogue of which is Kant's Transcendental Analytic, which was an analysis of the modes of knowing of objects by the cognitional aspect of man; as Kant described the structure of human knowing in order to determine its capabilities, modes, and defining limitations, so Heidegger's analogous analytic seeks to describe the structure of human be-ing in order to determine its capabilities, modes, and defining limitations as well as its cognitive functioning. Taken from the ground question of the Critical philosophy, Concern emerges as the central structure of human be-ing, just as the transcendental power of imagination was shown to be the central structure of human knowing. As the transcendental imagination animates our capacity to attain finite knowledge, so that apriori "primordial structural totality" termed Concern animates our general capacity to function as finite beings.[12]

We have, then, two approaches to this centrality of Concern. It has here been developed through Kant's question, 'What can I know?' which Kant had worked out in his Transcendental Analytic as one of the questions comprising the 'combined interest of human reason.' Alternatively, the centrality of Concern is developed in *Being and Time* by means of the phenomenological 'existential analytic.' We thus have an option of philosophic approach.[13] By either path we arrive at the central animating operational 'category' of Concern in which the ultimate unity of our transcendental structuring is to be found. Problem-solving and goal-oriented, it is essentially futural. Animating the whole man, it is to be even more strongly identified as 'original time' than the synthesizing imagination could be as the animating center of the cognitional aspect of man in the Kantian context.

---

capacity for the particular or ontic animating concerns, worries, hopes, fears manifested in our lives as focusing our interests and provoking our acts.

It must be noted that Heidegger uses the word 'existential' as an essential constituting structural element of human activity in much the same way that Kant used the word 'category' as an essential constituting structural element in the cognition of particular things. Accepting the Kantian use of the word 'category,' Heidegger creates the analogous word 'existential' to follow Kant in clearly differentiating 'people' and 'things.' [Cf. *B&T*, p. 73 (48).]

Time and temporality—as foreshadowed in the more restricted Kantian investigation—thus emerge more fully as the "concrete explication of Concern." [14] Man is not, as far as we can tell, the only temporal creature; for all the things-that-are for us are conceived by us to be essentially time-bound. But we do find that (whatever may be the case with other beings[15]) we are essentially temporal in our innermost structure, that we find ourselves "as temporality" itself.[16] To comprehend just what this means points us ahead (in the next section) to what Heidegger is to describe as the task of fundamental ontology—just because, as the ground of our ontological ascriptions, the time that we discover in every manifestation of our be-ing must have some ontological status.

Heidegger explicated the unity of the apriori grounds of knowledge in the comprehensive unity formed by the temporalizing transcendental imagination. Similarly, in the development of his own existential analytic, he finds the unity of our apriori transcendental structures in the comprehensive unity formed by the temporalizing manifestation of Concern.

In order to refute his thesis concerning the centrality of Concern in 'human existence' (the fuller meaning of which is explicated in the following section), Heidegger suggests three separate theses which would first have to be independently established: (1) our human finitude is not constituted by our transcendence—as, against Kant, one would need to demonstrate that our finite modes of knowledge are not structured by the kind of transcendental 'apparatus' Kant described; (2) metaphysics can be securely founded without taking into account its dependence on the nature of our finite way of be-ing the kinds of beings we are—as, against Kant, one would need to demonstrate that this range of metaphysical knowledge was not dependent on the nature of our finite capacity for knowledge; (3) the grounding of metaphysics is not preoccupied with the problem of understanding the meaning of the to-be as that by virtue of which all beings are—as, against Kant, one would need to demonstrate that the grounding of knowledge is not preoccupied with the problem of understanding the meaning of the to be 'in time' as that by virtue of which all the things-that-are for us are in inner sense as representations.

The parallelism with the Kantian structure is clear. What

Heidegger proposes is a transcendental investigation, which expands the Kantian, concerning the possibility of experience and which grounds human cognition in the possibility of be-ing an experiencing human being. The 'clues'—the transcendental grounding of the particular, the general mode of analysis which proceeds from 'elements' to their unifying ground, the priority of the temporal in the nature of any activity to which the adjective 'human' may be properly attached—all clearly emerge from the interpretation of the Kantian analysis of cognitional experience. As that interpretation found its center in the transcendental power of imagination, so Heidegger is to expand the focus to the essentially transcendental existential of Concern, an embracing 'category' whose roots are to be found in the motivating impetus of the Kantian structure.

This 'Concern' may be regarded, in retrospect, as implicitly grounding the Kantian inquiry itself. For it is Concern, the transcendental capacity for particular or ontic concerns or 'rational interests,' that would seem to animate and direct the particular selection of the criteria of relevance invoked in any empirical imaginative synthesis. It holds the key to a crucial question not even raised by Kant or by Heidegger: why do we and how do we, in an apprehended presentation, select certain aspects as important, as prior, as meriting interpretive attention and ignore the others? As I come upon a wooden glen, why do I focus my cognitive synthesizing on a towering oak while my companion does not notice it but directs his attention to the grassy bank of the stream running through it? If that tree holds out to me the prospect of resting under it, while the grass by the stream suggests access to a refreshing drink of water, we see that our immediate concerns, the ontic particularity of our reason in interpreting the same presentation, our motivating desires or immediate ends-in-view, are explanatory of this selective focus-as-interpretation. Thus the ontic question 'what are you concerned about, seeking out, in this specific perceptual presentation?' is the ontic determining principle of selective empirical focus-and-interpretation.

Such a specific questioning must have a transcendental ground of its possibility. To ask or presume an ontic question means that imagination, in the light of the categories, invokes certain empiri-

cal concepts instead of others as germane to the content of apprehension; doing so presupposes the transcendental capacity for
imaginative selection of relevant interpretive concepts, for search-
ing out of specific possibilities in terms of which imagination
renders the particular cognitive synthesis it does. These function as
guidelines for ontic imaginative synthesis and must emerge from
a transcendental capacity for them to emerge, to be chosen as
interpretive instruments. Such guidelines provide the standard of
objectivity by which to evaluate the judgment my cognition incorporates. They are essentially futural, for the guideline or rule
which the imagination invokes in an empirical (ontic) cognitional interpretation of a presentation suggests the meaning of the
presentation to me in terms of its instrumentality toward fulfilling
a present 'lack' I see myself as having. What I do not need I
barely notice or ignore; what I conceive myself as needing or
lacking attracts my attention, arouses my interest, stands out from
the background in my focus, and determines how I will 'read' the
presentation before me.

Such a specific guideline or rule for an empirical imaginative
synthesis rests on my capacity to relate my lacks, ends-in-view,
desires, momentary concerns, by an act of 'rational imagination,'
to the situation which I immediately define in terms of the possibilities, instrumental potential, or use as a tool which it seems to
offer to me as a solution of the problem, the fulfillment of the lack
in terms of which I assess the situation. I thus project or 'read
into' this presentation the interpretive concepts which define the
possibilities to which I want the situation to respond; I 'read it'
in terms of its responsiveness to the possibilities which I wish to
realize from it. This empirical procedure of my 'rational imagination' is predicated on that existential or transcendental capacity
of Concern, which enables me to bring into the Kantian cognitional synthesis, as its animating directive, the ontic concerns I
have.

Thus, Heidegger's 'category' of Concern does not only fill out
a notable gap in the Kantian explanation of cognition. It grounds
the functioning of transcendental imagination itself. It suggests
an additional justification for the priority of 'non-thing-ness': my
definition of a problem to be solved, an end-in-view to be attained,

a concern for a lack, all presuppose my postulation of the genuineness of a possibility that has not been transformed into something
present and actual, of the genuineness and present import of that
which is not now present. Insofar as all these characterizations of
any ontic concern are future-oriented, the priority of a transcendental of Concern substantiates Heidegger's insistence on the
precedence of futurity in defining the meaning and principle of
synthesis in any cognitional act. As the determination of ontic
concerns are essentially volitional in character, Concern provides
an additional ground for my suggestion that Heidegger's temporalization of the self opens the ground for reconciling cognitive
and moral reason; for Kant had defined the latter in volitional
terms and, by virtue of its alleged noumenal character, regarded
it as more real. This extension of Heidegger's Concern back into
the Kantian Critique implies that the temporalization of the self
establishes the precedence of the functional aspects of 'practical'
before 'cognitive' reason or the understanding.[17] It provides the
transcendental foundation upon which the possibility of ontic
moral as well as cognitive acts stand, and it serves, in effect, as
their 'common root.'

We can now see the significance to be drawn, either in Heidegger's own terms or by going beyond them, from Heidegger's focus
on Kant's 'reduction' of ontology or general metaphysics to the
human capacity for knowledge. This knowledge always involves
our transcendence of the dependence we have on discrete presentations of objects we do not create. The way in which we attain
knowledge, the kinds of knowledge we do attain, the limited
knowledge it always seems to remain—they arise from this transcendental capacity to select finite interpretive canons, and they
indicate the essential finitizing and finitude of the human knower.

The central 'category' in terms of which this cognitional finitude
of ours is manifested is the form of time. It enables us, by imaginative synthesis of the elements in a cognitional act, to bring together
sensory reports, the actuality of the presentation, conceptual categories of selected possibilities as interpretive tools, and (as the
Highest Principle demonstrated) the 'coexistence' of our be-ing as
knowers with the be-ing of the things to be known.

Central to the triune temporality we employ in cognitive synthesis is the manifestation of imagination as 'original time.' This temporality enables us to know the objects whose representations constitute the content of our knowledge and, thereby, that knowledge of our own selves which is revealed in our own experiential acts. Our essential temporalizing thus emerges, in Heidegger's explication of the Kantian analysis, as the ground of our own to-be, of the kind of finite being-status we are able to enjoy.

The nature of the temporality we employ in every cognitional and moral act enters into every kind of systematic inquiry we may undertake and is the foundation of any metaphysical investigation we might conduct. This Critical grounding of 'every possible metaphysics' in human time pursued definite stages of development. It began with intuition and proceeded through analysis of the elements contributing to the possibility of knowledge. In accord with Kant's fourth question, it is essentially what Kant had called a "study of our inner nature." [18]

What results, Heidegger suggests in pointing to his own work, is the philosophical duty of a systematic interrogation of man and man's way of be-ing. From the outset Kant had seen that metaphysics is necessarily linked to 'human nature'; his examination, conducted within the confines of his conception of man and human time, resulted in the explication of human finitude: what it is and what its limited realm of possibility includes. This essentially finite structure of man thus becomes the horizon within which such metaphysical knowledge which man can attain must be found.

Kant had undertaken his inquiry as one into the nature of human cognition. From his examination of what Kant had done and seemed to imply, Heidegger has achieved, as Martin points out, "decisive results as regards the ontological characterization of man, more particularly in bringing out the finiteness of man as grounded in his combination of receptivity and spontaneity." [19]

From his initial insistence on the essential unity of all elements of cognition, Heidegger has shifted the direction of philosophical inquiry to the essential unity of man—to the nature of man as a totally unified and unifying being. In man's be-ing, he is cognizing, acting, and providing the possibility for the appearing of the things-that-are for him, while depending on their appearing

[233]

within his experiential horizon for the knowledge he is capable of attaining. From the Kantian investigation into the transcendental (ontological) grounding of finite human knowledge, Heidegger has shifted the inquiry to the ontological (transcendental) grounding of the human being in the world of his experiential possibility. The comprehensiveness of human reason itself impels us to an ontological investigation into the finitude of human nature as such; for it is the way of be-ing of human nature that finds part of its mode of expression, of its self-manifestation, in the use of that theoretical reason in the quest for knowledge which Kant had been concerned to justify and explain.

2 · *And the Metaphysics of Dasein*

THE FULL DEVELOPMENT of fundamental ontology, a metaphysics of man, is the business of the existential analytic of *Being and Time*. But we can fruitfully preview Heidegger's own development of his thematic study from the legacy he accepts from Kant, which in large measure parallels, buttresses, and arises from his painstaking examination of Kant.

The point of departure is the nature of finitude itself—not mere reiteration of the fact but the attempt to determine in what this finitude consists. To attain such a determination, a random contingent cataloging of human imperfections cannot suffice. As any systematic interrogation requires a principle, so the operating principle is to be a concern for discovery of its essential structure, of the characteristic ways in which it is made manifest. Because human existing is the expression of the finite ways in which we are, it is an expression of the essential structure of our being-finite.

Our own understanding of be-ing, as revealed in our own modes of be-ing, provides the ground of all ascriptions of being-status to ourselves and the things-that-are for us. Just because any metaphysic emerges from human thought and the state of be-ing of the human thinker, clarification of the meaning of the verb 'to be' must precede any meaningful metaphysic. Philosophic thinking is the thinking of finite beings-that-are, of living humans. Thus, the foundation of metaphysical inquiry must rest on what we, as finite men-who-are, discover as the meaning of this crucial verb. The question of the meaning of the 'to-be' thus provides the center and ground of all philosophic thinking.

The import of Heidegger's ontological questioning of Kant thus emerges in the continuing parallelism between our knowledge of objects and of ourselves, the continuing reciprocity of the content of knowledge and its revelation of the nature of the knowing self, as suggested in Kant's Highest Principle (and in aspects of his "Refutation of Idealism"). Kant had made it manifest that all finite human knowledge involves a relationship with and a dependence on the ascription of being-status to the entities represented as objects in intuition.[20] This continuing and essential reference to the being-status of the objects of knowledge as reported by sensibility was developed into the 'sensibilization of concepts' and 'sensible reason.'

This is merely to assert the claim that there is, even if preconceptually, an ontological significance to any meaningful assertion; as Royce had suggested:

> to assert that God is, or that the World is, or even with Descartes, that I am, implies that one knows what it is to be . . . what the so-called existential predicate involves. . . . You deal constantly, and decisively, with the problems of the Theory of Being whenever you utter a serious word.[21]

Even, Heidegger pointedly suggests, in the mere exclamation "Fire!" we comprehend that a fire has broken out or come into be-ing, that a fire *is*. For that matter, one need not even speak: the be-ing of an object and a relationship with it is presumed "even when in silence we assume an attitude toward it";[22] we implicitly assume the truth of our judgment that it is and what it is: we assume at least something of the meaning involved "in the 'is' of every proposition . . . whether expressed or not."[23] We have, therefore, at all times a comprehension, if indeed preconceptual, of something of the significance of the verb 'to be.' It is this preconceptual comprehension, which underlies everything we think and say and do, that permits us to question the meaning of an assertion concerning the being-status of any thing. This preconceptual comprehension of the meaning of 'to be' has an ontological

[235]

significance: it points out that in advance of any ontic encounter we are invoking or utilizing what in Kant's terminology would be called an apriori transcendental 'category.'

Human knowledge does not arise or function in a vacuum. It depends, as Kant had shown, on the special human way of being within a world of others, of beings known and to be known. Their status as beings, and our own amongst them, is presupposed from the outset. To-be-in-the-world is an essential part of what is meant when we speak of being human. Just as a bird is the kind of thing it is by virtue of being in a world with air to sustain flight, ground upon which to alight, and insects to eat, so man is essentially at least the kind of a being who knowingly and self-consciously lives in a world of certain kinds of possible experiences. Man's to-be in the world is not a matter merely of physical location; it is essentially 'internal' to the kind of be-ing he is and has. Essential to man's being-in-the-world is the observation that it is not only misleading and distortive but also "impossible to consider man as an entity and the world as an entity and then put the two together to get man-in-the-world." Any such distinctions are not original but derivative. It is a constituent, original, and basic element of the essential nature of man "to be in the world in such a way that the world is of his essence." [24] The relationship is mutually implicatory: the kind of being I am implies the kind of world in which I see myself; the world in which I see myself implies the kind of being I am. *My* world is not merely that of physical nature but involves the whole web of relationships and concerns which animate my actually experiential area of operation; it is inseparable from *my* being.

Thus, in possible contrast to all other kinds of entities, Heidegger explains—carrying the Kantian moral distinction of 'persons' and 'things' into the heart of the matter—man is not an object, not a thing. As far as we know, man alone can *consciously and deliberately* relate things, relate himself to things, relate things to him, question the relationship of absent possibles to present actual states, anticipate the future, retrieve the past. This is to say that, as far as we know, man has the unique capacity to act in the present on the basis of consciously evaluated possibilities, that this capacity for awareness and appropriation of possibility is intrinsic to the construction of the temporal field within which he sees himself as functioning in a world. Man is, then, a self-questioning being who can ask about his own finite possibilities and his own relationship to them; this self-questioning is an essential element of his nature. To say, then, that "a man is" is a different kind of assertion from saying "a tree is." Man is that kind of being who is aware of be-ing among others 'in such a way that what-he-is and what-he-is-not are always already [if preconceptually] manifest to him.' [25] Man is, then, that kind of a being that is self-consciously present in a context with varied kinds of beings in the world of his concerns.

In order to avoid ambiguity by confusion with any of the many characteristics or connotations which have accrued in the philosophic traditions to the words 'man' and 'human,' Heidegger introduces a special term to describe just this precise meaning of what is the essence of being human: viz., the being-that-is-here-and-open-to-his-possibilities, the to-be-here-in-the-world-of-concern-and-to-be-self-aware—the 'Dasein.' *

'Dasein' does *not* refer to an abstract idea or entity; it is, be it noted, essentially a verb-form and refers to the *mode* of essential functioning in any real human existent. Thus, when we analyze the characteristics of Dasein, we find that 'We ourselves are the being to be analyzed. The to-be of any such being is in each case mine.' [27] Each of us deliberately or preconceptually is concerned in a multitude of ways with the question of what it means to-be. We

---

* The usual translation of *Dasein,* as Heidegger uses it, is as 'the being that is *there';* this translation is distortive as it is unduly external, object-oriented, remote in its connotation; it does not convey the essential looking-out from subjectivity that is crucial to Heidegger's understanding of the mode of human existing. It also overlooks the crucial threefold distinction in German (and some other languages) which is absent from English: *hier* ('right here'), *dort* ('way over there'), and *da* ('sort-of in between'). The import of the *da* is that a man is not merely *in* his body as an embodied soul with a physical world about him; a man is always in a context that is present to him, in a general environment which is inseparable in a real sense from his actions and his thoughts, from the way in which he conceives himself to be at any moment, from the way in which he looks-out *in* his world. Additionally, the significance of the *sein,* as the infinitive verb 'to be,' must be kept in mind as a reminder that 'to be here' *in* a world of one's concerns is an act of be-ing. Because this whole meaning cannot be concisely conveyed in translation, the word 'Dasein,' following general usage, is brought directly into English as a technical word, and should be understood as 'the being that is consciously here as the center of his environment of concerns.' [26]

continually ask Hamlet's question—about ourselves, about those things we encounter in our experience and to which our ideas claim to refer: *is* it real? *is* it possible? *is* it useful? *is* it true? *is* it pleasant? etc. Inasmuch as human questions are essentially questions about the being-status of what is of concern, the essential nature of being-human derives from its chief manifested concern, from what it inquires about, the meaning of the to-be questions it asks, the meaning of the to-be which permeates its questions and concerns. Thus, to assert that I 'exist' is to be aware of my self and, at least preconceptually, to raise the distinction of the nature of the being-status of what comes into view; rudimentary, for example, is the basic ontological distinction between what-*is*-my-being and what-*is-not*-my-being.

Existence, *qua* self-conscious questioning awareness of ontological distinctions, is the essence of what we mean by the be-ing mode of a human being—whose essence "lies in its 'to-be.' . . . *The essence of Dasein lies in its existence.*" [28] It is crucial to note that 'existence' is not taken in the traditional sense of opposition to 'essence'; the essence of Dasein 'in' man is Dasein's existence, Dasein's to-be-in-a-world of beings, of other people, and of things. In conformity with Kant's analysis of cognition, Heidegger notes that Dasein is essentially dependent for self-awareness on the beings that Dasein is not. This dependence is grounded on Dasein's prior projection of the possibility of the not-me object; but, in turn, this projecting is itself made possible by the apriori possibility of the distinction between my-being and not-my-being. [29]

Thus, as man's mode of be-ing, Dasein incorporates finitude into the heart of its essential way of manifesting and discovering the kind of being it is. As a self, Dasein is not merely finite in its cognitional dependence on other beings. One did not 'choose' to come into the world, into the particular existential situation in which one finds itself. 'Thrown into' a world not of its own choosing, a world inhabited by other beings over which it has little if any control but upon which it is essentially dependent, existential finitude is its foremost characteristic. [30] Man is what he is by virtue of the structure of the kind of to-be he has, the to-be in a context that is present to him and is designated as 'Dasein.'

The Dasein that is 'in' man is that center of his structure which

[238]

functions in much the same way as the Kantian transcendental power of imagination which it encompasses—for man's mode of be-ing manifests itself, in one way among others, by seeking to attain knowledge. As the center of the structure of man's mode of be-ing, Dasein manifests itself as Concern; it is the root of the capacity for transcendence, a capacity that is essentially temporal:

> Whenever Dasein tacitly understands and interprets something like the to-be, it does so with *time* as its standpoint. Time [is] . . . the horizon for all understanding of the to-be and for any way of interpreting it.[31]

Thus the transcendental imagination is transposed into the Dasein-in-man as the new Heideggerian formulation of 'original time'; similarly, its essential characteristics formulate ontology, the general metaphysics of Kant's concern. If we accept the rooting of ontology in the unifying transcendental imagination, we can then see the justification for Heidegger's contention that metaphysics can only be grounded in a Dasein-metaphysic, a systematic inquiry into the human mode of being-in-the-world and what it essentially involves. Such a metaphysic becomes a systematic delineation of the structure of human finitude; this foundation of metaphysical inquiry is, as Kant had suggested, the "metaphysics of metaphysics";[32] it is what Heidegger terms 'fundamental ontology,' the ground of the to-be as such in the human being, who asks the kinds of questions which we term metaphysical. As Heidegger explains it:

> The disclosure of the structure of the to-be of Dasein is ontology. So far as the ground of the possibility of metaphysics is established in ontology, the finitude of Dasein being its foundation, ontology signifies fundamental ontology.[33]

Just because the nature of Dasein is the source of all Dasein's ontological characterizations of the things that appear to it, its structure is foundational to any ontic discipline as well as to the nature of what it means to-be as such.

The Dasein-in-man is ontological (transcendental); it is in advance of any ontic event; as such it is apriori.[34] It is the constituent structure which permits and enables each one of us to be the kind of time-forming questioning beings we are. It broadens out transcendental imaginative synthesis from the restricted Kantian cognitive context to the whole operational mode of human nature of which cognition is but one aspect. This 'expansion' of the central human structure was indicated in the discussion of practical reason; it is, under this designation, carried to encompass the whole unity of an individual being. Heidegger is thus broadening Kant's problematic from the transcendental ground of human knowing to the transcendental foundation of human existing as such. The Dasein-in-man may be thus understood as the Kantian transcendental imagination broadened out and transformed into the defining operational structure of the unity of the whole man in his total comprehensive experiencing as a being-in-the-world in which he is.

As imaginative synthesis set the grounds for the be-ing of the objects in cognition, as well as of the mode of cognition itself, so it is in terms of a Dasein-analysis that Heidegger seeks to explicate the be-ing of objects in man's world as well as man's mode of relating to them. The essential unity of human cognition, pressed forward in the Kant interpretation, is transformed into the unity of the whole human being and the unified individual is seen as part of the world of concerns in which he finds himself.

In contrast to the implicit Kantian assumption that the categories were 'permanent' features of human cognition, Heidegger's Dasein-metaphysic is not conceived as a fixed doctrinal system; it calls for a continually dynamic process of re-reflection and reconstruction as our understanding of our own modes of be-ing changes: "metaphysics thus appears to us as an elan of questioning rather than as immobilization in a system." [35] The Kantian interrogation (of nature) which inspired the Copernican Revolution is thus brought into its own as something of a first principle of philosophical method.

Heidegger's one explicit starting point is "the transcendence of Dasein, namely being-in-the-world." [36] We are not concerned with the idle question of whether there is a world with which man deals; we recognize, at the outset, that we are already in a world of other people and of things. We find ourselves in activity, in the ways in which we relate to the world and the world to us.

The function of his detailed analytic is designed to unfold what this starting point involves, what follows from it.

As the Kantian cognitive structure grounded the be-ing of the object in the capacity of the knowing subject, so the relation between ourselves and the things-that-are for us is not reducible to a traditional subject-object dichotomy.[37] It is from Dasein's mode of be-ing, as from the elements of the synthesizing imagination, that the ontological grounds, of the things-that-are for us in our world, arise. Heidegger's analytic is to seek out not psychological description of human behavior but, following Kant's lead, an ontological (transcendental) investigation into the essential elements constituting the complex apriori structure of human ways of be-ing which are expressed in particular ontic activities.

As indicated, these various transcendental (ontologizing) characteristics are encompassed in the unifying structure of Concern; it is in terms of the comprehensive 'existential' of Concern, analogous to the unifying imaginative synthesis, that Heidegger sees the systematic expression of the Dasein-in-man, of the questioning being-within-the-world. Analogous again to imagination, Concern manifests itself as temporality. To understand the meaning of our way of be-ing *qua* time-forming temporality is *the* goal of fundamental ontology; as such it necessarily refers us again to the essential question of the meaning of 'to be,' which is always temporal for us. Time thus emerges as having a basic ontological status.

As historical beings who have the capacity to take up the lessons of what-has-been in human experience into their own, we should take cognizance of the way in which time was understood in the foundational period of classical thought. In the classical characterizations of the nature of time, we find that in the traditional distinction between the 'to-be' and 'beings,' the 'to-be' (*Sein*) was rendered as 'Being'; it was understood in terms of permanence, subsistence, an eternal present, an everlasting now. As such, 'Being' was understood from the outset in terms of temporal categories—as a "projection of 'Being' onto time." [38]

In the preceding discussion of Kant, references to the 'precursory,' or 'in advance,' or 'prior,' or 'anticipatory' nature of the transcendental or apriori were repeatedly designated as being used in a logical and not a temporal sense. This discrimination is somewhat at odds with Heidegger's rooting of the logical in the temporal, an outcome which he sees as rooted in Kant's Critique[39] but which is necessitated by the terms of ordinary linguistic usage in order to avoid misunderstanding.

Now that we approach his question concerning the ontological status of time itself, the 'To-Be' ('Being') of time, he raises the question of the 'why' of this usage which accords with our philosophic tradition and is embedded in our language. Why are references to apriori concepts repeatedly made by such essentially temporal terms as 'before,' 'prior to,' 'earlier than'? And why are we repeatedly reminding, as I have reminded, that these essentially temporal terms are not meant in anything but a figurative or metaphorical sense? Why do we persist in describing 'Being' in terms of time—as time-bound, or a-temporal, or beyond time, or time-less? 'Where is the ground for this spontaneous and self-evident understanding of the 'To-Be' ('Being') out of [or: in terms of] time'? [40]

The traditional delineation of time was based on the conception of 'Being' as permanence; the 'Being of time' was conceived, in one set of terms or another, in terms of the now. Even Kant tried to carry this on through the Copernican Revolution; as Heidegger points out, his delineation of time proceeded "from that character of time which in itself is constantly present and, hence, (in the ancient sense of the term) really *is*." [41] The nature of 'true Being' was then conceived as a continuing presence, "a permanent *now* conceivable only through time." [42]

Aristotle's characterization of time as the measure of motion has been taken as fairly axiomatic for most of our philosophic history. When we think about it, however, we can see even there an intimation that a source of time is in the mind of the measurer, the 'subjectivity of the subject'. Isn't this, Heidegger asks, possibly revealing concerning the ultimate source of the assessment of 'Being' in the essentially temporal characterization of 'permanence' —as that which 'always,' is, is 'at every time,' is present or conceived as necessarily being-present to anyone who would observe it at 'any time'?

If 'permanence' always is, it is now and in any now. Thus the now was implicitly taken as the temporal counterpart of a-temporality, as the abiding through change, as the change-less real. This essentially temporal nature of the notion of 'now' was suggested in the Kantian exegesis. Kant himself demonstrated that its inherent temporality is the schema of substance as "permanence of the real in time . . . itself non-transitory and abiding." [43]

This is to say that 'the understanding of the to-be in Dasein necessarily, as it were, projects the "to-be" onto time' [44] as its basic determination; we can only comprehend the meaning of what it is to-be, of 'Being,' in terms of time. Their relationship is so intertwined that even preconceptually we think of 'be-ing' and of 'time' as inseparable even when we claim to deny it—just as the Greeks did when they conceived the 'to be' (or 'Being') as that which is change-less and thereby time-less, as that which is then present at 'every time,' as an eternal and abiding now. Consciously or preconceptually, then, human thinking has always taken experiential time as its standpoint in every consideration of 'reality,' of 'Being,' of the things-that-are. In doing so it has postulated the essential nature of time as a series of moments, a sequence of nows. Untenable as this conception may be as basic, it is nevertheless revealing. For *implicitly,* I would add, it has pointed to the standpoint of primary experience as foundational in its temporal outlook: no matter how object-oriented the perspective may claim to be, the concept of 'now' is really meaningless without immediate reference to the experiencing of the speaker, the mind of the measurer, the subjectivity of the experiencing subject.

And the primacy of the now-sequence is untenable just because it does not accord with the authenticity of time-formation in primary experience. That it cannot be empirically foundational, that the now-sequence is essentially derivative from the ways in which we experience temporality in our primary experience, is a prime result of this reconsideration of Kant. Heidegger's re-reading of Kant has pointed beyond the now as the prime form of time. In place of the notion of disparate and nonexperiential now-points, it has urged the centrality of the integrating-present—that experiential presentation which joins the presently-possible-future and the presently-retrieved-what-has-been in a unified field of experience which encompasses the things-that-are which appear and the experiencing subject who permits them to appear in a interpretively selected temporal framework within which and by means of which he forms his experience and enables himself to be affected by it. Taken in this way, the traditional notion of time 'as the measure of motion' is certainly distortive if it is not regarded as wholly derivative; for the import of what Heidegger is saying is really the reverse: we use motion in order to measure the time of primary experience, the temporality which is the experiencing.

This re-reading of Kant, then, has also underlined the essential temporality of all be-ing, thought, and knowledge. Temporality, identified with transcendental imagination, emerges in Heidegger's analysis as the cognitive source of the "transcendental structure of Dasein as temporality." [45] Temporality is thus intrinsic to the structure in terms of which we function and manifest ourselves as human beings.

If all thinking is essentially temporal, then metaphysical thinking is necessarily temporal also. From the essentially historical nature of human thought, metaphysics arises as a retrieve of the question of the meaning of the to-be in terms of new perspectives. The goal of fundamental ontology, then, is to rekindle the insight —in its systematic elucidation of human thinking and acting— that all philosophical thinking is essentially temporal and time-forming. In the perspective of historical time, which arises from our modes of be-ing temporal, or from subjective temporality itself, the concepts of what it means 'to be' and of 'time' (as a derivative mode of measuring 'before and after') are fundamentally intertwined. In *Being and Time,* Heidegger thus seeks a more fundamental exploration of their meaning as revealed in those apriori categoreal existentials which seem to structure human existing in the context of which human thinking arises.

This dependence of human thought on the need to interpret and understand not only our own to-be but the idea of what it must mean to-be as such, in temporalist terms, is what can be regarded as the capsuled lesson of Kant's Critique. In effect Kant directed us to a more basic grounding of our everyday now-sequence conception of time. His preliminary doctrine, in the Aesthetic, described time as the prime form of intuition: alone, that would give it centrality as requisite not only for perception but as the catalytic framework for any conceptual synthesis (insofar as its representation provides the occasion for conceptual synthesis). The ultimate grounding of time emerged from its function as the transcendental foundation of all experience, as temporality, as our capacity to 'affect ourselves.' As such, it projects the conditions within which we enable ourselves to have any experience at all (and thereby to affect ourselves by that experience). Here is the heart of the essential unity of knowledge which Kant had sought: it unites perception and pure apperception and the understanding in the unity of the constitutive structure of pure sensible reason. It is no longer, then, merely the preliminary doctrine of the Aesthetic. Triune time-forming temporality grounds the possibility of knowledge out of the functioning of transcendental imaginative synthesis as the expression of Concern; as foreshadowed in the temporalization of practical reason, it grounds Concern itself as the capacity to seek knowledge, to pursue ends, to evaluate alternatives, to achieve and to be the possibility of an integrated living acting self, to be a person in a world whose meaning is framed for him by the temporal outlook he brings to it. That we are unable in our finitude to understand what it means to-be except in terms of temporality and time attests to its fundamental ontological centrality for us.

If we are, in the Kantian spirit, to interrogate nature and, in Heidegger's, to interrogate man; if we are to conduct such interrogation systematically and with understanding of what we are doing, we must do so as temporal beings who can anticipate the answers and their possibility. From Kant's First Critique, Heidegger has extracted a ground for anticipating the nature of time and temporality—as the mode of be-ing a human person. He has proceeded by an essentially internal critique, which sought to develop Kant's own reasoning further than Kant had done. He has pursued questions which he sees Kant as having raised but not having pursued far enough. The prime question he extracts is that of the nature and be-ing of time. The anticipated answer, which requires an existential analysis for its fuller development, is that time is pervasive in our experience of our being-in-a-world of other people and of things, that the temporal is the foundational 'category' of all that is meant when we pride ourselves on being human.

VIII

Retrospect

As we come to the end of this philosophic journey we look back and see that we have come a long way. We have passed through strange territory and find ourselves encamped in a new land. Many of the new perspectives seem hardly reminiscent of what we have been used to; before venturing out to explore them further it is well to consider the road just traveled. Before we can discern the new paths now open before us, we must be clear as to where we have been guided and just how we arrived here.

If one concedes any plausibility to arguments marking the road on which Heidegger has taken us, he must acknowledge the legitimacy of the starting point. Despite any reservations concerning the ways we have come, we must concede that this road, rocky and untraveled as it may be, has indeed led from Kant's analytic to Heidegger's.

We may look back on this unaccustomed route with some measure of incredulity and with wonderment: why the choice of this rough route instead of the broad and traveled highways leading from the same Kant in other directions all different from this one? We think back and, perhaps, remark that somehow the 'old' Kant had never before seemed quite like this. Why hadn't the possibility of this road from Kant been seen before? And why travel it? What is to be gained from the special effort? What makes it important?

Kant had seen the functioning experience of time as the center of cognitional synthesis; Heidegger has transformed it into the experiential center of human existing. In this light, we should reconsider this philosophic journey. We should, first, be clear about the temporalist problem Kant bequeathed which necessitated a new departure. We should quickly re-survey the landmarks we have passed. Finally, we should note some of the new philosophic perspectives which Heidegger has opened up for us by his journey from Kant.

1 · *Reluctant Temporalism*

THE IRONY posed by Immanuel Kant is precisely that focus on time which he brought into philosophy. Having discerned the requisite of time for all cognition, he made it the keystone of the structure of experience and promptly turned to adorning the columns of the arch it held together. He discerned its necessity, took it thereafter largely for granted, put it to use, and pursued it no further.

Kant's initial datum was awareness of the temporal context involved in even the most rudimentary experience. His thorough and often brilliant analysis of just what and how much this intrinsic temporality portends demonstrates the pervasiveness of time in the organization of human experience. Yet, the nature of this time remained virtually unexplored. Like a *deus ex machina* invoked to explain what could not be otherwise explicated, time was utilized as the keystone of the arch, pointed and referred to as the requisite center of the entire structure, but left rough-hewn and ignored in its own right.

When all is said and done, the Kantian arch of cognition, held together by its temporal keystone, appears as a solid, intricate, but static construction which barely indicates the temporal dynamicity implicit in its central and crucial segment. Most critics and commentators seem to have overlooked this unique Kantian discovery, this keystone of temporality. At first, this seems incomprehensible. Something is seriously wrong. Dewey's observation that there is nothing "temporal and historical in the Kantian machinery" [1] points to the heart of the problem.

Kant never seems to have come to terms with the time he saw

as the animating heart of human experience. It remains, in the end, not the pulsating heart of the dynamic being, but an abstract logical function which is continually pointed to as a necessary presupposition—as the keystone of a marble arch that endures. When we see this we can understand why those who have discussed Kant's work have so often not felt it incumbent to take the experience of time as seriously as its central place in the Kantian edifice suggests. His working conception of time has been criticized on a number of counts, and it comes as no surprise to find one of his prime commentators conclude that his conception of time "is the most vulnerable tenet in his whole system."[2] The reason may well be that the nature of time was not really what he saw himself setting out to determine.

A prime motive for the Critique was the grounding of the new scientific knowledge of things by the new Newtonian physics. In order to justify the objectivity of that system of 'non-transitory' laws of nature's operational procedures which the new science was bringing to light, Kant's analytic procedure was a 'vertical' slice-through of experience (as one cuts down through a layer cake) in order to determine the requisite structure of *what* is experienc*ed*. His categories, then, were primarily geared to what was presumed to be the structure of the experienc*ed* things as such. Implicitly taking the scientific structuring of the content of experience as given, his appointed task was to transplant it into the *cogito* inherited from Descartes. His working conception of time, then, comes not from an examination of the time of the subject's experienc*ing* but from the ordered structure of what is experienc*ed at any time*—the invariable laws in terms of which the content of experience is rendered intelligible regardless of the *when* of the particular cognizing act concerning it. The working conception of time is thus not the 'temporal flow' of the subject's inner sense but the requisite of a constructed unalterable ordered succession in what is experienc*ed*. Hence, the working conception of time, as distinguished from the doctrine of time, usually appears to be the sequential relationships of events (as formulated in the Analogies) rather than the time of pure intuition, of the synthesizing imagination, of the experiencing *cogito* or 'I think' invoked in its name as its ground.

[248]

But, in addition to justifying the new science, Kant was determined to ground morality also together with the freedom which it presupposes. The kind of time he derived from the causal sequence of scientifically understood events foreclosed the possibility of reconciliation with the self as an autonomous source of causal acts and thereby as temporally operative. Just because a normative ethic requires a 'spread' of futurity stretching ahead of any present moment, the knife-edge of the now-sequence cannot sustain the abiding-across-nows of the moral acting self. Consequently, the kind of time formulated in response to the first motive was at odds with that required for the second. As a consequence, Kant found himself constrained to postulate the ground of moral freedom in a somehow timeless noumenal self, just as he found it necessary to postulate the self of pure apperception in cognition as somehow distinct from the self revealed in inner sense as the knower of the 'external world.'

This dichotomous description of the self is curious in at least two ways relevant to the present concern. First, it suggests human action under a dual kind of causal-temporal order: as beings in the world which appears in time we are subject to cause-and-effect sequential determination and are not free; as noumenal we are somehow non-temporal but also somehow free causative agents in the phenomenal and rigorously determinist time-world. How these two aspects of the self are to be made intelligible, functionally related, or identified is never really made clear. The second and perhaps greater curiosity is the detemporalization of a normative ethic. However normative moralities may differ—in method, values, or doctrine—they are essentially future-oriented and time-bound and presuppose as a *sine qua non* some kind of temporal realism in which the moral agent is operative. If time is sheer illusion for my moral self, I cannot talk meaningfully about any ought; if time is nothing but an eternalized now, any change would be impossible. Whatever else may be called for, it would seem clear that some notion of the ultimate reality of time, *qua* related to the moral self, is a necessary condition for any imperative. That Kant implicitly recognized this would seem clear from the fact that an important argument he advanced in developing his moral doctrine is the human inability to foresee, with any certainty, the *future* consequences of a present act.[3] If one were to excise every temporal word, and especially every futural connotation, from Kant's moral writing, what is left would be near meaningless. This is to say that, despite the curious ontological framework he proposed for morality, he implicitly recognized the requirement for the reality of the temporal ground and the priority of futurity within it.

Whether developed on the cognitive or the moral level, it thus appears that the conception of time with which Kant found himself working created a problem of the nature of the self—in which he had planted the conditions of knowledge and the nature of time—which effectively subverts the structure he so laboriously built. If there can be no change in the real self, if that self which is the root of the 'I think' or the 'I will' as its principle of unity must remain wholly unaffected by its experience or by its creating the possibility of that experience, that real self becomes wholly irrelevant. If my own true self must remain "free from all influence of sensibility,"[4] if it cannot be affected by its own acts, cognitions, or judgments concerning the world appearing to it, my own self must remain totally ignorant of its own acts of cognition, of will, of serving as the ground of either. Any such awareness would constitute a change in my mental life and is subject to time determination in inner sense; if it is to remain totally unchanged and unaffected by its own activity, it must remain completely independent from that activity. This consideration is reminiscent of Aristotle's reasoning in restricting the thinking of his unchanging God to a 'thinking on thinking.' Perhaps the only other analogue to Kant's real self that is available is—not Plato's 'soul' (whose state in reincarnation was affected by its comportment on entering time) but—the Platonic Idea for which time and change did not exist and which was non-personal and non-conscious. Yet Kant's apparent motive for forbidding the real self to enter time is precisely that the sequential time of the now-succession forecloses the possibility of that reality of an abiding self which is presupposed in the experience it creates, enjoys, and by which it is thereby affected.

We can then see why Kant's failure to examine the conception of time, which he took for granted, confuses the structure and subverts it. For, however derived and however conceived, Kant planted time and our knowledge of time in the self, in the only aspect of that self which we are permitted to know. But if that time which provides the binding structure, the keystone of the cognitive arch, and the ground upon which that arch is standing, is itself unstable, then the entire arch is hopelessly insecure. Accept the *cogito* as the ground of experience, and the nature of the self which pronounces the crucial 'I think' is decisive. Yet as he left it, he failed to integrate the capacities of the self for pure, judgmental, and practical reason, will, desire, conscience, sensibility, imagination, and appreciation—which he saw as ways in which were manifested the equally unintegrated portraits of the transcendental and empirical egos, the knowing and acting selves which were themselves grounded in the essentially unreconciled two strata of the real.[5] In all of these ways he had seen the self disclosing its own be-ing but in each aspect he maintained a dichotomous division, which he never succeeded in bridging, so as to account for the *one self* that manifests itself in so many ways.

Crucial to the entire Kantian outlook is the moral distinction between 'persons' and 'things.' The central paradox is that Kant sought to ground time, as crucial to the person's knowledge of things, in the essential subjectivity of the person; but the time he planted there is the constructed time of the things knowledge 'speaks' about. Finding this kind of time incongruous with the nature of the person whose knowledge he had sought to guarantee, he found no alternative but to remove the person somehow from the time he projected as the condition of the knowledge he sought; the consequent is to insist on the necessary ignorance of the cognizing person in order to salvage his reality or being. For turning away from the primacy of this thing-time before it destroyed the autonomy of the cognizing and acting self, we can hardly blame him.

Yet, when all is said and done, Kant had discovered the permeating presence of *some kind* of temporality in the structure of our knowledge. We may criticize his derivation of his notion of time, point out the difficulties it created for him and, as we accept his insight into the subjective ground of cognition, for ourselves as well. Despite all criticisms we can offer and any hesitations he may have revealed, we must welcome his pioneering insight into the centrality of time in any inquiry we may pursue.

But, granted this epoch-making discovery, why was he so hesitant to pursue it? Why did he accept this rather impossible detemporalization of the self rather than pursue the examination of that time he had discovered as the prime ingredient and precipitating agency of all our knowledge and cognitional processes?[6] Why did he turn away from that time which he saw to be the keystone of the entire cognitional structure?

His reluctance to develop the Schematism and the Subjective Deduction—where, in the Kantian framework, the nature of time *qua* the time of the person would be revealed—is difficult to understand. For, as Kemp Smith observed, he left us at the end "with only three forms of experience—experience of self, experience of objects, and experience of time. The two former are open to question." They are problematic; but our experience of time, Kant's initial datum, is beyond question. What its 'essence' is may be debatable but that we are aware of it, that it is the one pervasive certainty, is the Kantian insight: for "consciousness of time is the *factual* experience, as conditions of whose possibility the apriori factors are transcendentally proved."[7]

Despite his discovery of the centrality of time, he seems to have been unhappy and ill at ease with it. Perhaps the rationalism which nurtured him had a hold that he could not or would not give up. Or perhaps he could not come to terms with the only conception of time he knew, a time that could not ground the cognitive and moral selves in the unity of the living person.

We find this temporal bifurcation of the self, and the turning away from the temporal priority, in the distinction between knowledge that is *merely* historical from the non-temporal purely rational.[8] The fact that we are not unchangeable is regretted.[9] Hopefully, he anticipates that period when 'we shall be freed from dependence on historical knowledge and empirical determinations and be ruled by nothing more than reason itself.'[10] *

The reluctance before the dynamic contingency of time, its

---

* Lessing's assertion, in its pathos and revealing confession, seems to epitomize Kant's own personal stance: "Contingent truths of history can never prove necessary truths of reason. That is the horrible wide ditch which I cannot cross, often and earnestly as I have made the spring."[11]

magnetic attraction and the resistance to it, combine to form the underlying subjective dynamic which gives the Critical inquiry, as a whole, the life it has. The Preface to the B Edition (in which the import of time is diminished as it is more explicitly invoked) speaks of "that notable characteristic of our nature, never to be capable of being satisfied by what is temporal." [12] The temporal is the unknown, the unstable, the changeable, the locus of our hopes and our fears, the ultimate definition of our finitude. The hope—albeit futural—remains Platonic, the entry into the company of the gods, the vision of unchanging Truth, the eternality of the perpetual now.

Kant took us to the discovery of the central reality of time for us. But he was unable to explore what he had come upon. He took with him in his discovery the inherited notion of time as the burden, the mark of frustrating limitation. Unable to temporalize his experiencing self as the creator of its experiential possibilities in a causal sequence of disparate nows, he sought liberation from the slavery of now-time in order to find his own true self in an eternity.

But apparently he saw beyond the limitations of his own perspective; for the time he discovered in us, the time we project, and in the framework of which we achieved knowledge and self-fulfillment is itself the mode of personal liberation in the perspective of the possible. From Kant's construction of the essential nature of knowledge, from the transcendental focus on conditioning possibility, from the insightful analysis of practical reason, we can see that he laid the ground for that positivity of freedom which sets out time not as a chain to be broken but as an offering of opportunity to be realized, of possibilities to be achieved, of fulfillment in which the selves we are may find themselves.

2 · From Kant to Heidegger

IN EXAMINING Kant's temporalism, it is easy to forget that this discovery itself took place in a temporal context. His own statement was thus conditioned and qualified by the concerns he shared with his contemporaries.

Kant would not have been human had he not taken something

of the old with him, defended himself in terms of his own contemporary context of discussion, or failed to foresee all the implications of the new insights he had achieved. Even the most systematic and dispassionate study is, in a historical context, something of a polemic; it is then fair to expect that corrective features of the new perspective may be overstated, unnecessary burdens from the past may be retained, and the controversial nature of points not central to what is conceived as the revolutionary new thesis may be deliberately or unconsciously minimized. For this reason a later consideration may more clearly reveal the significance of a pioneering thinker than he was able to do. As Kant himself observed in writing of Plato:

> it is by no means unusual, upon comparing the thoughts which an author has expressed in regard to his subject, whether in ordinary conversation or in writing, to find that we understand him better than he understood himself. As he has not sufficiently determined his concept, he has sometime spoken, or even thought, in opposition to his own intention.[13]

The central issue for Kant was the Copernican Revolution. Heidegger has started here; he has proceeded on the implicit thesis that 'Kant had not sufficiently determined his concept of time and consequently had often thought in opposition to his own intention.'

Kant's prime definition of time is that it is the form of inner sense, of pure intuition. He never retreated from this but expanded upon it. The significance of this opening thesis, and the subsequent elaboration of its meaning, provided Heidegger with the principle determining his field of focus; he has sought to take this basic Kantian insight into the fundamental priority of time, as a subjective condition imposed by the self, to deeper ground than Kant was able to do.

Heidegger began with the thesis that knowledge presupposes the synthetic union of sensory reports of particular presentations with interpretive concepts arising spontaneously from the understanding within the self. The resultant cognition is thus not reducible to the merely passive reception of particular presentations although they constitute its originating source. Beginning with these perceptual impressions which are received by the self, by its own necessary fiat as temporal, the human mind integrates them with temporalized concepts into meaningful cognition. This integration is effected by an imaginative synthesis of the sensory report and the intellectual concept by means of the one universal characteristic they both manifest, amenability to temporal form.

This human cognition, rooted in the human capacity to produce it, bears the limitations intrinsic to what that cognitional capacity can do. In order for this product of cognitional synthesis of percept and concept to be knowledge and not illusion, the human mind is able to ascribe ontological counterparts of its own transcendental modes of knowing as valid characterizations of the things it knows. This means that, basic to our ability to have knowledge and for things to be known insofar as they are known, there is requisite a mutual amenability to the establishment of a functional relationship within the binding form of time. The activation of the possibilty for these elements to be brought together in a cognitional act is effected by the synthesizing power of imagination. In effecting such a synthesis of percept and concept in a cognitional act, time is manifested by the imagination as the center of our way of cognizing.

Our way to know is to know *qua* temporal; temporality is thus involved in any cognition. The priority of the temporal, revealed by Kant in his analysis of the 'how' of our knowledge, was developed in the Deduction and made explicit in the Schematism; it is augmented by Heidegger in the interpretation of the Deduction, the priority of the Schematism, the insistence on the Highest Principle, the recasting of the ethic, the sensibilization of concepts and the temporalization of the human self. To-be, then, is not only to-be-in-time for objects; our own to-be is also essentially temporal. The temporality imposed by intuition thus emerges as the meeting place of percept and object, of my 'I think' and the object I think about; for the object to-be for me, it must be represented in my thought, in my inner sense; and my thinking must meet it as and when it comes into my awareness as temporally marked appearance to be understood as such.

In order for this temporality to function as Kant portrayed its functioning, it cannot be constituted as a sequence of knife-edge nows. That traditional view of basic time thus emerges as a vestigial remain from a pre-Critical metaphysic, which took its cues from the supposed independence of things-as-such and not from the ways in which we must apprehend their appearing to us within the limitations marking the manner in which we are able to respond to their being.

As Kant had shifted the center of ontological description from presumably outer things to the subjective ground of human cognition, so Heidegger has argued that insofar as this human cognition is pervasively temporal and time-forming, it, too, must find its center in that same subjective cognitive ground. However we may project and utilize the construction of an unalterable dating of the things we know for public communication, our consciousness of time arises from the temporal modes integrally expressed in the imaginative synthesis from which any particular cognition must arise.

In any specific act of cognition, the three distinguishable modes of perceptual time are brought together into a unified focus on the problem or situation before us; this present situation is itself not a point but a field in which the what-is-as-having-been, the what-is-as-can-be and the what-is-as-presenting-itself can all join together in the interpretive awareness that we call cognition. Without derogation of the import of either the 'present' or the 'past,' the emphasis is emphatically shifted to the element of futurity. This futural priority in temporal synthesis most clearly marks Heidegger's original contribution to the development of a philosophy of time.

This priority of futurity has been explicitly extracted from the Kantian inquiry in terms of the conceptual aspect of cognitive synthesis. A concept is essentially a futural referent because it is predictive and prescriptive. Even in terms of a now-sequence, it defines the limitations on any possible presentation in any future now. As transcendental time determination, it states essential characteristics which must be perceivable in any entity before that entity can enter our future experience; it marks out the realm of what is experientially possible for us. What cannot accord with the temporalized concepts comprising our schema of interpretive tools cannot be included in any future we may reasonably anticipate.

[256]

Likewise, our empirical concepts delimit the realm of future experience: as long as my concept 'horse' does not include horns, I know that a horned horse is not a possible object of my future experience.

This suggests that any concept is ontically predictive. A concept is a rule specifying how characteristics may be related to each other in terms of a possible 'embodiment'; it sets out essential 'attributes' by which I may recognize and verify its relevance to an object appearing before me. As such, a concept includes a criterion for verification, for evaluating its applicability. If I am told that brown cows are grazing in the field and I see brown animals that are not cows, I know that the concept 'cow' does not apply because its constituent elements do not describe the kind of 'embodiment' before me. But if the concept 'horse' does apply, I correct the statement and excuse its maker for conceptual confusion. If, however, those 'horses' start to climb trees or feast on a carcass in their midst, I would again revise my judgment about applicability, because a concept describes not only what its 'embodiment' looks like but also *the kinds of acts it performs,* what kind of *behavior* I can reasonably anticipate from the kind of animal to which the concept 'horse' does rightfully apply. 'Tree climbing' or 'meat eating' are not included in my concept of 'horse'; my likely response to such a spectacle would be "what kind of an animal is it which looks like a horse but doesn't *behave* like one?"

A concept is not something, however, Heidegger emphasizes, which 'waits' in a not-yet future. The concept *is* present *qua* future possibilities. It is essentially involved in my present cognitional act. It enables my thinking to look ahead to what it does and does not portend. Under its futural arrows, I am empowered to interpret the present presentation and invoke the relevant what-is-as-having-been in my experience ('do I now recall ever having seen tree-climbing horses?'). In terms of the concept and because of the concept, I regard the object before me as offering a nest of reasonable expectations, a limited range of behavioral patterns, a number of uses to which I can put it and thereby the kind of significance or meaning I see it as portraying.

Whether in transcendental or empirical terms, Heidegger has

elicited his reinterpretation of the manifestation of time in the triune cognitive synthesis as dominated by its future conceptualizing mode.*

Two additional grounds, deriving from Kant, have been suggested in the foregoing discussions for arriving at this same priority of futurity:

1. In strictly Kantian terms, the functioning of imaginative synthesis has been left with the serious gap of omitting any principle by which certain empirical concepts are incorporated into that synthesis instead of others. By what principle does my imagination select one concept for my 'recognition' of an object instead of another? If I am buying a dog, I may ask if it barks very loudly; but if I am buying a stuffed dog or a living canary, the concept of barking would appear ludicrous. Although Heidegger does not appear to discuss this problem of the gap in Kant's cognitive synthesis, his 'category' of Concern supplies it and thus provides the missing transcendental principle for empirical concept selection, a futural principle by which imaginative synthesis invokes future-referring concept A together with past recollection A and not future-and-past D or M or Z.

Any particular presentation can be interpreted in terms of a variety of interpretive predictive concepts. Which one(s) do I choose? This choice among available concepts is made in terms of my present interest. But my present interest is, again, futurally referent. What is the problem with which I approach this object? What is my end-in-view for which its usefulness is considered? In what frame of reference am I operating when the object comes into my perspective? Which is to say that I invoke those concepts —all future in reference—in terms of my 'concern' of the moment. I use these available concepts, as I use tools, to discern the relevance of what appears before me in terms of a possibility I want to pursue. The 'combined interests of my reason,' my 'concern' in a

---

* In developing the significance of the conceptual element in that synthesis, there is a radical shift: Kant had pointed it to a kind of non-temporal rationalistic ground of intelligibility, whereas Heidegger has shown that for cognitive conceptualization itself to be intelligible, it must not only buttress but also enter into and help to form the time of pure intuition. In contrast, then, to all kinds of Platonism, Heidegger has effectively argued that intelligibility, far from involving any escape from temporality, necessarily is permeated by it.

particular situation, the kind of as-yet-unobtained resolution I seek out of a problem constitute a futural orientation in terms of which I approach the content of any presentational field.

2. If we accept Heidegger's temporalization of the human self and of practical reason or his 'category' of Concern, we are, in effect, accepting the primacy of Kant's practical reason, identified with will and volition, as prior to and undergirding theoretical or cognitive reasoning. That this is consistent with the futural reference of concepts (and Concern) seems apparent.

In each of these distinguishable ways of grounding the priority of futurity, there is to be found the thesis that present interpretive awarenesses, i.e., cognitions, are necessarily structured in terms of a future which is not yet but is nevertheless presently crucial as possibility that is conceived as genuine. This is to say that cognition as such, limited within possible experience as Kant described it, has as its concern the determination of those particular possibilities which are presently open to it in the light of the concerns and the interests of the individual knower.

Kant had taken Descartes' bare *cogito* and transformed it into the self of a living being which was to be described in terms of certain distinctions: on a cognitive level, between the 'I think' and the representations of objects in the thinking; on an operational level, between thought and sense; on the rational level, between moral reason and understanding; on the ontological level, between the noumenal and phenomenal sides of its nature. In each of these dichotomous divisions, (now-)time was the principle of separation and discrimination. Heidegger has done little more than to continue insistence on seeing the one person as a unified act of be-ing thus rendering these Kantian dichotomies as nothing more than analytic distinctions which may be useful as mere tools for comprehending aspects of the kind of a self each one of us is. The human self which emerges from this development of thought is a unified being who is to be discerned within the continuing situation of 'his world,' in which he functions as a creative center of interpretive experience. This functioning is the continuing activity in which he manifests and brings forth the individual being he is; his continuum of activity is marked by his moving focus of triune temporal synthesis, which he 'embodies' within his field of attention; he is moved in its moving focus by the rational interests and concerns which he projects and by the volitional synthesis he formulates from the possibilities he sees as presented to him.

The empiricism that stimulated Kant had interpreted ideas in terms of the sensory experiences which presumably had produced them; Kant grounded them in the possibility which allowed them to arise. Heidegger carries this development forward by seeing the source of our ideas not in what has been or in what is but in the future *qua* a 'beckoning' of temporal possibilities. These are interpreted by the knowing being, who is assessing the presentation before him, in terms of the present meaning of his possible future and in the light of presently remembered experiences selected as relevant to those possibilities of the future.

The individual present is not a point; it is a temporal spread of interpretive synthesis, a dynamic spread which brings into the present presentation, by imaginative thinking, the future possibility it presently incorporates and the past experience which helps to verify it. In the traditional language of traditionally conceived but (in the light of Heidegger's explication) actually constructed time, the future brings the past into any perceptual 'now' so that that 'now' can be discriminated, its import for action evaluated, its content understood, and the experience itself discussed with others.

3 · *The Perspective of Futurity*

"ALL STATEMENTS ordinarily made about time seem to imply that time is something which we know it is not, and make assumptions about it which we know to be untrue." [14] This sage observation by Collingwood points out well the problem Kant raised by identifying time, as the objective serial order of events, with the time of our subjectively apprehended experience of them.

Heidegger avoids this confusion between the time of things and the time of our apprehendings by his thesis, in full fidelity to the principle of the Copernican Revolution, that thing-time is a derivative construction from the primacy of subjective experience. In developing his analysis, he has remained on essentially Kantian ground and rejected specific doctrines as he saw them in conflict with the Critical outlook. He has, therefore, not really discussed time as such, events as such; he has spoken of time only insofar as it is manifested as an aspect, albeit the crucial aspect, of human experiencing. In examining the nature of time *qua* operative in that immediate apprehending of sensory reports from which both trace all cognition, Heidegger has effectively argued that to reduce this experiential time to a line of now-points is to make 'an assumption that we know to be untrue.'

Heidegger's entire discussion—and to insist on this is to forestall a number of misunderstandings—is within the Kantian priority of the internality or subjectivity of the grounds enabling, limiting, and prescribing the conditions confining human knowledge. He has presumed the Kantian framework wherein 'empirical reality' is a reality of experience designed and structured by an apriori transcendental idealism. Basic to every point he has made is this fundamental Kantian thesis: the 'is' of any assertion is only within the context of human thought; 'objects' = 'objects for us,' 'things' = 'things as we can perceive them,' 'time' = 'our form of constituting and relating those entities which appear in our temporalizing outlook.' Every statement referring to the 'external world' has been implicitly prefixed by some qualification such as a 'for us' or a 'within our (possible) cognition.'

Within this context he has accepted a second Kantian thesis as well, that the human mind is in some sense a free causal agent. In cognitive terms it makes an essential contribution to its own knowledge. Dependent though it is on the sensory report to activate a cognitional act and to have something to cognize about, human cognition is not to be reduced to mere awareness of passive sensory-report reception. A cognitional act is a dynamic interpretive synthesis of that report of what appears and the transcendental forms and categories in terms of which that appearance is structured, related, made intelligible, understood.

He thus starts from the essentially Kantian assumption that "man's essence is completely inseparable from the world in which it finds itself";[15] both the human mind and the world-as-experienced are presupposed in any interpretive act. Both insist that knowledge only arises in a context—for Kant, the context of the transcendental modes of interpretive knowing of appearances; for Heidegger, the context of the transcendental modes by which the essence of being a whole man, not merely a cognizing being, is manifested.

Beginning with Kant's own formulation, he has tried to unify the Kantian dichotomies: in human terms, the Kantian distinction between a world of knowledge and a world of activity; in temporal terms, the Kantian distinction between our consciousness of succession and the succession of the states of our consciousness. This unity of consciousness has served as his prime interpretive tool. The unity of conciousness has been taken as essential just because it is requisite to having any kind of connected experience in which discrete perceptions are brought into relationship; reduced to discrete successive apprehensional states, the mind would be unable to relate one moment to the next, one content to another. Instead of Kant's virtual abandonment of the Critical enterprise by his postulation of 'substance' as the mode of connection (as the *external* 'permanent in time'), Heidegger has grounded this necessary unity of the whole person and his experience in that prime 'category' of time in which Kant had originally lodged every human thought or awareness. In examining the nature of this experiential time, Heidegger has urged that it is, as temporality, in some sense at least, the 'form' of the self; as such it cannot be manifested merely in discrete moments; thereby, the traditional primacy of the now-succession is groundless. As the 'form' of the self, temporality must reflect or ground the unity of the one self that serves as a unified center of experiencing.

To 'look' at the time of my experiencing, as contrasted with the time of the things experienced, is to place a priority on that interpretive mode which is necessarily a dynamic continuum irreducible to a line of discrete now-points and which expresses the out-look of the subject, viz., the mode of future-past-present (as distinguished from the object-oriented mode of before-and-after). The usual transliteration of the now-point conception of time into this subjective out-look is to focus on the so-called present *qua* the momentary now before me. Heidegger has argued that effectively this is still object-oriented, that the focus need be shifted to futurity in order to comprehend the unified mode of activity of a unified experiencing human being. We function in terms of concerns, purposes, goals, intentions, anticipations, desires: looking-out from the 'interior' of a person means that the prime out-look is always essentially futural: the out-look is always essentially forward to what is yet to come, to what is not yet but is now seen as what can be. This means that it is from out-look in thought—from my forward-looking perspective—that I render something as present to me as my thinking recognizes the selected content of a presentational field as 'embodying' certain possibilities I bring to what is before me from my vision of what can be. The object before me is seen by me as present to me under the 'light' of the possibilities I see it as 'offering' in terms of a possible future which I want to achieve or avoid. Insofar as the presentation is thus 'lighted' by the possibilities which I focus upon it, I also bring to present awareness past experiences that are relevant to these possibilities and bring them, too, into this light under which I discern the object before me.

This is to say that, like a dual searchlight in the dark, my out-look picks out objects to recognize as the 'lights' of possibility-of-interest to me and of past experience deemed relevant to it focus on it. My present is not then primary; it is primarily formed by future possibilities which interest me and which, by an act of thinking, I bring into a time-spread which, in a non-point sense, I might call a 'now' as constituted in terms of future-past-present.

Analogously to a good camera, I can only experience (photograph) what appears before me: within the field of vision my focus is drawn to a variety of different objects as the mechanism of the camera permits. Within a field of vision, some particular object arouses my attention in terms of its response to some interest of mine; it becomes my object of focus as it stands out against the background formed by the rest of the scene. The object stands out against its background for me just because it seems to embody some conceptual description of interest, exemplify the denotation of a conceptual prediction, suggest possibilities relevant to my interest or concern; it 'offers' certain possible uses, experiences, satisfactions, relevant to my defining interest. The depth-of-field of the camera is adjusted—thus determining how much of the

[263]

background (the past against which the object stands out as a center of focus) is directly related to my interest in the object and how much is merely distracting and should be blurred out. Having selected in the perspective of (future-referring) interest (a) the object of focus and (b) the degree of relevant background, I adjust the camera in terms of the available light (providing the horizon of possibility for the picture itself) so that shutter speed and lens opening integrate all these considerations into the synthesis effected in the 'I think' click of the shutter button, which exposes the film and 'takes' the picture. The resulting good photograph, like a sound cognition, does not suggest a representational dualism as much as an interpretive report of a deliberately selected aspect of the presentational field. What renders that field, as the camera records it, 'present' to the 'film' (the conscious cognizing awareness) is precisely this synthesis of temporally defined considerations manifested in the various camera settings which enable this particular picture to have been taken.

From this kind of reinterpretation of experiential time, Heidegger looks to two conceptually distinct 'categories' with which it is intrinsically involved. From the perspective of this essentially temporal out-look, which is always forward-seeking, future-oriented, the sometimes baffling notions of 'possibility (*Möglichkeit*)' and 'non-thingness (*Nichts*)' emerge into a new light of comprehension.

If futurity in any sense 'creates' or essentially constitutes that cognitive synthesis of 'what is present,' it does so in terms of the 'possible.' It cannot do so from the fleeting knife-edge of the actual now because a discrete now is, in itself, inherently unintelligible. My selection of what is before me for focus and my understanding of the meaning which I take it to suggest are in terms of the 'why' of my interest with which I approach it, in terms of the possibilities I see 'suggested' or 'embodied' as genuine in the presentation itself.

How then is possibility to be related to actuality? Kant had defined the possible as that "which agrees with the formal conditions of experience, that is, with the conditions of intuition of the concepts." [16] Possibility, therefore, would seem to take a priority before actuality; for possibility, corresponding to the whole area of 'possible experience,' is the defining limitation within which those things that are actual and necessary must be confined: for the actual is that which is "bound up with the material conditions of experience" [17] and the necessary is connected with it. Insofar as any cognition arises from the synthesis of intuition, in the form of time, and from apriori concepts, it would seem that the actual and the necessarily-actual derive from the broader area denominated as the possible.[18]

But, as foreshadowed in the Schematism, Kant explicitly declined to follow this through.[19] The B Edition but emphasized the thesis that time must be represented as a line of now-points[20] and the distinction between the 'possible' and the 'actual' was effectively reduced to one of temporal sequence. The 'actual' was identified with the determinate and necessary; it refers to what 'is' (or 'was'), and the 'possible' then becomes merely another name for the equally determinate (if not determin*able* by finite human cognition) 'will be.' The only apparent reason for his use of 'possible' instead of 'future actuality' thus seems to have been our limited ability to foresee the particular future causal effects of present things and events. But if this is all that was really meant by 'possible experience,' the whole tenor of this meaning would have been better conveyed by using from the outset the more accurate and less ambiguous '(probable) future actuality.' Heidegger is quite right in maintaining that when Kant spoke of the 'real' or 'existent,' he did so in the sense of identification with the actual,[21] that whatever Kant may have implied in his formulation, he retained in his doctrine the traditional priority of actuality before possibility.

But the priority of the actual is the priority of the now; it is derived from the experienc*ed,* not from the experienc*ing.* What is actual is now; what is not yet actual is either possible or not-possible (a distinction which Kant had described as the highest concept underlying transcendental philosophy).* In the actual

---

* Note that Kant regarded the distinction between the "possible and the impossible" as the supreme ground concept of any transcendental philosophy; but he suggested as his own contribution to the development of transcendental philosophy the priority of the concept of the transcendental object, "the concept of an object in general" regardless of "whether it is something or nothing" [*ob er Etwas oder Nichts sei*].' [22]

functioning of my temporal out-look, a range of alternative possibilities is present to me now as 'actual possibilities,' in the same sense as memory is also actual for me. The point of distinction is the matter of determination: in contrast to the now or the past the specific content of the future is, for finite human minds at least, not determinable.

In the identification of the actual with the now in which it is presumably perceived, the same argument concerning the essentially illusory nature of the now can be extended to the myth of moving across the knife-edge of momentary actuality. If actuality is merely the content of the specious present now, it shares that same speciousness. The actual and the now would seem to be reciprocal concepts which necessarily go hand in hand. The distinction between them is that the actual refers to the content of the now-perception (as 'ontological'), and the now claims to characterize the perceiving out-look itself (as subjective or transcendental).

Both seem wholly out of keeping with the Kantian subjective ground of all cognition; both appear as essentially derived from a pre-Critical metaphysics which claimed competence regarding things-in-themselves. If one has no place within the Critical context, neither does the other. The thesis concerning the priority of the actual is an object-priority: what my pencil can do is constituted by the nature of what it actually is. But the pencil only enters my experience *qua* pencil as I regard it as embodying a real or genuine possibility for me. The priority of the actual emerges from the assertion of a causal-metaphysic that 'something cannot come out of nothing'; but for a 'thing' to be cognized as a 'thing' it must first be represented by me in terms of the kind of temporal determinations which Kant had portrayed as the grounds permitting any entity to become an object for me. If Heidegger's interpretation of the conceptual element of the cognitive synthesis has any validity, that transcendental time-determination procedure is logically prior to any particular object appearing within its framework, and it proceeds in organizing sensory reports in terms of futural considerations; ontic appearances appear within its out-look, an out-look which looks out toward possible futures and yet cannot know precisely what any ontic future will be; hence my individual out-look, within which my pencil appears as a writing implement, comports itself within the range of future-pointing possibilities which it 'now' accepts (even if preconceptually or non-reflectively) as genuine.[23]

Heidegger's interpretation of the nature of experiential time, a triune temporal synthesis organized under the aegis of futurity, thus brings the traditional priority of actuality into the same question as it brought the parallel priority of the now. His analysis of the nature of experiential time has demonstrated the priority of futural consideration to manifest itself as dominating human thinking. This thesis, emanating from Kant's Copernican Revolution, is bound up with and grounds Heidegger's own revolution, the reversal of the traditional priority of the actual. Because that traditional priority is incompatible with the grounding of knowledge in the experiential structure of the individual self,* it is essentially pre-Critical and the priorities need be reversed; hence, "Higher than actuality stands *possibility*." [25]

Startling as this pronouncement might have appeared before Kant, it is fully implicit in the Critical philosophy. Kant did not ask about the actual things which do appear in my experience but about the possibility for me to have an experience of them. His central question was 'what are the apriori conditions defining the *possibility* of any specific knowledge I may attain?' He answered this question by his analysis of the transcendental structure of knowledge *qua* defining *enabling possibility*.

Such actual experiences as I do have must each meet these requisites of their possibility but cannot be determined solely by them; within the range of the defined genuinely possible, any ontic actuality is to be found. What is actual, then, first must have been possible—and the whole point of the distinction is lost if the two are declared a mere identity. The things I experience are understood by me not merely as particular presentations, not merely by their place in a serial time-order, but in terms of the possibilities which I see them embodying and which give them their meaning. What transpires in my 'actual' experience, what

---

* Compare Dewey: "While it is necessary to revive the category of potentiality as a characteristic of individuality, it has to be revived in a different form from that of its classic Aristotelian formulation." [24]

comprises my world or area of operation and concern, is not merely the collection of fleeting presentations before me, the ontic factual data of which I become aware. My world of actual experiencing includes all of these; but it also includes a determining range of possibilities I take as genuine; these serve me as my instruments to use in interpreting and integrating discrete experiential events into my one continuum of experience.

If this were not so, it is hard to see how I could possibly connect one presentation, one present actuality, with another, one moment with the next. The possibilities with which I 'work' maintain the 'connection' *between* me and the object-world I see; they also seem to enable me to connect and relate my apprehending-content of ten minutes ago with the 'same' content I will see ten minutes hence. In terms of the possibilities I 'read into' and thereby 'read from' the object, I can understand its 'abiding' through 'change.' It is in terms of a continuum of possibility that I am able to apprehend changes as such, instead of mere awareness of merely similar-but-discrete apprehendings. The continuum of possibility presupposes my continuum of future-past-present as grounding the continuity of my apprehending self; as such it enables me to verify the cognitional integrations that I term knowledge, which is essentially predictive and sets forth criteria of verification of those possibilities to which I see them pointing.

But this is to suggest that the possibility of change, as of experience, depends upon possibilities, upon the genuiness of what-is-not-actual. If a possibility is really a possibility, it involves more than merely 'determinate future actuality'; it encompasses the realm of 'what will be' within the broader range of 'what can be.' This is to say that if something is truly possible it may well not-be and never-be even though it could-be. If my possibility-selecting, which is the expression of my transcendence and the ground of my freedom, has any efficacy, I am participating in the decision as to which possibilities shall and which shall not be brought, as the future moves into the present, from the 'realm' of the 'can-be' to the 'realm' of the 'is.'

All of this is to say that the concept of 'negation' is included in the concept of the 'possible.' But this negativity is included not only in the concept of the 'possible' but in any intelligible concept at all. By definition a concept necessarily includes-out while it includes-in. As James neatly stated it, "When we conceptualize, we cut out and fix, and exclude everything but what we have fixed. A concept means a *that-and-no-other*." [26]

It is in this sense that Kant seems to have suggested the priority of the possible; in the conclusion of the Analytic, for example, he has told us that the most "the understanding can achieve apriori is to *anticipate* the *form of* a *possible* experience." [27] It cannot determine a specific actuality but it can look into the limitations of the future and see the kinds of things that may eventually be rendered present—which is to say that it can determine what can *not* be rendered present also. "Negation is that the concept of which represents not-being (in time)," [28] which is to say that any experiential object, to be regarded as real, must "exhibit in itself that combination of being and not-being which is known as degree"; for any object to be regarded as real, we must know not only its reality as 'filling time' but also its negativity regarding the 'time it doesn't fill.' [29]

Thus, "Reality is *something;* negation is *nothing,* namely, a concept of the absence of an object, such as shadow. . . ." [30] But shadows *are,* as possibilities *are,* real in my experience and help constitute it. These absences, these non-objects, these 'lacks' are essential ingredients of the intelligibility of my experience; they define my interests, my aims, my obligations, my ends-in-view, my concerns. They are constituent of any possibility as such. They are constituent of the particular possibility of dynamicity or change. For, any change presupposes a temporally prior negation which it 'overcomes'; to pronounce something as 'possible' is to pronounce a defining limit on any relevant future, as well as present, actuality. As Aristotle suggested long ago, the possibility of change depends upon 'privation,' on what-is-not, on a lack of completed development, on need, on a negative condition. If something is pronounced as 'possible,' there is at once implicit the present lack, the futural reference, and the reality of change.

In the cognitional act I maintain a dynamic relationship with objects known in a field of experience that is structured by the non-thing temporal modes of my cognitional capacity. To know, to be a knower means *that* going-beyond myself, which is termed transcendence, into the non-thingness of the possible which enables me to know. It is this capacity to face the non-thingness, the "negation of the totality of what is," [31] which turns me ahead to what-is-not but is possible, that makes theoretical reason and science itself possible. It is this capacity to face that ontological non-thingness grounding the apprehension of particular lacks, privations, negations that makes possible the call of conscience, resoluteness, and the morality of an I-thou relationship.[32] It is this capacity to face non-thingness as such that enables me to unify my personality in that unity of theoretical and practical reason to which Kant had looked in the capacity to form judgments "apriori by principles." [33] It is this possibility that enables me to become and to be what I am.

These considerations show us why Heidegger, in taking the meaning of experiential time in fullest seriousness, insists on recognizing the 'positivity' of the negative—the inclusion of negativity in any finite being, in any finite apprehending, judging, cognizing, acting, in any finite object, as "integral to the Being of what-is." [34]

In the structure of the knowing self who I am, as in the structure of the things-that-are-for-me, there is thus included the defining lacks, the determinate negativity, the presence of the 'not.' To be human, then, is to have an experience that is pervasively temporal and self-interpretive. It is formed by time which is not a thing, as 'in time,' and the principles of interpretation are primarily denominated and selected in terms of what-is-not-actual, what is anticipated, hoped for, or feared as the genuinely possible that the future offers. The what-is-not-actual-but-can-be is thus the primary mode of our interpretation of the actual, of the 'is,' and of 'the-what-has been.'

In the traditional sense of time, the only reality is the actuality of the immediate now. As Augustine had wondered, what *is*, then, comes out of non-being and disappears back into it; thus the 'cause of its being seems to be that it shall cease to be.' As the actuality of the now arises only to disappear in a 'split second' over the knife-edge of the now-point, the traditional view of time seems to presuppose a view of the real as a hairline of true actuality somehow suspended over and dependent upon an abyss of negativity and non-being on both sides. It is thus exceedingly strange that despite Heidegger's emphatic rejection of this traditional notion of time, the charge of 'nihilism' is so frequently heard.[35]

It would seem that in the explicit recognition of the 'not,' it is granted its due and the essential finitude of negativity-as-such is thereby explicitly affirmed. For, if to-be = to-be-finite, i.e., to be within limits, and, if the 'not' is not a *nihil absolutum* but an aspect of the real, of to-be as such, then that negativity is also limited, finite, and it is no longer consuming. To recognize that non-being is essential to the possibility of change is to recognize the reality of change; to recognize that non-being is essential to the possibility of experience, of knowledge, of morality, is to recognize their reality. To recognize that the possible is defined in contrast to the not-possible is to recognize the possible scope of possibility. To recognize what is excluded by a concept is to recognize what the concept *does* mean and does predict. To recognize the negation of possibilities ('the nihilation of non-thingness') as they are transformed, selected, and 'funneled' into actuality is to recognize the determinate and irrevocable nature of the actual (as it is to recognize the unchangeableness of the past, of the actuals that have been). To recognize the degree of non-being in a thing is to recognize what the being is and can be. To recognize what the future cannot include is to perceive what it may include.

If, as Kant said, "Everything that is in time is actual," [36] then those possibilities which I presently see in my temporal synthesis are possibilities-that-are, possibilities which are real for me *qua* possibilities 'now.' These 'actual' or genuine possibilities constitute my cognition; it is in their terms that my imaginative synthesis relates one disparate event to another; they thus constitute my experience. In a real sense, these possibilities claim to represent negative affirmations; as future, their content is not 'now.' This is to say that the content of the future is denominated as something-which-is-not; the concept of any future, as Kant had indicated, 'is nothing, a concept of the absence' of a certain state of affairs.

If Kant's questions that 'combine the interests of my reason,' if Heidegger's notion of animating Concern have any meaning at all, their meaning is derived from the what-is-not-present, from what-is-absent, from the state of affairs which-is-not-yet. If we are thus animated by that non-actual state of affairs called the future, if the possibilities that are currently present are representations of non-existent things, in that future which is-not-yet, and if these present possibilities are essential and crucial ingredients in present cognition—then the notion of everything implicated in the concept of negativity is crucial to any current affirmation. If it is in the cognitional act that the be-ing, the to-be, of the object is constituted, then it would seem to follow that a 'not' is included in every act of be-ing, in every thing that is. In accord with Kantian transcendentalism, a transcendental capacity to create and apply a 'category' of 'not-ness,' of 'non-being,' of 'non-thingness,' of *Nichts,* is prerequisite for any such empirical utilization of a principle of negation.

By bringing a non-actual but possible future into the present by an act of imaginative thought, we constitute the present cognitional field and the objects seen in it. In bringing a no-longer existent past into the present presentational field, we are 'binding' time together in and by thought. By doing both and doing them together, the present presentational field can be interpreted, known, and understood. But this is to say again that my present cognition, as the objects present within it, derives its 'empirical reality' from my temporal synthesis, from my transcendental capacity to synthesize the nature of experiential time itself.

Time as such is not a 'thing'; it remains, for us at least, 'something,' an *etwas,* which can *not* appear to us as an object of sensory perception. But this is not to suggest that it is thereby merely nothing-at-all. It is, as the discussion has urged, a non-thing in terms of which a system of relationships constituting knowing, acting, and be-ing is constituted. These relationships, the structuring they comprise, as the time of their relating, are not 'things'; they are presupposed modes, possibilities enabling us to bring perceivable things into intelligibility. Kant had finally yielded to the temptation to posit the intelligible as opposed to time. But, from Kant's insight into time *qua* the structuring of knowing and of things *qua* known, Heidegger has derived the insight that time is crucial to intelligibility as such. It permeates the knower, the knowing, and the known. It necessitates a priority of that which appears in its form as the focus of our experiencing; it is, then, the dynamic center of our experiencing and directs our concerns to render that experiencing intelligible.

If we take the ultimately necessary empirical sensory reference of meaningful cognition seriously, as Kant had urged in commencing the Critique, then our cognitions and the structure of the 'things' to which they ultimately refer depend upon an unperceivable transcendental structure; we project this non-thing structure on the 'realm' of entities in order to constitute their appearing and to comprehend them as things-for-us. This transcendental structure, as a system of time determinations and thereby the whole ground of any meaningful sense of what it means to-be for us, is dependent upon the non-thingness, the *Nichts,* of time.

This non-thingness of time is, then, the ground relationship of my experiencing and my experience. To know myself, to act, to think, to relate to the world or to the things with me in the world, I necessarily relate in a temporal framework, a framework which I necessarily presuppose and cannot see. It is the necessary condition for my experience of temporality and temporal distinctions. It is the non-thing that must somehow be the crucial 'some-thing' for my unity of consciousness, for my capacity to 'unfreeze' particular nows into a dynamic presentational field that I take as real, for the continuum of the experience I enjoy. It is requisite for my unification of moments into events, and in turn this unification presupposes my capacity to comprehend these moments and the events that give them their meaning for me. All of which is to say that time is the prime possibility in which I find my be-ing, the individual self that I am, the self that I am continually in the process of becoming.*

But then, what is 'ultimate' or 'original' time? So far Heidegger has taken us, so far but no further. On Kantian grounds he rightly stops here. He has shown that the what-is-not, the open future, and the genuineness of unfilled possibilities are essential characteristics of the be-ing of man and of human cognition. He

* Compare Dewey: "[An individual does not] exist in a time which externally surround[s] him, but time [is] the heart of his existence. . . . Genuine time, if it exists as anything else except the measure of motions in space, is all one with the existence of individuals as individuals, with the creative, with the occurrence of unpredictable novelties." [37]

has underscored the need to include the idea of what-is-not in the idea of what-is, to ground actuality in the reality of possibility and time in temporality—if the idea of the to-be, of be-ing-for-us, is to become meaningful. Through the Kantian analysis of the nature of human knowledge, he urges on us a candid recognition of just what is involved in the essential finitude of man and in the nature and pervasiveness of temporality in man's way of knowing and be-ing.

Postscript:
Being, Possibility, and Time

HEIDEGGER, as Kant, has understood a philosophic inquiry to be essentially a systematic interrogation. The organizing principle of Heidegger's interrogation has been the meaning of what it is to-be in the light of the Copernican Revolution. Its outcome points us to the intrinsic relationship between his fundamental ontological question and that of the nature of Time as such. So far Heidegger has taken us. It remains to posit some core questions, suggested by his inquiry, which hopefully should take us further.

To say that temporalization, whatever else it may be, is the form of the human self is to focus on it as a function and not as a 'thing.' But is this functioning merely hallucinatory or does it reflect something beyond itself? Is it rooted in the transcendental power of imaginative synthesis, or is transcendental imagination rooted in it? In both questions it would seem that the latter is the case. As manifested in human Concern, temporalization is the form of human be-ing, of the imaginatively constituted acts of cognitive and practical reason which manifest its essential core. Yet the question arises as to whether this human sensible reason is self-sustaining and essentially autonomous—or does it point to something beyond itself? What is the ground relation between Time as such and human temporality?

In the first Kant-book, the terms 'time' and 'temporality' were used as virtually mutually implicatory. In *Being and Time* 'temporality' has been taken to designate the human mode of constituting its general experience; 'time' has been reserved as the designation for the derivative constructive sequential orderings of events in terms of clocks and calendars; 'world-time,' only briefly alluded to, can be taken as ultimate Time itself, as the ontological 'real' referent of our subjective temporal modes. The reason for this ambiguity is due to the fact that the Kant study focused on the ways in which we constitute our knowledge of objects, and *Being and Time* focused on the ways in which we constitute our own subjective be-ing. Both point toward an intentional referent, the ultimately 'objective' 'world-time' (of *Being and Time*), that objective Time which constitutes the be-ing of those entities which can appear to us as temporal objects in terms of the temporalizing structure which enables us to know them. This 'objective' orientation is carried forward into Heidegger's 1962 lecture "Time and Being" [*Zeit und Sein*]," in which 'world-time' or Time-itself is referred to as "authentic Time [*eigentliche Zeit*]." [1] The question remains, however, of just how our subjective temporality may conceivably disclose the nature of objective Time.

We are forced back to the ground question, "What then is Time?" We are obligated to pursue the question—which Kant would foreclose, but Heidegger cannot—of the ontological meaning and status of ultimate Time as such. In this vein we should ask whether, in a curious negation of Kant's result, Heidegger's conclusion has pointed us not to the unknown root but to the need of unearthing it on a yet deeper level—to the 'original source' of the form of the human self *qua* an act of temporalizing be-ing within a world not of its own making. If temporalizing is the form of the human self; if the self projects temporality onto the world which appears to it as a world of independently appearing things; if, from this knowledge and from our relations in and with this world, we come to know ourselves as dynamic centers of experience in terms of the time-embodying ontological predicates we accord to the objects of our knowing; if our moral selves are essentially future-possibility oriented—then we are forced back to the ground of possibility, the ultimate nature to which we respond in our form-ing, to the primordial referent which permits us to form the selves we find ourselves to be. We find that this

[276]

imperative to 'go beyond' our own temporality arises from both cognitional and practical reason.

If our experience somehow reflects, within our finite perspective, the nature of the world to which it refers, then the presentation of Time in human apprehension happens as a temporal event, and Time-as-such is a necessary condition for the necessary experiencing of temporality. In the most minimal terms, the world of entities appearing to us must be amenable to representation in temporal form. Our success in dealing with the world, in both cognitional and actional terms, seems to confirm that our temporalizing modes of thinking do indeed relate to the nature of that world-time in which entities can appear to us as cognizable things and utilitarian instruments. If our essential temporality is a legitimate response to an existential situation in-a-world not of our own making, then the subjective grounding of human time cannot be taken to imply that its 'be-ing' is illusionary. As Heimseoth has pointed out, in the Critical philosophy "time is not illusion but appearance. Temporal relations represent in their sensuous limitation real aspects of being itself." [2] Throughout both the Kant-book and *Being and Time,* Heidegger has presumed, on the ground of Kant's Highest Principle, some kind of parallelism between the forms of subjective experience and the entities that appear as objects in it, between the structure of subjective temporalization and world or ultimate Time. Especially prominent in his developed discussions of the transcendental object as well as of the Highest Principle, it is clear that somehow human temporality reflects, or is oriented to, ultimate Time as such. Time, then, is somehow related to the question of Being. And, as Heidegger has often stated, the 'and' between them expresses the central philosophic problematic. [3]

That this is true of moral reason is also evident. If one accepts Heidegger's insight that "temporality first showed itself in anticipatory resoluteness" which in itself unlocks the possibility of morality; [4] if one accepts Kant's thesis that moral reason offers the possibility of transcending the limits of phenomenality; if one appreciates the force of Heidegger's temporalization of human practical reason—then the implicit reference to some sense of ultimate Time would seem apparent. For, in full accord with Heidegger's conception of temporality, moral reason *qua* normative is essentially future-oriented and constitutes its temporal field most explicitly in terms of the future-referring 'should.' As such it necessarily transcends the notion of time as a series of discrete now-points and presupposes temporal continuity while bringing the future into the present. Whether taken in these terms, or in Heidegger's own term of Concern, the priority of volitional reason seems preeminent in defining the temporal present. It is then strange that, aside from providing an ontological grounding of morality in the transcendental capacities of resoluteness, guilt, and conscience, Heidegger has not been concerned to develop the implications or significance of moral practical reason for his own temporalizing fundamental ontology.

Nevertheless, we do find this essential intentional reference to ultimate Time in both cognitive and practical reason. If time-forming is the essential core of what it means to be, we find ourselves oriented to the nature of that ultimate Time in response to which we form the selves we are and which we manifest in that subjectively grounded temporality which binds us to the world we claim to know and in which we find ourselves compelled to act. If our subjective temporalizing constitutes our cognitive objectivity, we find ourselves in a world that is essentially constituted in terms of Time. If Kant conveyed any basic insight in seeing human practical reason as at least a clue to noumenal reality as well as providing the essential context for the functioning of speculative reason and the understanding; if Heidegger's interpretations of the steps in Kant's Analytic essentially hold; if his renunciation of the *mere* subjectivity of the subject and the focus (in the Kant-book) on the nature of the constituted object are accepted; if his temporalization of the moral self makes any sense—then the essential temporality of human practical sensible reason, whether in cognitive or practical employment, must point to the primordial nature of ultimate Time itself.

What, then, is the ontological status, the be-ing of Time as such? Has this ultimately intentionally referent Time-itself any being-status? Does 'world-time' have any Being? It grounds our 'subjective' and 'objective' concepts; it is essentially prior; but, what and how is it? In the Kant-book Heidegger has left the question open; in *Being and Time* he explicitly closed off the query as taking us against the 'boundary' which is imposed by our understanding of it as temporality. But he has also told us that "contrary to Kant's opinion," it cannot be reduced to the psychical, that *"World-time is 'more Objective' than any possible Object because, with the disclosedness of the world, it already becomes 'Objectified' in an ecstatico-horizonal manner as the condition for the possibility of [beings]-within-the-world."* [5] If entities are independently existent prior to their appearances in our apprehension as objects; if our knowledge of them is dependent not only on our cognizing capacities but also on their coming into view; if the temporality in terms of which we understand the world is somehow dependent on that world-time in which they appear; if our "understanding of time . . . [depends upon] the possibility of our understanding in terms of primordial Time what is meant by this conception—that is, the possibility of understanding it as *temporality"* [6]—then, human temporality somehow depends on the 'reality' or 'given-ness' of Time as such.

The question of the Being of Time, which Heidegger has accepted as legitimate, needs to be raised again. Heidegger's prime interest in exploring experiential time and temporality has been because it seemed to offer a clue to unraveling the mystery of Being. As he found this inquiry leading to a 'boundary,' he turned his attention directly to the question of Being as such. That these subsequent inquiries have been fruitful is certainly an open question. But, in investigating the nature of temporal experiencing, he had succeeded in elucidating the way in which temporality functions as essentially constitutive and, in so doing, points beyond itself to some kind of ultimate or authentic Time; the nature of this referential Time-as-such has, however, been left as a basic, but side-stepped ontological problematic.

The curious thing is that, for the most part, Heidegger has pursued, in subsequent work, neither the problem of the nature of Time nor the question of its 'and' with Being. Apparently turning his attention away from both, he focused on the question of Being-as-such. Kant had largely passed over this question and focused his attention in the First Critique on the pervasiveness of time-forming in human apprehension. Perhaps Heidegger has sought to redress the balance, to point out the correlative nature of Time and of Being. Indeed, he identified them to the extent of saying that "Being is not something other than Time: 'Time' is called the first name of the truth of Being, and this truth is the presence of Being and thus Being itself."[7] Rather than pursuing this insight, he moved from the analysis of the pervasiveness of temporality in human experience to the question of Being itself—to the nature of which he had originally thought that temporality would provide a key. But in turning away from their identity or necessary conjunction, he also has turned away from his essentially temporalist empiricism which we have been examining.

And, indeed, the progression of his thinking seems to parallel the kind of development which he has charged on Kant. Even in the 1962 lecture "Time and Being," when he returns to the question of the 'and' between them, Being and Time are seen as paired and as requisite to each other. But, revealingly enough, in the 1969 published version of the lecture, an insertion suggests a repudiation of the transcendental priority of the temporal which was the doctrine of the Kant-book and of *Being and Time*. He specifically dismisses, without explanation, Section 70 of *Being and Time,* where, in a Kantian strain, he had seen the notion of spatiality as derivative from temporal constitution; apparently he leaves them as equal 'coordinates' of a 'time-space' which is not really further clarified.[8]

The increasingly 'rationalist' preoccupation with Being-as-such instead of with Time seems to culminate in this late disowning of the priority of the temporal in favor of a 'time-space' coordinate. Significantly enough, this movement of thinking is not accompanied by a renunciation of Kant; rather it seems to parallel Heidegger's increasing use of the previously rejected B edition, which analogously followed much the same direction. May this suggest that, in some sense, Heidegger's charge against Kant now applies to Heidegger as well? That as he has increasingly shied away from the essentially sensate-temporality of the First Edition, the charge of 'recoil' or 'retreat' from the temporal problematic is symptomatically justified? In our retrieve of Heidegger, how then shall we regard the 'later' Heidegger in his implicit disavowal of his own essentially Kantian thesis of the priority of the temporal in human experience?

For, if the principle of the Copernican Revolution holds, if the transcendental method is fundamentally valid, then the mode of our knowing precedes metaphysical speculation regarding the nature of the things that appear in that knowing. Things that are known are indeed known as spatial as well as temporal; but our knowing of them, as both Kant and Heidegger have insisted, is essentially time-bound—and being time-bound is precisely what our knowledge has in common with the objects that are known. If our essential temporality is *our* key to the nature of 'reality' as it appears to us, then we can only construe that 'reality' in terms of its Time, which is the counterpart of our temporality. And everything else notwithstanding, in this late essay Heidegger still somehow holds on to this prime principle. It is, he points out, just because man somehow stands in "authentic Time," that man can apprehend events, experience Being and raise the question of its meaning.

Indeed, in this 1962 lecture he has returned, not to the nature of Time-as-such, but to the question of the 'and.' In doing so, he picks up the tradition of the Kant-book and of *Being and Time* and extends it by explicating the necessary reference of temporalization to ultimate, primordial, or, now "authentic Time."

For, here, he admonishes us not to think of Time, or of Being, as a 'thing'; each is 'given'; they are both 'given' together, and nothing more can really be said about either. Being is not a being; Time is nothing temporal. Time is not; Being is not. The only becoming expression is the very indefinite German: 'It gives Time; it gives Being' (*"Es gibt Zeit; es gibt Sein"*—with the *'es gibt'* usually rendered into English as 'there is' and into French as *il y a,* 'it has there'). Time, as Being, is given—but we are warned not to reify one or the other. What is apparent is that both are 'given' together in what we call an 'event (*Ereignis*)'; but an 'event' should not be thought of in substantive terms: 'an event events' (*"das Ereignis ereignet"*);[9] an event is not merely an occurrence; it is a dynamic structured 'happening' which brings the 'forces' of Being and of Time into ontic synthesis.

So, despite any other directions investigated in the meantime, Heidegger here still carries forward the Kantian Critique in terms of its ontological implications. On an ultimately ontological level, he even parallels the Kantian cognitional dialectic: as Kant had pointed out, a specific cognitional act is a synthesis of sense and thought, which are separably distinguishable only as mere analytic distinctions within their imaginatively rendered organic unity. So here we find that an event is a presentational field in which the what-has-been and the what-is-not-yet are 'held apart' to constitute that present in which the things-that-are for us are constituted as beings-in-time; both Being and Time, as such, are apparently to be taken as analytic distinctions of the unified ontological ground of that synthesis which renders possible the event-as-such which is apprehended in our knowledge.

In the end, then, as in the beginning, we are left with Being and with Time. In "Time and Being" we are reminded that they are named together, that neither is a 'thing,' that they determine themselves reciprocally, that they are known to us in much the same way but that we cannot clarify either by a direct examination of its own separate properties.[10] We are told that they appear together in an event, that 'an event events,' that an event is a dynamic concrete synthesis of Being and of Time, that neither can appear to human apprehension without the other. But we are left with the mystery, not only of the nature of Being which can only appear in terms of Time, but with the nature of Time itself which is requisite for the appearing of Being.

If neither Being nor Time is to be reified, if neither is a 'thing,' if both together provide the ultimate ground of the event-ings in which particular things appear to us as objects of temporal apprehension, we are reminded of the priority of the transcendental object, the object-in-general which Kant had proposed as the most basic of all concepts—just because our categories must refer to it. For Heidegger's interpretation has suggested the identification of the transcendental object with the ultimate non-thingness (*Nichts*) of Time, and of the necessary structuring of the experiential field in which objects appear to us as temporally constituted beings. Both in terms of the 'given-ness' of Time and of Being, and in terms of the necessary reference to the transcendental object, we are pointed to this ultimate non-thing reference of all human experience. But, if this is the case, one is tempted to suggest that, whatever one may think of Hegel's Absolute Idealism, his insight deserves consideration: for Hegel, identifying pure Being as an abstraction saw it as the 'Nothing'; as such, he observed, "Nothing, if it be thus immediate and equal to itself, is also conversely the same as Being is. The truth of Being and of Nothing is accordingly the unity of the two: and this unity is Becoming." [11]

If a concrete event is the concrete synthesis of Being and of Time; if neither can appear to us without the other, outside of the event-ing which brings them together—then they can only be apprehended in the apprehension of a definable becoming. But the concept of Becoming is notoriously absent from Heidegger's work and yet his dynamic concept of the To-Be, or Being-as-such, seems to imply its meaning. Perhaps a root-source of the problem is that the concept of Becoming has been 'collapsed' into that of Being; Becoming as an ultimate ontological characterization has not been explicitly explored, and the focus has been wrongly placed on its two 'component' elements.

But 'becomings' or 'event-ings,' as the entire Kantian exegesis demonstrated, are apprehended in terms of possibilities. And the question of the nature of possibility is pronounced as central but unexplored. In side-stepping the problematic of the nature of the possible-as-such, Heidegger has followed a perhaps mistaken Kantian lead. For both have been concerned with spelling out the essential possibilities of human cognizing and experiencing; but neither has really faced the question of the ontological meaning of possibility-as-such.

If the analyses of cognition and temporality, as of moral reasoning, make any sense, events can only be apprehended by us in terms of possibilities; futurity and thereby all temporal experience is constituted in terms of the possible. This is to say, as Kant had also suggested, that the prime principle at the basis of any "transcendental philosophy is the division into the possible and the impossible." [12] The question of the nature of Time (as of Being), as revealed in our temporalizing experience, is, as Heidegger has insightfully developed it, shrouded in the nature of the possible. Perhaps the reason for the inconclusive yield of his existential analytic regarding the nature of Time (or of Being) is that Heidegger had turned away from this essential insight and problematic of transcendental philosophy, the need for a systematic elucidation of the nature of possibility-as-such. He himself enunciated the principle which, on the level of human temporalizing, he pursued: "Higher than actuality stands *possibility*." [13] This principle, which defines Kant's cognitive and Heidegger's existential investigations, has not been itself directly investigated.

If transcendental method has any pragmatic validity, I would suggest that Being appears to us, in Time, as the Becoming of the Possible, that futurity comes into our ken in terms of possibilities, that the question of the nature of Time is transcendentally the question of the ontology of the Possible. In pursuing the question of the nature of Time (as of Being), and not pursuing the ground question of the nature of the Possible-as-such, which he has succeeded in exposing to our view, Heidegger has not pursued his most brilliant insight.

Yet it is to this problematic that Heidegger points us; it is a problematic that is inextricably tied not only to the question of Being but also to the question of Time. If possibilities are indeed prior; if, in contrast to momentary actualities, possibilities constitute the time-bound-and-binding reality of our experience and of the things we seek to know; if some possibilities are truly genuine or real, even if never actualized, and others are illusory—then the primal question would seem to be the nature, the ontological status, the to-be of the Possible-as-such.

That, ontologically speaking, this is Kant's essential Critical thrust Heidegger has pointed out well. For, Kant, after setting out the three groups of cognitive Principles which govern our knowledge of the thingness of things appearing to us (the Axioms of Intuition, the Anticipations of Perception, and the Analogies of Experience), then turned to the fourth set of Principles, the Postulates of Empirical Thought. These set out the modalities of possibility, actuality, and necessity. These Postulates, Kant clearly pointed out, do not refer to the objects of knowledge as they do to how "the object, together with all its determinations, is related to understanding and its empirical employment. . . ." [14] As Heidegger has pointed out, this fourth group, though presented last, is, in the Critical perspective, indeed first. By the principle of the Copernican Revolution, it is the ground of the other three sets of Principles in that *all* the other Principles of human knowledge presuppose these modalities of human knowing which they apply in ontic cognitive acts.[15] Of these three modalities, that of possibility is prior just because, as Kant said, possibility "requires that the concept of the things should agree with the formal conditions of an experience in general . . . [which] contains all synthesis that is required for knowledge of objects."[16] Indeed, as Paton has urged, even "necessity is existence (or being) given through possibility itself."[17] It is this modality of possibility that determines, as Heidegger suggested, that essential reality which is a condition for the given-ness of any ontic actuality.[18]

In a pre-Critical out-look, with a philosophic focus on the 'external' world of things, which are continually passing away, we were pointed to the destructive nature of 'temporal flow' and tempted to hold on to the momentarily present actuality as the only temporal reality on which we could anchor ourselves. But Kant had unveiled the immanent transcendental structure of man; what emerges from re-thinking his efforts is the insight that the sustaining nature of Time forms the reality of the continuing self which finds itself by facing the possibilities constituting its existence and its experience. Kant's Aesthetic, which raised the question of the nature of Time, commenced with the essentially ontological query of its nature. His preliminary statement that it is the essentially pervasive form of all cognitive experiencing pointed ahead to the further ramifications of this initial thesis. As argued in the Deduction, the pervasive reference to Time justifies that triune synthesis which we call cognition. As argued in the Schematism, it is because we are capable of temporalizing-thinking that we can form and employ the specific cognitive Principles in the construction of knowledge. As Heidegger has argued, despite Kant's disclaimer, this capacity is central to our whole moral experience and the be-ing of the practical self. By virtue of the Highest Principle, it enables us to deal with the world that is given in terms of our own cognitive temporally organized Principles. This necessary temporalizing which permits us to know, to act, and, thereby, to be the selves we are, is rooted, as Heidegger has urged, in the first Postulate, the concept of possibility itself.

To face the nature of the Possible is to face the continuum of experience and of the things that are experienced. It is to ground the time-binding nature of events, our experiences of them, and the 'moments' in terms of which we conceptualize their elements. For we experience the linkages of temporality, space, and causality in the world of nature and of our own be-ing in a continuum of possibilities. This continuum of possibilities, as contrasted to a series of momentary discrete actualities, permits the unity of experience in both outer and inner sense. But this is to suggest that the Possible is somehow identifiable with Being, in the sense of 'Reality,' and can only appear to us in a temporally constituted field.

As Heidegger has suggested, to point to the priority of the possible is to point to the essence of things in terms of the apriori; it is to point to the essence of human experiencing as well, for the "apriori is what belongs to the subjectivity of the subject." [19] It thus points to the ground of human experience and, by virtue of ontological projection, to the essential nature of what can appear in that experience. It points to the fact that possibilities are presented in the given and also brought to the given by us; that possibilities come into temporal be-ing for me in the encounter between my self and all that is not my self in the world in which I find myself.

The priority of the concept of the Possible is then fundamental. Yet it has remained a very ambiguous notion throughout Western thought. It is often referred to as 'mere possibility' in contrast to the fleeting momentary actualities which are, oddly enough, taken to be more real. Since Aristotle, it has been generally confused with the notion of potentiality or been confined, as both Leibniz and Wolff presented it in logical terms, as signifying lack of contradiction.

But perhaps this ambiguity may be traced to the fact that the notion of the Possible is inextricably wedded to the concept of Time, which has also defied precise description. Kant's Critique, as Heidegger's elucidation, would seem to have revealed their intrinsic relationship. As Heidegger has urged of the concept of Being, so the concept of the Possible has always been thought as 'projected' onto Time. And the concept of the Possible is subject to all the predicates which Heidegger has used to delineate Time—it is a crucial non-thingness which is certain not nothing-at-all but which somehow constitutes the actuality of any ontic thing appearing to us. Possibility, as Time, seems to be a kind-of dynamic non-thing structuring which constitutes the continuum of our experience and the reality of the world which we experience.

Kant's effort in the First Critique was largely directed to establishing this first principle of possibility as the delimiting ground of finite human knowledge. The concept of the Possible is, then, the ground concept of the transcendental; it defines the scope of what Heidegger has called 'transcendence.' It is, to use Heidegger's terms, not merely ontic but, more importantly, ontological. As the outcome of the Copernican Revolution, Kant demonstrated the essential temporality of human cognition by examining the ground of its possibility. By means of his incisive study of Kant's work, Heidegger has explicated this priority of possibility, suggested ways in which to distinguish it from potentiality, to free it from a merely logical context, and to see it as existentially manifest in human transcendence and human freedom.

Yet Kant had urged, without really developing the thought, that the concept of the object-in-general, as the ultimate referent of our categories, is yet more basic than the concept of possibility, which he described as the supreme transcendental idea. Heidegger's discussion has been developed to suggest that this transcendental object, which is necessarily presumed as grounding any ontic content of knowledge, is to be identified as the referent of the temporalizing structure of our being and intentionally with ultimate or authentic Time itself. It then may be suggested that Heidegger has sought to unearth it and bring it into view, as Being, as Time. But, however much may have been accomplished, the To-Be of one as of the other remains obscure. They remain obscure because they are both grounded, and grounded together, in the question of the essence and Being of the Possible-as-such, which seems to be their common root and which has been left unexplored in the realm of the unknown. For it is in the realm of the Possible that man's reality is found as the reality of that world which he brings into his own be-ing. If our concepts, as our obligations, are normative, their ontological status is at least intentionally in the realm of possibilities, the possibilities which define reality for us, as well as our futurity, our actions and our knowledge which bring aspects of the Possible into view.

The concept of the nature of the Possible is, as Kant's Critique effectively argues, the root concept of human experiencing. It is, as Heidegger has urged, "higher than actuality." It is yet a concept which philosophy has largely named only in passing. Yet what Heidegger has effectively brought out of Kant is its central import as constitutive of all that *is* in the human out-look.

As Heidegger has said, Being is given, Time is given. But they are given, to man at least, as apprehended in temporalizing imaginitive synthesis enabled and structured in terms of constituting possibilities. What, then, is the meaning of Being? What is the Being of Time? What is the nature of the Possible-as-such? Beyond all that has been accomplished, perhaps the central lesson of Heidegger's retrieve of Kant is the retrieve of the primordial problematic of the nature and Being of the Possible, the Possible which shows itself to us as be-ing in time.

LIST OF WORKS CITED

Aristotle. *De Generatione et Corruptione, De Interpretatione,* and *Physica,* trans. & ed., W. D. Ross. London: Oxford University Press.

Augustine, St. *The Confessions,* trans. Rex Warner. New York: The New American Library, 1963.

Barrett, William. "Introduction, Part Four, Phenomenology and Existentialism," W. Barrett & H. D. Aiken (eds.), *Philosophy in the Twentieth Century,* Vol. III. New York: Random House, 1962. Cited as *PTC.*

———. *Irrational Man: A study in Existential Philosophy.* Garden City: Doubleday, 1958.

———. *What Is Existentialism?.* New York: Grove Press, 1964.

Beck, Lewis White. *Early German Philosophy: Kant and His Predecessors.* Cambridge: Belknap Press of Harvard University Press, 1969. Cited as *EGP.*

———. *Studies in the Philosophy of Kant.* Indianapolis & New York: Bobbs-Merrill, 1965.

Biemel, Walter. *Le concept de monde chez Heidegger.* Louvain: E. Nauwelaerts & Paris: J. Vrin, 1950.

Boas, George. "The Acceptance of Time." *University of California Publications in Philosophy,* XVI, 12, 1950, pp. 249–70.

Borgmann, Albert. "The Transformation of Heidegger's Thought," in Jerry H. Gill (ed.), *Philosophy Today No. 1.* New York: Macmillan, 1968.

Brock, Werner. "Introduction," in Martin Heidegger, *Existence and Being.* London: Vision Press, 1956.

Cassirer, Ernst. "Kant and the Problem of Metaphysics," in Moltke S. Gram (ed.), *Kant: Disputed Questions.* Chicago: Quadrangle Books, 1967.

[289]

Cerf, Walter H. "An Approach to Heidegger's Ontology." *Philosophy and Phenomenological Research,* Vol. I, pp. 177–90.

Collingwood, R. G. "Some Perplexities About Time: With an Attempted Solution," *Proceedings of the Aristotelian Society.* London: Williams & Norgate, New Series, XXVI, 1926, pp. 135–50.

De Ruggiero, Guido. *Existentialism, Disintegration of Man's Soul.* New York: Social Science Publishers, 1948.

de Vleeschauwer, H. J. "A Survey of Kantian Philosophy," *Review of Metaphysics,* XI, 1, 1957, pp. 122–42.

———. *The Development of Kantian Thought: The History of a Doctrine,* trans. A. R. C. Duncan. London & New York: Thomas Nelson & Sons, 1962. Cited as *DKT.*

de Waelhens, Alphonse & Walter Biemel. "Introduction," in Martin Heidegger, *Kant et le problème de la métaphysique,* Fourth Edition. Paris: Gallimard, 1953.

Dewey, John. *Art as Experience.* New York: Capricorn Books, 1958.

———. *Experience and Nature.* New York: W. W. Norton, 1929.

———. *The Quest for Certainty: A Study of the Relation of Knowledge and Action.* London: George Allen & Unwin, 1930.

———. "Time and Individuality," in Harlow Shapley (ed.), *Time and Its Mysteries.* New York: Collier Books, 1962. Cited as "T&I."

Gelven, Michael. *A Commentary on Heidegger's "Being and Time,"* Harper Torchbooks. New York: Harper & Row, 1970.

Gilson, Etienne. *God and Philosophy.* New Haven & London: Yale University Press, 1941.

———. *The Philosophy of St. Thomas Aquinas,* trans. Edward Bullough. Cambridge, Eng.: W. Heffer & Sons, 1929.

Gray, J. Glenn. "Heidegger's Course: From Human Existence to Nature." *The Journal of Philosophy,* LIV, 1957, pp. 197–207.

———. "The New Image of Man in Martin Heidegger's Philosophy," in George L. Kline (ed.), *European Philosophy Today.* Chicago: Quadrangle Books, 1965.

Grene, Marjorie. *Martin Heidegger.* New York: Hillary House, 1957.

Heidegger, Martin. *Being and Time,* trans. John Macquarrie & Edward Robinson. London: SCM Press, 1962. Cited as *B&T.* n.b. See entry for *Sein und Zeit.*

———. *An Introduction to Metaphysics,* trans. Ralph Manheim. New Haven: Yale University Press, 1959. Cited as *ItM.*

———. *Kant and the Problem of Metaphysics,* trans. & introd. James S. Churchill. Bloomington: Indiana University Press, 1962. Cited as *KPM.*

———. *Kant und das Problem der Metaphysik.* Frankfurt am Main: Vittorio Klostermann, Second Edition, 1951. Cited as *KPM/G.*

————. *Kants These über das Sein.* Frankfurt am Main: Vittorio Klostermann, 1962. Cited as *KTS.*

————. "Letter on Humanism," trans. Edgar Lohner, in Barrett & Aiken (eds.), *Philosophy in the Twentieth Century,* Vol. III. New York: Random House, 1962.

————. *Sein und Zeit,* 8th Edition. Tübingen: Max Niemeyer Verlag, 1957. Cited as *SuZ.* N.B. Insofar as all pagination is indicated in the English translation, citations are made to *B&T* with *Sein und Zeit* pages indicated in parentheses.

————. *Vom Wesen des Grundes,* Fifth Edition. Frankfurt am Main: Vittorio Klostermann, 1965. Cited as *WdG.*

————. "The Way Back into the Ground of Metaphysics," trans. Walter Kaufmann, in Kaufmann (ed.) *Existentialism from Dostoevsky to Sartre.* New York: Meridian Books, 1958. Cited as "WBGM."

————. "What Is Metaphysics?," trans. R. F. C. Hull & Alan Crick, in Brock, *op. cit.* Cited as "WIM."

————. *What Is a Thing?,* trans. W. B. Barton, Jr., & Vera Deutsch, with Analysis by Eugene T. Gendlin. Chicago: Henry Regnery, 1967. Cited as *WIT.*

————. "Zeit und Sein," in *Zur Sache des Denkens.* Tübingen: Max Niemeyer Verlag, 1969. Cited as "ZuS." (Also, in *L'endurance de la pensée,* Paris: Plon, 1968.)

Hegel, G. W. F. *The Logic of Hegel* (from *The Encyclopaedia of the Philosophical Sciences*), trans. William Wallace. London: Oxford University Press, 1892.

Heimsoeth, Heinz. "Metaphysical Motives in the Development of Critical Idealism," in Moltke S. Gram (ed.), *Kant: Disputed Questions.* Chicago: Quadrangle Books, 1967.

James, William. *A Pluralistic Universe.* New York & London: Longmans, Green, 1943.

Kant, Immanuel. *Critique of Judgment,* trans. James Creed Meredith. London: Oxford University Press, 1952. Cited as *CJ.*

————. *Critique of Practical Reason,* trans. & ed., Lewis White Beck. Chicago: University of Chicago Press, 1949. Cited as *CPrR.*

————. *Critique of Pure Reason,* trans. Norman Kemp Smith. New York: The Humanities Press, 1950. Cited as *CPR.*

————. *Groundwork of the Metaphysic of Morals,* trans. H. J. Paton. New York & Evanston: Harper & Row, 1964. Cited as *GMM.*

————. *Kritik der reinen Vernunft,* Raymund Schmidt (ed.). Hamburg: Verlag von Felix Meiner, 1956. Cited as *KRV.*

————. *Kant: Philosophical Correspondence 1759–99,* ed. Arnulf Zweig. Chicago: University of Chicago Press, 1967. Cited as *PC.*

————. *Prolegomena to any Future Metaphysics,* trans. & ed. Paul Carus. LaSalle: Open Court Publishing Co., 1947. Cited as *PAFM.*

————. *Religion Within the Limits of Reason Alone,* trans. & introd. Theodore M. Greene & Hoyt H. Hudson. Chicago & London: Open Court Publishing Co., 1934. Cited as *RLR.*

Kroner, Richard, *Kant's Weltanschauung,* trans. John E. Smith. Chicago: University of Chicago Press, 1956.

Langan, Thomas. *The Meaning of Heidegger, A Critical Study of An Existentialist Phenomenology.* London: Routledge & Kegan Paul, 1959.

Lawrence, Nathaniel. "Kant and Modern Philosophy." *Review of Metaphysics,* X, 3, 1957, pp. 441–56.

Little, William et al. *The Oxford Universal Dictionary on Historical Principles,* Rev. & ed. C. T. Onions et al., Third Edition. London: Oxford University Press, 1955.

Lovejoy, Arthur O. *The Reason, the Understanding, and Time.* Baltimore: Johns Hopkins Press, 1961.

Löwith, Karl. "Heidegger: Problem and Background of Existentialism." *Social Research,* XV, 1948, pp. 345–69.

Martin, Gottfried. *Kant's Metaphysics and Theory of Science,* trans. P. G. Lucas. Manchester University Press, 1955.

Paton, H. J. *Kant's Metaphysic of Experience: A Commentary on the First Half of the "Kritik der reinen Vernunft,"* Two Volumes. London: George Allen & Unwin, & New York: Macmillan, 1961.

Plotinus. *The Enneads,* trans. Stephen MacKenna, P. S. Page (ed.), Second Edition. London: Faber & Faber, 1956.

Randall, John Herman, Jr. *The Career of Philosophy,* Vol. II, *From the German Enlightenment to the Age of Darwin.* New York & London: Columbia University Press, 1965.

Richardson, William J., S.J. *Heidegger: Through Phenomenology to Thought,* Preface, Martin Heidegger. The Hague: Martinus Nijhoff, 1963.

————. "Kant and the Late Heidegger," in James M. Edie (ed.), *Phenomenology in America.* Chicago: Quadrangle Books, 1967.

Ryle, G. "Review of *Sein und Zeit." Mind,* XXXVIII, 1929, pp. 355–70.

Royce, Josiah. *Lectures on Modern Idealism.* New Haven: Yale University Press & London: Oxford University Press, 1919.

————. *The World and the Individual,* Two Volumes. New York: Macmillan, 1904.

Schaper, Eva. "Kant's Schematism Reconsidered." *Review of Metaphysics,* XVIII, 1964, pp. 267–90.

Seidel, Georg Joseph, O.S.B. *Martin Heidegger and the Pre-Socratics: An Introduction to His Thought.* Lincoln: University of Nebraska Press, 1964.

Smith, Norman Kemp. *A Commentary to Kant's 'Critique of Pure Reason,'* Second Edition. New York: The Humanities Press, 1950.

Spiegelberg, Herbert. *The Phenomenological Movement: A Historical Introduction,* Vol. I. The Hague: Martinus Nijhoff, 1960.

Thevenez, Pierre. *What Is Phenomenology?,* ed. & introd. James M. Edie, Preface by John Wild, trans. James M. Edie, Charles Courtney, Paul Brockelman. Chicago: Quadrangle Books, 1962.

Werkmeister, W. H. "An Introduction to Heidegger's 'Existential Philosophy.'" *Philosophy and Phenomenological Research, II,* 1941, pp. 79–87.

Whitehead, Alfred North. *The Concept of Nature.* Ann Arbor: University of Michigan Press, 1957.

Windelband, W. A. *A History of Philosophy, with Special Reference to the Formation and Development of its Problems and Conceptions,* trans. James H. Tufts, Second Edition. New York: Macmillan, 1901.

Wolff, Robert Paul. *Kant's Theory of Mental Activity: A Commentary on the Transcendental Analytic of the Critique of Pure Reason.* Cambridge: Harvard University Press, 1963.

Wyschogrod, Michael. *Kierkegaard and Heidegger, The Ontology of Existence.* London: Routledge & Kegan Paul, 1954.

NOTES

Frequently cited references are indicated by the name of the author or by the abbreviations given below. More complete information may be found in the List of Works Cited.

B&T—Heidegger: *Being and Time*
CJ—Kant: *Critique of Judgement*
CPR—Kant: *Critique of Pure Reason*
CPrR—Kant: *Critique of Practical Reason*
DKT—de Vleeschauwer: *The Development of Kantian Thought*
EGP—Beck: *Early German Philosophy*
GMM—Kant: *Groundwork of the Metaphysic of Morals*
ItM—Heidegger: *Introduction to Metaphysics*
KPM—Heidegger: *Kant and the Problem of Metaphysics*
KPM/G—Heidegger: *Kant und das Problem der Metaphysik*
KRV—Kant: *Kritik der reinen Vernunft*
KTS—Heidegger: *Kants These über das Sein*
PAFM—Kant: *Prolegomena to any Future Metaphysics*
PC—Kant: *Philosophical Correspondence*, Zweig (ed.)
PTC—Barrett & Aiken (eds.): *Philosophy in the Twentieth Century*
RLR—Kant: *Religion Within the Limits of Reason Alone*
SuZ—Heidegger: *Sein und Zeit*
T&I—Dewey: "Time and Individuality"
WBGM—Heidegger: "The Way Back into the Ground of Metaphysics"
WdG—Heidegger: *Vom Wesen des Grundes*
WIM—Heidegger: "What Is Metaphysics?"
WIT—Heidegger: *What Is a Thing?*
ZuS—Heidegger: "Zeit und Sein"

I. Prospect

1. Augustine, pp. 167–68.
2. Dewey, "T&I," p. 156.
3. Boas, p. 250.
4. Thevenez, p. 133.
5. De Ruggiero, p. 86.
6. Ryle, p. 370.
7. Heidegger, *KPM*, p. 245 & *B&T*, p. 487 (436). N.B. In citations to *B&T*, the first number refers to the English translation, the number in parentheses to the 8th German edition of *SuZ*.
8. See Richardson, p. 28.
9. Langan, p. 71.
10. Brock, "Introduction," p. 128.
11. See *WdG*, p. 27.
12. Spiegelberg, I, p. 307.
13. "Letter to Marcus Herz, February 21, 1772," *PC*, p. 71. Cf. also, "Letter to J. H. Lambert, September 2, 1770," *PC*, p. 59: "A quite special, though purely negative science, general phenomenology (*phaenomenologia generalis*), seems to me to be presupposed by metaphysics."
14. For a discussion of various phases of this debate, the following among others may be consulted: Heidegger, "Preface to Second Edition, *KPM*, p. xxv; "Preface," Richardson, pp. xxii–xxiii; Langan, p. 10; Richardson, p. 623; Spiegelberg, p. 291.

See also: Barrett, *What Is Existentialism?*, p. 177; Barrett, *Irrational Man*, p. 188; Barrett, "Introduction, Part Four, Phenomenology and Existentialism," in *PTC*, III, p. 128; Borgmann, pp. 139–57; Richardson, "Kant and the Late Heidegger," pp. 125–44; Wyschogrod, pp. 70, 74, 120.

15. *B&T*, p. 63 (39); cf. "ZuS," pp. 18–20 & "Letter to Christian Garve," *PC*, p. 101.
16. Aristotle, *De Interpretatione*, 16a19–20, 16b6–7. Cf. p. 26n.

II. The Project of Retrieve

1. Cf. *KPM*, p. 240, *B&T*, pp. 184–85 (145), *WIT*, pp. 88–89n.
2. See *WdG*, p. 15, n. 14; cf. *WIT*, p. 61.
3. See *KRV*, pp. x & 767.
4. *KPM*, p. 238.

5. Quoted, *KPM,* pp. 206–207 (italics mine); cf. *CPR,* A314–B370, p. 310.

6. Cf. Richardson, p. 89, n. 181.

7. *KPM,* p. 211.

8. Richardson, p. 159.

9. *KPM,* p. 133.

III. The Retrieve of Kant

1. This fundamental departure from Husserl should not be overlooked. See *B&T,* p. 228 (270), 358 (310); and *WIT,* p. 180.

2. *CPR,* A1 & B1, p. 41.

3. *CPR,* B2f., p. 43.

4. Smith, pp. 75, 74.

5. For an explication of the inherent relationship between 'transcendence' and 'subjectivity,' see *WdG,* pp. 19 & 50, and Gendlin in *WIT,* p. 281.

6. Smith, p. 79.

7. Cf. *B&T,* p. 96 (129), & *WIT,* pp. 95n., 143, & 197. Also *The Oxford Universal Dictionary,* p. 1037, col. 2.

8. *CPR,* A19 = B33, p. 65.

9. See *B&T,* pp. 53–54 (30–31); Smith, p. 83; Paton, I, p. 61; and *EGP,* p. 408.

10. Smith, p. 1; cf. *WIT,* p. 147.

11. Smith, p. 2.

12. *CPR,* B21, p. 56 (quoted, *KPM,* p. 4).

13. See *KRV,* Avii, p. 5; cf. *CPR,* p. 7.

14. *CPR,* B22, p. 57; cf. Paton, I, p. 82.

15. *EGP,* p. 445.

16. *CPR,* Bxxiv, p. 26.

17. *KPM,* p. 4.

18. See *KPM,* p. 4.

19. *KPM,* p. 5.

20. Smith, p. 89.

IV. The Copernican Revolution as Ontology

1. *CPR,* Axiii, p. 10; cf. Bxxxvi, p. 33.

2. See *KPM,* p. 10, n. 2.

3. See *KPM*, p. 16.

4. See Gilson, *The Philosophy of St. Thomas Aquinas*, p. 268.

5. Gilson, p. 272.

6. Gilson, p. 21.

7. Gilson, *God and Philosophy*, p. 114.

8. Thevenez, p. 149.

9. *CPR*, Bxvii, p. 23.

10. With reference to the import of the priority of the verb, note Aristotle's comment on p. 8 above. Regarding the translations of *sein* and *Seiende*, see *SuZ*, p. 42: "Das 'Wesen' dieses Seienden liegt in seinem Zu-sein;" cf. *B&T*, p. 67: "The 'essence' of this entity lies in its 'to be.'" Also, cf. Gelven, p. 18. Also, cf. Gilson's translation of the Latin *esse* as "the to-be": *esse Dei* = "the 'to-be' of God," in *God and Philosophy*, p. 142 (see also p. 63). Regarding Heidegger and the form 'is' see *ItM*, pp. 71ff. Regarding the use of the word 'object', see Seidel, p. 5, n. 6.

11. *CPR*, Bxiii, p. 20 (quoted, *KPM*, p. 15).

12. See *KPM*, p. 10. N.B. These distinctions are essentially Wolffian: cf. *EGP*, pp. 263 & 481.

13. *CPR*, Bxiii, p. 20 (quoted *KPM*, p. 15), (italics mine).

14. *KPM*, p. 17.

15. See de Waelhens & Biemel, p. 16.

16. *CPR*, Bxxiii, p. 15 (quoted, *KPM*, p. 21).

17. Smith, p. xlv.

18. Martin, p. 133.

19. Cf. Martin, p. 134 & Royce, *Lectures on Modern Idealism*, p. 55.

20. *DKT*, p. 154.

21. *CPR*, A12 = B25, p. 59.

22. *CPR*, A155 = B194, pp. 192–93.

23. *CPR*, A156 = B195, p. 193.

24. *CPR*, A158 = B197, p. 194.

25. *CPR*, A158 = B197, p. 194. Smith translated *zugleich* as 'likewise' and Churchill as 'at the same time'; the latter more literal translation is essential to Heidegger's point: see *KPM*, p. 123.

26. *CPR*, Bxxiii, p. 25.

27. *KPM*, p. 21.

28. Werkmeister, p. 83.

V. The Execution of the Retrieve

1. *CPR*, A51 = B75f, p. 93, (quoted, *KPM*, p. 40).

2. *CPR*, A15=B29, p. 61, (quoted, *KPM*, p. 41).

3. *CPR*, A835 = B863, p. 655, (quoted, *KPM*, p. 41).
4. *KPM*, p. 26.

1. Cognitional Finitude

5. *CPR*, A19 = B33, p. 65, (quoted, *KPM*, p. 28).
6. *KRV*, A51 = B75, p. 95; cf. *CPR*, p. 93 (quoted, *KPM*, p. 39); cf. *CPR*, A19 = B33, p. 65.
7. *KPM*, p. 29 & *CPR*, B305-06, p. 266.
8. *WIT*, p. 135; cf. *KPM*, p. 29.
9. *KPM*, p. 28; cf. *WIT*, p. 135 & *CPR*, A19 = B33, p. 65.
10. *WIT*, p. 148.
11. *WIT*, p. 135 (citing *CPR* A719 = B747, p. 581).
12. *KPM*, p. 28.
13. *WIT*, p. 135; cf. *EGP*, p. 458.
14. *CPR*, A51 = B75, p. 93.
15. *KPM*, p. 31.
16. *CPR*, A68 = B93, p. 105 (quoted, *KPM*, p. 33).
17. *KPM*, pp. 35, 34.
18. *CPR*, A89 = B121, p. 123 (quoted, *KPM*, p. 37); cf. *CPR* A249, p. 266.
N.B. If there is any doubt about the argument which follows this quotation, see *CPR*, Bxxvi, p. 27; *CPrR*, p. 155; *KPM*, p. 38; *WdG*, p. 29; *B&T*, p. 53(30); *WIT*, pp. 5, 194, *ItM*, p. 108; Paton I, p. 61; Heimsoeth in Gram, pp. 167-68; Zweig in *PC*, p. 16.
19. WIT, pp. 165-66 (citing Leibniz' letter to Volder, 21 January 1704).
20. *EGP*, p. 480.
21. See *KPM*, p. 43 (& *KPM/G*, p. 42): cf. *CPR*, A80 = B106, p. 113.
22. *KPM*, p. 47.
23. *KPM*, pp. 45-46 (quoting *CPR*, Axx, p. 14).
24. Gray, "Heidegger's Course: From Human Existence to Nature," p. 200; cf. *B&T*, p. 418 (366).

2. The Priority of Pure Intuition

25. *CPR*, A19 = B33, p. 65; cf. B305-306, p. 266.
26. *CPR*, A22 = B36, p. 67.
27. *CPR*, A22 = B36, p. 67.
28. *CPR*, A23 = B37, p. 68 (italics mine).
29. Martin, p. 154; cf. *CPR*, A35 = B52, p. 78.
30. *KPM*, p. 55; cf. *B&T*, p. 410 (358) (quoting *CPR*, B33).
31. See *KPM*, pp. 52, 193-95; cf. *WIT*, p. 201.
32. Cf., e.g., *CPR*, A77 = B102, p. 111; A101, pp. 132-33; B160-61, pp. 170-71; A143 = B182, p. 184; A156 = B195, p. 193; A163 = B203, p. 198; A182 = B225, pp. 212-13.

33. *KPM*, p. 49.
34. *KPM*, p. 50 (citing *CPR*, A32 = B48, p. 76 & A25 = B40, p. 70).
35. *CPR*, A34 = B50, p. 77.
36. *CPR*, A33 = B49, p. 77 (cf. *KPM*, p. 51); cf. "Letter to Marcus Herz, February 21, 1772," in *PC*, p. 75, & *EGP*, p. 459.
37. *WIT*, p. 147.
38. *KPM*, p. 89.
39. Cf. Wyschogrod, p. 71 & Gendlin in *WIT*, p. 281.
40. *KPM*, p. 61.
41. *KPM/G*, pp. 51–52; cf. *KPM*, pp. 53–54.
42. See "Letter to Marcus Herz, February 21, 1772," *PC*, p. 75.
43. *CPrR*, p. 153; cf. *KPM*, pp. 53–54.
44. *WIT*, p. 166; cf. *WdG*, pp. 16 & 42 n. 59; & *B&T*, p. 418 (366).

3. Unification of Thought and Sensibility

45. Martin, p. 120.
46. Martin, p. 65.
47. *CPR*, A57 = B82, p. 97.
48. *CPR*, A63 = B88, p. 100.
49. *KPM*, pp. 56–57.
50. Barrett, *PTC*, p. 161.
51. See *CPR*, A67–68 = B92–93, p. 105.
52. *CPR*, A65f = B90, p. 103.
53. *KPM*, p. 60; cf. p. 59.
54. See Smith, p. 194 & *KPM*, p. 62.
55. *CPR* A77 = B102, p. 111 (italics mine).
56. *KRV*, A77 = B103, p. 116; cf. *CPR*, p. 111.
57. *CPR*, A78 = B103, p. 112.
58. *KPM*, p. 61.
59. Kant used 'time' and 'pure intuition' as virtually interchangeable; he often wrote them as "pure intuition (time)"; this identification follows from the 'reduction' of all representations to representations in inner sense; e.g., "But all perceptions are grounded apriori in pure intuition (in time, the form of their inner intuition as representations). . . ." Its root, of course, is the Aesthetic doctrine especially insofar as "Time is nothing but the form of inner sense. . . ." See *CPR* A115, p. 141 & A33 = B49, p. 77; also *KPM*, pp. 56–57 & *WIT*, p. 147.
60. *KPM*, p. 64 (citing *CPR* A95, p. 127); cf. *CPR* A97, p. 130 & Paton, I, pp. 347, 358, & 358 n. 3.
61. *CPR*, A77 = B102, p. 111 (quoted, *KPM*, p. 65).
62. *KPM*, p. 65.

63. *KPM/G*, p. 63 (quoting *KRV* A78 = B103, p. 116); cf. *CPR*, p. 112 & *KPM*, p. 66.

64. Paton, I, p. 469.

65. *CPR*, A119, p. 143.

66. Paton, I, p. 572; cf. n. 34.

4. Possibility of Ontological Synthesis

67. *CPR*, A78 = B104, p. 112.

68. *CPR*, Axvii, p. 12.

69. *CPR*, A86 = B118, p. 121.

70. See *CPR*, Axvi, p. 11.

71. Martin, p. 96.

72. Barrett, *What Is Existentialism?*, p. 170.

73. Paton, I, p. 547.

74. *CPR*, A94 = B126, p. 126.

75. *CPR*, A88 = B121, p. 123.

76. *CPR*, A99, p. 131.

77. *CPR*, A143 = B182, p. 184.

78. *CPR*, A102, p. 133.

79. *CPR*, A104–105, pp. 134–35.

80. *CPR*, A106, p. 135.

81. *CPR*, A108, p. 137.

82. *CPR*, A107, p. 136.

83. *CPR*, A94, p. 127.

84. *CPR*, A111, p. 138.

85. *CPR*, A111, p. 139.

86. *CPR*, A113, p. 140.

87. *CPR*, A111, p. 138. N.B. The discussion of "The Highest Principle of All Synthetic Judgments" in V.6 highlights its import; but its first appearance here in the Deduction must be noted.

88. *CPR*, A110, p. 138; cf. A143 = B182, p. 184.

89. *KRV*, B136, p. 146a; cf. *CPR*, p. 155. Also see *B&T*, p. 366 (319) & note xvi, p. 496; cf. *KTS*, p. 22. N.B. Heidegger takes it as the point at which to start the analysis of selfhood.

90. Paton, I, pp. 431, 434, 442 (italics mine).

91. N.B. For examples of Heidegger's essential equation of 'ontological' and 'transcendental' see, e.g., *KPM*, p. 93; *WdG*, pp. 32–34; & *KTS*, p. 24.

92. *KPM*, p. 74; cf. n. 71 re translation of *entgegenstehen (lassen)*.

93. See *KPM/G*, p. 70; cf. *KPM*, pp. 74–75 & Richardson p. 114.

94. Cf. J. Glenn Gray, "The New Image of Man in Martin Heidegger's Philosophy," in Kline, pp. 34–35.

95. See, e.g., *CPR*, A92 = B124–25, p. 125.

96. See *KPM*, p. 79 & *B&T*, p. 95 (67)–114 (83); cf. Dewey, *The Quest for Certainty*, p. 160, & Barrett, *PTC*, p. 161.

97. See *CPR*, A795 = B823, p. 629.

98. *CPR*, A19 = B33, p. 65.

99. *CPR*, A104, p. 134.

100. *CPR*, A104, p. 134 (quoted, *KPM*, p. 76).

101. *CPR*, A104, p. 134; cf. *KRV*, p. 151a.

102. *CPR*, A250–51, p. 268; cf. A290 = B340, pp. 294–95.

103. Paton, I, p. 418.

104. See *KPM/G*, p. 71: "Wenn aber nicht Seiendes, dann eben ein Nichts." Cf. *KPM*, p. 76.

105. See *KPM*, p. 77.

106. See *KPM/G*, p. 47: "Das in der reinen Anschauung Vorgestellte ist kein Seiendes (kein Gegenstand, d.h. kein erscheinendes Seiendes), aber gleichwohl nicht schlechthin nichts." Cf. *KPM*, pp. 71 & 76.

107. See *KPM/G*, p. 71: "Sichhineinhalten in das Nichts." Cf. *KPM*, p. 76. Also cf.: "WIM," p. 370: "Hineingehaltenheit in das Nichts." Cf. "WIM," p. 369 & p. 399 n.

108. Cf. *B&T*, pp. 145 (110)–148 (113).

109. Smith, p. 270.

110. See *CPR*, A104, p. 134 (quoted *KPM*, p. 77). Cf. *KPM/G*, p. 72 & *KPM*, p. 78.

111. *CPR*, A104, p. 134.

112. *KPM*, p. 79.

113. Thus, in *B&T*, p. 367 (321), Heidegger says, "The 'I' is not just an 'I think,' but an 'I think something. . . .' "

114. *KPM*, pp. 79–80.

115. *CPR*, A94, p. 127.

116. Cf. *CPR*, Axvii, p. 12.

117. Paton, I, p. 465.

118. Paton, I, p. 469.

119. *CPR*, A118, p. 143.

120. *CPR*, A119, p. 143.

121. *KPM*, p. 84.

122. *KPM*, p. 84.

123. *CPR*, A118, p. 142 (quoted, *KPM*, p. 84).

124. *CPR*, A118, p. 143; cf. *KPM*, p. 85.

125. *KPM*, p. 86.

126. *CPR*, A99, p. 131 (cited in *KPM*, p. 86); cf. Paton, I, pp. 241f, n. 4.

127. *CPR*, A119, p. 143.

128. *CPR*, A123, pp. 145–46.
129. *CPR*, A124, p. 146.
130. Paton, I, p. 487 & n. 2.
131. See Paton, I, p. 241.
132. See, e.g., Paton, I, p. 475 & n. 2.
133. *KPM*, p. 89.
134. *KRV*, A110, pp. 160a–161a (italics mine); cf. *CPR*, p. 138.
135. *KPM*, p. 89.
136. *CPR*, A124, p. 146.
137. See *CPR*, A240 = B299, p. 260.
138. *KPM*, p. 92.

5. *Ground of Ontological Synthesis*

139. Cf. deWaehlens & Biemel, p. 28.
140. KPM, p. 118; cf. p. 206.
141. Cassirer, "Kant and the Problem of Metaphysics," in Gram, p. 139.
142. *KPM*, p. 94.
143. *KPM*, p. 97.
144. *KPM*, p. 113.
145. *KPM*, p. 118.
146. *PAFM*, pp. 76–77; cf. *KPM*, p. 118.
147. Paton, II, p. 20 (italics mine).
148. *PAFM*, pp. 76–77; cf. *CPR* A132 = B171, p. 177.
149. *See CPR*, B160 n.a, pp. 170–71.
150. See *PAFM*, pp. 76–77.
151. *CPR*, A139 = B178, p. 181 (italics mine).
152. *CPR*, A139 = B178, p. 181.
153. *CPR*, A140 = B180, p. 182. N.B. The word 'image(s)' should not be taken in any literal sense, as the discussion which follows indicates.
154. *CPR*, A145 = B184, p. 185.
155. Cf. Paton, II, p. 69, and *KPM*, p. 114.
156. *CPR*, A145 = B185, p. 186.
157. Windelband, pp. 79–80.
158. *CPR*, A146 = B186, p. 186 (italics mine); cf. A240 = B299, p. 260 & A258 = B314, p. 274.
159. *CPR*, A140 = B180, p. 182.
160. *CPR*, A142 = B181, p. 183 (quoted, *KPM*, p. 107).
161. *CPR*, A137 = B176, p. 180 & A138 = B177, p. 180 (quoted *KPM*, p. 107).
162. See pp. 63–64 above.

163. Cf. *CPR*, A124, p. 146.
164. *CPR*, A142 = B181, p. 183.
165. Cf. *CPR*, B163, p. 172.
166. Smith, p. 64.
167. Paton, II, p. 67.
168. *DKT*, p. 159.
169. *KPM*, p. 114.
170. *KPM*, pp. 114-15.
171. de Vleeschauwer, "A Survey of Kantian Philosophy," p. 133.
172. Martin, p. 85.
173. *CPR*, A240 = B299, p. 260; cf. A258 = B314, p. 274.
174. *KPM*, p. 96.
175. *KPM*, p. 97.
176. *KPM*, p. 101.
177. *KPM*, p. 101.
178. *KPM*, p. 106.
179. *KPM*, p. 106.
180. See *KPM*, p. 106.
181. N.B. Even mathematics, Kant had argued in the Aesthetic, is rooted in the pure forms of intuition; hence mathematical principles enter into constituting the temporal manifold.
182. *CPR*, B305f, p. 266.
183. *CPR*, A147 = B187, p. 187; cf. Paton, II, p. 69.
184. *CPR*, A147 = B187, p. 187.
185. Martin, p. 142.
186. Cf. *CPR*, A143 = B182, p. 184 & A110, p. 138.
187. Martin, p. 151.
188. Cf. *KPM*, p. 109 & *KPM/G*, p. 99.
189. *KPM*, p. 110.
190. *CPR*, A139 = B178, p. 181 & A140 = B179, p. 182.
191. *KPM*, p. 111.
192. *CPR*, A143 = B183, p. 184. As Heidegger makes clear, the fuller explication of this point necessitates reference to the First Analogy: cf. *WIT*, pp. 228-36.
193. *KPM*, pp. 112-13 (quoting *CPR*, A143 = B183, p. 184).
194. *B&T*, pp. 63-64 (40); cf. *KPM*, p. 113.
195. Paton, II, p. 76 (italics mine).
196. See *KPM*, pp. 94 & 116.

6. *The Transcendental and Ontological*

197. *KPM*, p. 118.
198. *WIT*, p. 124.

199. See *WIT*, pp. 182–83, 201; cf. Richardson, "Kant and the Late Heidegger," p. 134.

200. See *WdG*, pp. 16–18.

201. *WIT*, p. 183.

202. *CPR*, A154 =B194, p. 192.

203. *CPR*, A155 = B194, p. 192.

204. *CPR*, A155 = B194, p. 192.

205. *CPR*, A156 = B195, p. 193.

206. *CPR*, A158 = B197, p. 194.

207. *CPR*, A158 = B197, p. 194 (as in *KPM*, p. 123).

208. *CPR*, A156 = B195, p. 193 (quoted, *KPM*, p. 121).

209. See *WIT*, p. 181.

210. See *CPR*, A176 = B218, p. 208.

211. Cf. *WdG*, pp. 18–19; cf. pp. 26n. & 92n. above.

212. Cf. *KTS*, pp. 18 & 20; *WdG*, pp. 16–17. Also, Gendlin in *WIT*, p. 281.

213. *KPM*, p. 124.

214. See *KPM*, p. 125 & *B&T*, p. 418 (366).

215. See *KPM*, p. 125, *CPR* A108–109, p. 137 (quoted, *KPM*, p. 126), & A250, p. 268 (quoted, *KPM*, p. 127).

216. *CPR*, B303, p. 264.

217. Karl Löwith, "Heidegger: Problem & Background of Existentialism," *Social Research*, XV, p. 355.

218. See Biemel, p. 142.

219. *KPM*, p. 126.

220. *KPM*, p. 128.

221. *KPM*, p. 93.

222. *KPM*, p. 22; cf. p. 93.

VI. The Result of the Retrieve

1. *WIT*, p. 55.

1. The Basis of Interpretation

2. Cf., as examples, *CPR*, A33 = B49–A34 = B50, pp. 76–77; A115, p. 141; A123–24, p. 146.

3. *CPR*, A19 = B33, p. 65.

2. The Established Ground

4. *CPR*, B151, p. 165 (cited, *KPM*, p. 138). n.b. Although suggested by, and implicit in, the A Deduction (cf. Smith, p. 265) and the Schematism,

the productive imagination was explicitly developed only in the B Deduction.

5. *CPR*, A143 = B183, p. 184.

6. *KPM*, p. 138; cf. *KPM*, pp. 112–13, 139; & pp. 116–18 above.

7. *KPM*, p. 140.

8. *CPR*, A124, p. 146 (quoted, *KPM*, p. 141). See *KPM*, p. 122.

9. *CPR*, A78 = B103, p. 112 (quoted, in part, *KPM*, p. 142).

10. See, e.g., *CPR*, A94, p. 127 (cf. *KRV*, p. 135, n. 1), (quoted, *KPM*, p. 143). Also *CPR*, A94, p. 127 & A115, p. 141 (quoted, *KPM*, p. 143).

11. *CPR*, A15 = B29, p. 61 & *KPM*, p. 144; cf. pp. 37–38 above.

12. Smith, p. 77.

13. Smith, p. 265; cf. *CPR*, A124, p. 146 & B151–52, pp. 164–65; & Paton, I, p. 572.

14. Smith, p. 337. N.B. Smith further suggests that this characterization be read in the light of the Third Critique, where he finds the reassertion of the central position of transcendental imagination. Cf. Smith, p. 77, n. 8 & p. 265; & *CJ*, I, sec. 57, p. 209 (341).

15. *CPR*, A835 = B863, p. 655 (cf. *KRV*, p. 751), (quoted, *KPM*, p. 41); see p. 37 above.

16. *CPR*, A141 = B181, p. 183.

17. *CPR*, A138 = B177, p. 181.

18. *KPM*, p. 142.

19. To the interpretation which follows here, compare the contrary view, which propounds the question: "the Schematism . . . is unnecessary, and its presence merely obscures the connection between the Deduction and the Principles of Pure Understanding. However [!] Kant has managed to include in passing in the section some of the most important insights of the entire Critical Philosophy." Wolff, p. 43.

20. *CPR*, A90–92 = B122–24, pp. 124–25.

21. See *PAFM*, pp. 76–77.

22. See Paton, II, p. 20 & *KPM*, p. 94 & pp. 120, 128–29 above.

23. *CPR*, A132 = B171, p. 177.

24. *CPR*, A135 = B175, p. 179.

25. *CPR*, A140–141 = B180, p. 182.

26. *CPR*, A143 = B182, p. 184.

27. *CPR*, A147 = B186, p. 186.

28. *CPR*, A146 = B186, p. 186.

29. *CPR*, A158 = B197, p. 194 (as quoted, *KPM*, p. 123); see p. 78 n. 87 above.

30. See *WdG*, pp. 43–45.

31. Quoted, Eva Schaper, p. 286n. (italics mine).

32. *KPM,* p. 94. Note, however, that in later works such as *WIT* and *KTS* he increasingly throws the focus on the Highest Principle, not on the Schematism.

33. Cf., e.g. Heimsoeth, & Cassirer, in Gram, pp. 131–214.

34. Schaper, p. 281. N.B. Cf. CPR A141 = B181, p. 183, re " 'real modes of activity,' " & *KPM,* p. 65, re the last sentence in the first paragraph quoted. Also cf. Kant's explanation that the necessity of my being in a world of objects, of 'my existence in the time in which representations change,' and the necessity of the permanent outside of me must be included, as existent, in the determination of my own existence, 'which comes from inner intuition and is bound up with the condition of time.' This whole theme, which Heidegger is to take up as 'being-in-the-world,' is somewhat ambiguously forecast by Kant's "Refutation of Idealism," which appears as an insert in the B Edition of this same Analytic of Principles. See *CPR,* Bxla, pp. 34–36; B276ff, p. 245ff; & *B&T,* p. 247 (203).

35. See *KRV,* A140 = B179, p. 199; cf. *CPR,* p. 182.

3. The Common Root

36. *CPR,* A142 = B181, p. 183.
37. *CPR,* A145 = B185, p. 185–86.
38. *KPM,* p. 145; cf. *KPM/G,* p. 127.
39. *KPM,* p. 146.
40. *CPR,* A271 = B327, p. 283.
41. *KPM,* p. 144.

a. Of Pure Intuition

42. *CPR,* B160–61, pp. 170–71 (italics mine).
43. *KPM,* p. 152; cf. *CPR,* A268 = B324, p. 281.
44. *CPR,* A39 = B56, p. 80; cf. *KPM,* p. 148.
45. *CPR,* A77 = B102, p. 111.
46. *KPM,* p. 148.
47. *KPM,* p. 148. N.B. The full explication of this theme would take us far afield at this point; see VI.5.b, where this subjective grounding of the experience of time as an 'existential' of human be-ing is further developed.

48. *KPM,* p. 149 (citing CPR A94f, p. 127); cf. *CPR,* A97, p. 130 & Paton, I, p. 37.
49. *KPM,* p. 149.
50. *CPR,* A99, p. 131.
51. *CPR,* A32 = B48, p. 75.
52. See note 48.

53. *KPM*, p. 151.

54. See *CPR*, A291 = B347, p. 295 (quoted, *KPM*, p. 150) & *KRV*, p. 332: "Die blosse Form der Anschauung . . . wie der reine Raum, und die reine Zeit, *die zwar Etwas sind* . . . aber selbst keine Gegenstände sind, die angeschaut werden (ens imaginarium)" (italics mine); cf. *KPM/G*, p. 132. Cf. *KRV*, p. 332, n. 3 & *KPM*, p. 150, n. 21.

55. *KPM*, p. 150. N.B. In this instance, Heidegger's word for 'imagination' is not *Einbildungskraft* but *Imagination;* cf. *KPM/G*, p. 132.

56. See p. 127 above.

57. See *CPR*, A292 = B348, p. 295 & *KRV*, p. 333.

58. See *CPR*, A290 = B346 & A292 = B349, pp. 294–96.

59. *CPR*, B160, note a, p. 170 (cited, *KPM*, p. 152).

60. *KPM*, p. 152.

b. Of Pure Thought

61. See *KRV*, A124, p. 181a (quoted, *KPM*, p. 153); cf. *CPR*, p. 146.

62. See pp. 38ff. & 110–14 above.

63. *KPM*, p. 154.

64. *CPR*, A118, p. 143. As Kant stated the matter in the B Deduction: "This synthetic unity of apperception is, therefore, the highest point to which we must ascribe all employment of the understanding, even the whole of logic, and conformably therewith, transcendental philosophy. Indeed, *this faculty of apperception,* is the understanding itself." *CPR* B134, p. 154 (quoted, *KPM*, pp. 155–56).

65. *CPR*, A126, p. 147; cf. *KPM*, p. 156.

66. *CPR*, A141 = B180, p. 183 (quoted, *KPM*, p. 157); cf., Lewis White Beck, *Studies in the Philosophy of Kant*, p. 65: "Kant is saying . . . we make at least a problematical existential judgment and state the conditions under which this judgment could be verified so that the *definiendum* will be seen to have 'objective reference.' " See also John Dewey, *The Quest for Certainty*, p. 160: " 'Thought' . . . is a mode of directed overt action. Ideas are anticipatory plans and designs. . . ."

67. *KPM*, p. 157 (quoting *CPR*, A142 = B182, p. 183).

68. N.B. 'Freedom' is taken, in accord with Kant's discussion of it, as the presupposition of morality, as the "placing oneself under a necessity which is *self*-imposed." *KPM*, p. 162; see *WdG*, III, esp. pp. 43–45, where 'freedom' is identified as 'transcendence' and primal grounding.

69. *KPM*, p. 158.

70. *KPM*, p. 161; cf. *CPR*, A94, p. 127.

71. *KPM*, p. 161.

72. Cf. pp. 64, 72–73, 110–14 above.

73. *CPR*, A474 = B502, p. 429 (quoted, *KPM*, p. 161).
74. *KPM*, p. 162.

c. And Practical Reason

75. See *CPrR*, p. 177.
76. Cf. *GMM*, pp. 119–20.
77. See *CJ*, II, pp. 58–59. But note that moral practical reason takes priority; cf., e.g., *CPrR*, p. 153.
78. *CPrR*, p. 177.
79. *GMM*, p. 119.
80. *GMM*, p. 120.
81. *GMM*, pp. 119–20.
82. Cf. *CPR*, A795 = B823, p. 629.
83. *CPR*, A800 = B828, p. 632; cf. A796 = B824, p. 629.
84. See *GMM*, pp. 89–90.
85. *GMM*, p. 79.
86. *GMM*, p. 105.
87. See *CJ*, II, p. 59.
88. See *KPM*, p. 162, *GMM*, p. 96, & *CPrR*, p. 193.
89. *RLR*, p. 21.
90. *GMM*, p. 103. N.B. Churchill, Beck, and Friedrich translate *Achtung* as 'respect,' Paton as 'reverence.'
91. See *CPrR*, pp. 181–83; cf. Cassirer's attack on Heidegger's citation of this identification of 'respect' and morality, Cassirer, in Gram, p. 146.
92. *RLR*, p. 23; cf. *KPM*, p. 163.
93. *CPrR*, pp. 193–94.
94. *KPM*, p. 165.
95. *KPM*, p. 166; cf. *KPM/G*, pp. 145–46.
96. *B&T*, pp. 322–23 (278); *B&T*, p. 67 (41), *WdG*, p. 38.
97. *CPrR*, pp. 224–25 (italics mine).
98. *CPrR*, p. 235 (italics mine).
99. *KPM*, p. 166.

4. Allegation of Retreat

100. Paton, I, p. 260.
101. *CPR*, A158 = B197, p. 194 (as quoted *KPM* p. 125).
102. *CPR*, A78 = B103, p. 112 (quoted, in part, *KPM*, p. 134).
103. *CPR*, A15 = B29, p. 61; cf. *KPM*, pp. 166–67.
104. See *DKT*, pp. 90, 92.
105. *DKT*, p. 98.
106. *DKT*, p. 107.

107. *DKT*, p. 109.
108. *DKT*, p. 106.
109. Paton, I, p. 147.
110. *DKT*, p. 83.
111. Randall, p. 83; cf., *DKT*, pp. 83–86; Kant's "Letter to Marcus Herz (about May 11, 1781)," in *PC*, p. 96. Cf. *EGP*, p. 415, n. 77 & p. 468, n. 112.
112. Paton, I, p. 500.
113. See *DKT*, p. 114.
114. *KPM*, p. 173.
115. *KPM*, p. 174; cf. *CPrR*, pp. 153, 193 & *GMM*, pp. 79–80, 92, 94, 98. N.B. It should be noted that Heidegger's own development has followed a course similar to the one condemned here—from focus on the Schematism to focus on the transcendental unity of apperception, from 'being and time' to 'being and thought'; cf. *KTS*, which draws its Kant from the B Edition as does most of *WIT*. Cf. "Postscript."
116. *CPR*, A94–95, p. 127; cf. B127–29, pp. 127–28.
117. *KPM*, p. 167.
118. *CPR*, B154, pp. 166–67 (quoted, *KPM*, p. 169).
119. *CPR*, B152, p. 165.
120. *CPR*, A118, p. 143; cf. B153, p. 166 & *KRV*, p. 169b.
121. *KPM*, p. 202.
122. *DKT*, p. 106.
123. *CPR*, Axvii, p. 12 (quoted, *KPM*, p. 171).
124. *KPM*, p. 172.
125. *CPR*, A98, p. 131 (cited, *KPM*, p. 172).
126. *KPM*, p. 172.
127. *KPM*, p. 221.
128. *KPM*, p. 173.
129. See *KPM*, p. 173 & *KPM/G*, p. 153.
130. *KPM*, p. 175.
131. *DKT*, p. 111.
132. de Vleeschauwer, "A Survey of Kantian Philosophy," p. 128.
133. Lawrence, p. 448; cf. *WIT*, p. 135.
134. *KPM*, p. 176.

5. Time and Temporality

135. *KPM*, p. 178.
136. Spiegelberg, p. 307. N.B. We have had a preview of this existential analysis in the elucidation of the 'existential' of 'respect' in the temporalization of the moral ego and the 'placing' of practical reason into imaginative synthesis.

a. *Temporality of Imagination*

137. *KPM*, p. 178 (quoting, *CPR*, B291, p. 255); cf. *CPR*, A163 = B203, p. 198.

138. *Abbildung, Nachbildung, Vorbildung:* see *KPM/G*, p. 159 & *KPM*, p. 180; cf. *B&T*, p. 373 (325).

139. *KPM*, p. 180.

140. *KPM*, p. 181.

141. *KPM*, p. 182.

142. *CPR*, A99, p. 131 (quoted, *KPM*, p. 184).

143. *KPM*, p. 182.

144. *CPR*, A120, p. 144.

145. *CPR*, A102, p. 133 (quoted, in part, *KPM*, p. 188).

146. *KPM*, p. 189; see *CPR*, A551 = B579, p. 475, A152 = B191–92, p. 191 (all cited, *KPM*, p. 189).

147. *CPR*, A103, p. 133 (quoted, *KPM*, pp. 189–90).

148. *CPR*, A106, p. 135.

149. See *KPM*, p. 190 & *KPM/G*, p. 168.

150. See *CPR*, A126, p. 147 (cited, *KPM*, p. 191).

151. See *KPM*, p. 191.

152. *KPM*, p. 191; cf. *B&T*, sec. 65. N.B. Emerson, in his essay "History," expressed more poetically an essential aspect of this thought: "A man is a bundle of relations, a knot of roots, whose flower and fruitage is the world. His faculties refer to natures out of them and predict the world he is to inhabit, as the fins of the fish foreshow that water exists, or the wings of an eagle in the egg presuppose air."

153. See, e.g., *CPR*, A107–114, pp. 136–40.

154. See *CPR*, A231 = B284, p. 250; cf. *B&T*, p. 63 (38).

155. Cf. *B&T*, pp. 182–88 (142–48) & 401 (350).

156. See Gelven, pp. 184, 191–92.

157. *KPM*, p. 192.

158. *KPM*, p. 192.

159. *KPM*, p. 192; see p. 181 above.

160. *Physics*, 219a20–219b15, Ross translation. Cf. *B&T*, pp. 45 (24) & 49 (26).

161. *Physics*, 223a25; see *B&T*, p. 499 (427), n. xiv.

162. Lovejoy, p. 75.

163. See, e.g., *CPR*, Bxxx, p. 29 & A840 = B868, p. 658f; & Beck, *Studies in the Philosophy of Kant*, pp. 11–21. N.B. This is somewhat reversed or augmented in Heidegger's new grounding of the Critique in the nature of temporal experience; as he points out, "Temporality first showed itself in

anticipatory resoluteness," which provides the grounding of morality and thereby of selfhood; cf. *B&T*, p. 380 (336).

164. "T&I," pp. 146–47; cf. Aristotle: "since time is continuous, movement must be continuous, inasmuch as there can be no time without movement. Time, therefore, is a 'number' of some continuous movement," *De Generatione et Corruptione*, 337a23; Ross translation; cf. note 161.

165. See *KPM*, p. 187, *KPM/G*, p. 166, *B&T*, p. 373 (326) & Gelven, pp. 185–87.

166. Dewey, *Experience and Nature*, p. 352; cf. *Art as Experience*, p. 18.

167. James, p. 254.

168. Whitehead, p. 73.

169. Spiegelberg, p. 336.

170. Cf. Biemel, p. 125, & Dewey, *Art as Experience*, p. 18.

171. *B&T*, p. 401 (350); cf. p. 387 (337).

172. Plotinus, p. 225.

173. See *B&T*, pp. 472 (420)–480 (428) & esp. p. 478 (426).

174. Wyschograd, p. 64.

b. *Temporality of the Self*

175. See *KPM/G*, p. 52 & *KPM*, p. 54; cf. *B&T*, p. 418 (366).

176. *CPR*, B67–68, pp. 87–88 (quoted, *KPM*, p. 196), italics mine; with regard to the bracketed 'their' in the seventh line, see *KRV*, B68, p. 88, n. 2 & *KPM*, p. 196, n. 88.

177. *CPR*, A77 = B102, p. 111 (quoted, *KPM*, p. 193); cf. pp. 39–41, 49, 111–14 above.

178. *CPR*, A143 =B192, p. 184.

179. *CPR*, B67f, p. 87.

180. See *KPM/G*, p. 172 & *KPM*, pp. 194–95.

181. *KPM*, p. 194.

182. *KPM*, p. 195.

183. See Paton, II, p. 414.

184. See *KPM*, p. 195.

185. *KPM*, p. 196.

186. Paton, II, p. 404; cf. Paton, I, p. 571 & *B&T*, secs. 12, 25, 26, 32.

187. *KPM*, p. 197.

188. *KPM*, p. 197.

189. See *CPR*, A123, p. 146, A143 = B183, p. 184, A182 = B225, p. 213 (cited, *KPM*, p. 197). N.B. Heidegger's essential argument here is basically Leibnizian but note that he implicitly invokes the Principle of the Identity of Indiscernibles (*within* the Copernican Revolution); with particular reference to Leibniz' Principle of Sufficient Reason and Heidegger's concept of Transcendence, see *WdG*, especially pp. 16–17; also, *WdG*, esp. pp. 7–18.

190. *Cf. CPR*, A348f, p. 333f (cited, *KPM*, p. 198).
191. *KPM*, p. 199.
192. *B&T*, p. 367 (319); cf. pp. 366 (319), n. xvi, & 368 (**321**).
193. *KPM*, p. 199.
194. *KPM*, p. 198.
195. *KPM*, p. 201.
196. *KPM*, p. 200.
197. Plotinus, pp. 234–48. N.B. Heidegger cites a passage from Augustine's *Confessions*, XI, 26: "Hence it seemed to me that time is nothing else than an extendedness; but of what sort of thing it is an extendedness, I do not know; and it would be surprising if it were not an extendedness of the soul itself." *B&T*, p. 499 (427), n. xv.
198. See *B&T*, pp. 36–37 (15–16) & 63 (39).
199. "T&I," pp. 152–53.
200. *B&T*, p. 45 (23).

6. *The Meaning of the Retrieve*

201. Martin, p. 133.
202. Cf. *B&T*, p. 418 (366) & *WdG*, pp. 51f, 111.
203. *ItM*, p. 108.
204. *KPM*, p. 202.
205. Martin, pp. 150–51; cf. pp. 55 & 154.
206. See *KPM/G*, p. 178 & *KPM*, p. 201.
207. We can now see more clearly just why Heidegger has regarded changes in the B Edition as a 'recoil' from the doctrine and meaning of the A, as a reversion to rationalism. By abandoning the Subjective Deduction, Kant had abandoned the ground of his own structure. In the abandonment of the integrating nature of imagination, the reduction of pure imagination to pure thought, the essential dynamism and empiricism were lost; as such the B Edition became the source of inspiration for the development into Hegel's Absolute Idealism. In many ways the question can now be asked whether Heidegger himself has not in his later thought (cf. e.g., *KTS*) followed a somewhat similar route.

At any rate, we should note that a prime reason, which Heidegger might have developed in *KPM*, for the rejection of the B Edition Analytic is that it tends to bring space into the forefront. Space, *qua* intuition, is rooted in time as the self-affecting projection of the self; in accord with the temper of the A Edition, space 'belongs' to the finite space with which we can deal just because, as a condition of 'outer' representations, it is rooted in inner sense, as Kant steadfastly maintained, i.e., as Heidegger puts it, in ultimate or "authentic Time." Cf., e.g., *B&T*, Sec. 24 & 70 & my "Postscript."

VII. Kant and Fundamental Ontology

1. Martin, p. 55.
2. Kant, "Letter to Marcus Herz [about May 11, 1781]," in *PC*, p. 95, (cited, *KPM*, p. 238).

1. The Legacy from Kant

3. Spiegelberg, p. 307.
4. *KPM*, p. 221.
5. Cf. *KPM/G*, p. 94 & *KPM*, p. 221.
6. Did Kant have any intimation of this impending 'collapse'? Heidegger thinks so. See *CPR*, A244 = B302, pp. 262-63 (quoted, in part, *KPM*, p. 252); also A245-46, pp. 263-64 & A246 = B303, p. 264.
7. *CPR*, A804f = B332, p. 635 (cited, *KPM*, p. 214).
8. See *KPM*, p. 214.
9. *KPM*, p. 223.
10. *KPM*, p. 224.
11. Cf. *B&T*, p. 83f (57).
12. See *B&T*, Sec. 41, esp. p. 238 (193).
13. See *KPM*, pp. 244-45 & *B&T*, p. 487 (436) and p. 5 above. N.B. If one remembers that a decade before publication of the Critique Kant had conceived of it as a "general phenomenology" (as indicated in his "Letter to Marcus Herz, February 21, 1772," see *PC*, p. 71), then perhaps these are not such different approaches after all; in this light, one could regard the approach of Heidegger's 'existential phenomenology' as but the development of the 'Critical phenomenology' which Kant had originally undertaken.
14. *KPM*, p. 247.
15. See *B&T*, p. 396 & n. 2 (346) & *WIT*, p. 221, which suggests that a differentiation between humans and animals is to be found in their modes of temporality; cf., Josiah Royce, *The World and the Individual*, II, p. 124.
16. *KPM*, p. 247.
17. Cf. Kroner, esp. Chap. V.
18. *CPR*, A703 = B731, p. 570 (quoted, *KPM*, p. 225).
19. Martin, p. 139.

2. And the Metaphysics of Dasein

20. Cf. *CPR*, e.g., A245-46, pp. 263-64.
21. Royce, *The World and the Individual*, I, pp. 12 & 14.
22. *KPM*, p. 234.

23. *KPM*, p. 231. N.B. Heidegger refers here to the first section of *WdG*.

24. Wyschograd, p. 55.

25. See *KPM/G*, p. 205 & *KPM*, p. 235; also *WdG*, p. 111, "WBGM," pp. 206–221, esp. p. 214.

26. Cf. Gelven, p. 23, n. 3.

27. See *B&T*, p. 67 (41); also p. 27 (7). Cf. p. 168 above.

28. *B&T*, p. 67 (42). N.B. Note the German: "Das 'Wesen' dieses Seienden liegt in seinem Zu-sein. . . . Das 'Wesen' des Daseins liegt in seiner Existenz." As pointed out on p. 26n., the first sentence prompts part of the reason for insisting on the translation of *das Sein* as 'the to-be' instead of the more abstract, traditional, and nonexistential 'Being.'

29. Cf. "Letter on Humanism," in *PTC*, III, p. 278.

30. See *KPM/G*, p. 207: "*Ursprünglicher als der Mensch ist die Endlichkeit des Daseins in ihm*" (all italics); cf. *KPM*, p. 237.

31. See *B&T*, p. 39 (17).

32. See above, pp. 222–23 n. 2.

33. See *KPM/G*, p. 209; cf. *KPM*, p. 240.

34. Cf., e.g., *B&T*, p. 244 (199).

35. Thevenez, p. 159; cf. Cerf, p. 188.

36. *KPM*, p. 243; cf. *B&T*, p. 358 (310).

37. See *KPM*, p. 243.

38. See *KPM/G*, p. 217: "*Entwurf des Seins auf die Zeit*" (all italics); cf. *KPM*, p. 249.

39. Cf., e.g., *KPM*, p. 252.

40. *KPM/G*, p. 217: "Wo liegt aber der Grund für dieses spontane und selbstverständliche Verstehen des Seins aus der Zeit?"; cf. *KPM*, p. 249.

41. *KPM*, p. 250.

42. *KPM*, p. 248.

43. *CPR*, A143 = B183, p. 184.

44. See *KPM/G*, p. 219 & *KPM*, p. 251.

45. *KPM*, p. 250.

VIII. Retrospect

1. Reluctant Temporalism

1. Dewey, *Quest for Certainty*, p. 275.

2. Smith, p. 137.

3. See, e.g., *GMM*, pp. 70 & 86.

4. *CPR*, A541 = B569, p. 469.

5. As indicative of the essential Platonism underlying this aspect of

Kant's thought, one should note his insistence on the distinction "between the *sensible world* and the *intelligible world* . . . which is its ground, [and] always remains the same." *GMM*, p. 119.

6. For example: "The categories . . . are nothing but *forms of thought,* which contain the merely logical faculty of uniting apriori in one consciousness the manifold given in intuition; and apart, therefore, from the only intuition that is possible to us, they have even less meaning than the pure sensible forms." *CPR*, B305f, p. 266; cf. A19 = B33, p. 65 & A246, p. 264.

7. Smith, p. 241.

8. See, e.g., *CPR*, A836 = B864, p. 655.

9. See *RLR*, p. 61.

10. See *RLR*, p. 112; also p. 59.

11. Quoted, "Introduction," *RLR*, p. xx; cf. Heimsoeth in Gram, p. 199.

12. *CPR*, Bxxxii, p. 31.

2. From Kant to Heidegger

13. *CPR*, A314 = B370, p. 310.

3. The Perspective of Futurity

14. Collingwood, p. 138.

15. Gray, "Heidegger's Course: From Human Existence to Nature," p. 200.

16. *CPR*, A218 = B265, p. 239.

17. *CPR*, A218 = B266, p. 239.

18. See *CPR*, A227 = B280, pp. 248–49, A290 = B346, p. 294, & Paton, I, p. 306.

19. See *CPR*, A144–45 = B184, p. 185 & A231 = B284, p. 250.

20. See, e.g., *CPR*, B292, p. 255.

21. See "Letter on Humanism," p. 278, & *WIT*, pp. 239 & 278.

22. See *CPR*, A290 = B346, p. 294 & *KRV*, p. 332.

23. Cf. Heidegger's discussion of the description of a piece of chalk in *ItM*, p. 30.

24. "T&I," p. 153.

25. *B&T*, p. 63 (38). N.B. One might say that Heidegger discerns possibility as 'idea,' not as 'matter,' and thereby his reversal of the Aristotelian priority consists in 'idealizing' the concept of possibility.

26. James, p. 253.

27. *CPR*, B303, p. 264 (italics mine).

28. *CPR*, A143 = B182, p. 184.

29. See Paton, II, pp. 52 & 149.

30. *CPR*, A291 = B347, p. 295; cf. *KRV*, p. 332: "Realität ist *Etwas*, Negation ist *Nichts*, nämlich, ein Begriff von dem Mangel eines Gegenstandes, wie der Schatten. . . ."

31. "WIM," p. 362; cf. pp. 378–79; & *B&T*, sec. 69(b).

32. Cf. *WdG*, pp. 38, 46–47; *B&T*, pp. 322–23 (278), 381 (332), & "WIM," p. 370.

33. See *CPrR*, pp. 224–25.

34. "WIM," p. 377.

35. Cf., e.g., Grene, p. 120.

36. *CPR*, A79 = B104, p. 112.

37. "T&I" pp. 146–57.

Postscript: Being, Possibility and Time

1. See "ZuS," esp. pp. 15 & 18.

2. Heimsoeth, in Gram, p. 198.

3. See, e.g., *KPM*, p. 251 & Spiegelberg, p. 336.

4. *B&T*, p. 368 (321).

5. *B&T*, p. 471 (419); cf. pp. 458 (406) & 471–72 (419–20).

6. *B&T*, p. 472 (420).

7. "*WBGM*," p. 215.

8. Cf. "ZuS," p. 24, with the 1962 version in *L'endurance de la pensée* (Paris: Plon, 1968), p. 66.

9. "ZuS," p. 24.

10. See "ZuS," p. 10.

11. Hegel, par. 88, p. 163; But, see "WBGM," p. 215.

12. *CPR*, A290 = B346, p. 294; cf. *KRV*, p. 332.

13. *B&T*, p. 65 (38).

14. *CPR*, A219 = B266, p. 239.

15. See *WIT*, pp. 165f. & p. 241.

16. *CPR*, A220 = B267, pp. 239–40.

17. Paton, I, p. 306.

18. See *WIT*, p. 239.

19. *WIT*, p. 166.

INDEX

INDEX